CW01261187

EU–ASEAN Relations in the 21st Century

Studies in the Political Economy of Public Policy

This series presents cutting-edge research on the origins and impacts of public policy. It takes as its starting point the recognition that public policy and its outcomes are shaped by and shape the political–economic context within which they exist. It accepts that conflicts and cooperation between public and private interests and how they are reconciled are crucial determinants of public policy and its impact on society. Titles in the series focus on the competitive and cooperative dynamics operating in increasingly complex policy spaces in a range of diverse settings. The series is being launched with a set of books on emerging and frontier markets, failed states and crisis-afflicted developed countries. Fundamentally pluralist and interdisciplinary in nature, the series is designed to attract high-quality original research of both a theoretical and empirical nature that makes sense of contemporary public policies as well as of their determinants and impacts in novel and relevant ways.

Series editors

Toby Carroll, Senior Research Fellow, Lee Kuan Yew School of Public Policy, National University of Singapore, Singapore

M. Ramesh, Chair Professor of Governance and Public Policy, Hong Kong Institute of Education, China

Darryl Jarvis, Associate Professor and Vice-Dean, Lee Kuan Yew School of Public Policy, National University of Singapore, Singapore

International Advisory Board

Michael Howlett, Simon Fraser University, Canada
John Hobson, University of Sheffield, UK
Stuart Shields, University of Manchester, UK
Paul Cammack, City University of Hong Kong, China
Lee Jones, Queen Mary, University of London, UK
Kanishka Jayasuriya, University of Adelaide, Australia
Shaun Breslin, University of Warwick, UK
Kevin Hewison, University of North Carolina, USA
Richard Stubbs, McMaster University, Canada
Martin Painter, City University of Hong Kong, China
Dick Bryan, University of Sydney, Australia
Kun-Chin Lin, University of Cambridge, UK
Apiwat Ratanawaraha, Chulalongkorn University, Thailand
Wil Hout, Institute of Social Studies, Erasmus University, The Netherlands

---

Studies in the Political Economy of Public Policy
Series Standing Order ISBN 978–1–137–00149–8 (hardback)
ISBN 978–1–137–00150–4 (paperback)
(*outside North America only*)

You can receive future titles in this series as they are published by placing a standing order. Please contact your bookseller or, in case of difficulty, write to us at the address below with your name and address, the title of the series and one or both of the ISBNs quoted above.

Customer Services Department, Macmillan Distribution Ltd, Houndmills, Basingstoke, Hampshire RG21 6XS, England

EU–ASEAN Relations in the 21st Century

Strategic Partnership in the Making

Edited by

Daniel Novotny

and

Clara Portela

palgrave
macmillan

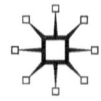

Editorial matter, selection and introduction © Daniel Novotny and
Clara Portela 2012
All remaining chapters © respective authors 2012

All rights reserved. No reproduction, copy or transmission of this
publication may be made without written permission.

No portion of this publication may be reproduced, copied or transmitted
save with written permission or in accordance with the provisions of the
Copyright, Designs and Patents Act 1988, or under the terms of any licence
permitting limited copying issued by the Copyright Licensing Agency,
Saffron House, 6–10 Kirby Street, London EC1N 8TS.

Any person who does any unauthorized act in relation to this publication
may be liable to criminal prosecution and civil claims for damages.

The authors have asserted their rights to be identified as the authors of this
work in accordance with the Copyright, Designs and Patents Act 1988.

First published 2012 by
PALGRAVE MACMILLAN

Palgrave Macmillan in the UK is an imprint of Macmillan Publishers Limited,
registered in England, company number 785998, of Houndmills, Basingstoke,
Hampshire RG21 6XS.

Palgrave Macmillan in the US is a division of St Martin's Press LLC,
175 Fifth Avenue, New York, NY 10010.

Palgrave Macmillan is the global academic imprint of the above companies
and has companies and representatives throughout the world.

Palgrave® and Macmillan® are registered trademarks in the United States,
the United Kingdom, Europe and other countries.

ISBN 978–1–137–00749–0

This book is printed on paper suitable for recycling and made from fully
managed and sustained forest sources. Logging, pulping and manufacturing
processes are expected to conform to the environmental regulations of the
country of origin.

A catalogue record for this book is available from the British Library.

A catalog record for this book is available from the Library of Congress.

10 9 8 7 6 5 4 3 2 1
21 20 19 18 17 16 15 14 13 12

Printed and bound in Great Britain by
CPI Antony Rowe, Chippenham and Eastbourne

Contents

List of Figures and Tables   vii

Notes on Contributors   viii

Acknowledgements   xii

Prospects for EU and ASEAN Relations in the 21st Century: Growing Closer Together or Drifting Further Apart?   1
Daniel Novotny and Clara Portela

Part I ASEAN and the EU Today

1 The Context of EU–ASEAN Relations: Trials and Tribulations of Regionalism in Post-Cold War Europe and Asia   7
  Douglas Webber

2 The EU and Non-Traditional Security in Southeast Asia   26
  Naila Maier-Knapp

Part II (Inter)Regionalism in Danger?

3 Democratisation and Indonesia's Changing Perceptions of ASEAN and its Alternatives   45
  Marshall Clark and Juliet Pietsch

4 The EU's Asia Strategy in Trade and Investment: Externalities, Interdependencies and the Prospects for Coordination with ASEAN   62
  David Treisman

Part III Shifting Perceptions: Can the EU be a Model for ASEAN?

5 The EU in Southeast Asian Public Opinion: Public Diplomacy Case   87
  Natalia Chaban, Lai Suet-yi and Karima Abidat

6 Law and Policy: A Useful Model for ASEAN?   108
  Rachminawati and Anna Syngellakis

7 Energy Security in Southeast Asia: A Role for the EU?   124
  William Kucera

Part IV EU–ASEAN: Practitioners' View

8 ASEAN and the EU: Natural Partners 139
   Jan Willem Blankert

9 Bringing Europe and Southeast Asia Closer Through
   ASEAN and the EU 155
   Ong Keng Yong

10 EU–ASEAN Relations in the 21st Century: In Search for
   Common Values to Forge a Partnership 166
   Xavier Nuttin

11 The EU, ASEAN and the Challenges of the 21st Century:
   Conclusions and Recommendations 179
   Pascaline Winand

Index 193

Figures and Tables

Figures

4.1	Percentage EU-27 exports to major Asian economies: 2004–2008	67
4.2	Percentage EU-27 imports from major Asian economies: 2004–2008	68
4.3	Per capita FDI outflow from the EU: 2004–2006 (euros)	72
4.4	Per capita FDI inflows to the EU: 2004–2006 (euros)	73
4.5	Per capita total portfolio investment outflows from the EU-27: 2004–2006 (US$)	75
4.6	Per capita total portfolio investment inflows to the EU-27 (US$)	76
5.1	Personal and professional links with individual EU member states	97
5.2	The type of connections between the ASEAN public and the EU member states	98

Tables

4.1	Comparison of UN and EC methods of calculating percentage EU-27 exports to major Asian economies: 2004–2008	69
4.2	Comparison of UN and EC methods of calculating percentage EU-27 imports from major Asian economies: 2004–2008	70
4.3	Summary of relative importance rankings for ASEAN and other major Asian economies from an EU perspective	78
5.1	Perceived importance of the EU: in the present and in the future	92
5.2	Spontaneous images of the EU	93
5.3	Issues recommended by the public to be stressed when their local governments formulate policy towards the EU	94
5.4	Personal/professional connections with EU member states	96
5.5	The ten EU member states that feature most personal/professional links with the Southeast Asian public	98

Contributors

Karima Abidat holds a Master's degree in European studies from the Université de Provence, France. She collaborated with the National Centre for Research on Europe (NCRE) at the University of Canterbury (New Zealand) to work on the perception of the EU as a global actor. Ms Abidat is currently European and International Project Manager at College de France in Paris.

Jan Willem Blankert is special adviser for the relationship of the EU with ASEAN in the EU delegation in Jakarta. He is an economist from the University of Amsterdam and a veteran of economic and political reform and regional integration. He started his career working in Latin America and Africa. Since 1985, he has worked for the European Commission, always on issues related to European integration. He worked first in Brussels and then in EU delegations in Poland, Bosnia and Serbia. Between 2003 and 2007, back in Brussels, he worked on EU–China relations. In the academic year 2007–2008 he was a senior fellow at the Lee Kwan Yew School of Public Policy of the National University of Singapore, where he wrote his book *China Rising: Will the West Be Able to Cope?*

Natalia Chaban is deputy director at the National Centre for Research on Europe, University of Canterbury, New Zealand, and co-editor of *Australian and New Zealand Journal of European Studies*. Natalia is actively pursuing her research interests in the fields of cognitive and semiotic aspects of political and mass media discourses, image studies and EU external identity, widely publishing and advancing methodological training in this regard. Since 2002, she has led (together with Professor Martin Holland) a comparative transnational project on EU external perceptions comprising a multicultural team from 20 Asia-Pacific locations.

Marshall Clark is senior lecturer at Institute for Professional Practice in Heritage and the Arts (IPPHA), College of Arts and Social Sciences at the Australian National University (ANU). Prior to his appointment at the ANU, Dr Clark was a senior lecturer at the School of International and Political Studies, Deakin University, for four years. Between 1999 and 2007 he was a lecturer in Indonesian and Asian studies at the University of Tasmania. Recent publications include *Maskulinitas: Culture, Gender and Politics in*

Indonesia (2010); a monograph on Indonesian literature, *Wayang Mbeling* (in Indonesian, 2008); and a chapter on Indonesian cinema in *Popular Culture in Indonesia* (2008). His doctorate in Southeast Asian studies is from the ANU. In spring 2010, he was a visiting scholar at the Shorenstein Asia-Pacific Research Center at Stanford University, where he worked on a joint research project with Dr Juliet Pietsch, 'Indonesia-Malaysia relations: culture, politics and regionalism in Southeast Asia'.

William Kucera is a research analyst at the Institute of Defence and Strategic Studies, S. Rajaratnam School of International Studies at Nanyang Technological University, Singapore, where he works on Southeast Asian security issues with a focus on Indonesia.

Naila Maier-Knapp is a visiting fellow at the Griffith Asia Institute in Australia. She completed her PhD at the National Centre for Research on Europe in New Zealand. She has specialized in the EU's foreign and security relations, international security concepts, regionalism and interregionalism with particular focus on ASEAN and the EU. She is currently a member of the CSCAP New Zealand Forum.

Daniel Novotny is director of the 'Global Europe' think-tank (www.globaleurope.org), editor of 'EU External Affairs Review' and also adjunct fellow at the Monash European and EU Centre, Monash University, Melbourne, Australia. Previously, he was deputy director of the Research Centre at the Association for International Affairs (AMO) and taught International Relations at the Metropolitan University and Anglo-American University in Prague. He holds a PhD from the University of New South Wales, Sydney, Australia. He has recently published a monograph entitled *Torn between America and China: Elite Perceptions and Indonesian Foreign Policy* (ISEAS, 2010). In the past, he has held fellowships with The Habibie Centre in Jakarta, the Institute of Defense and Strategic Studies and Institute of Southeast Asian Studies (ISEAS) in Singapore, Australian National University, Monash University and Deakin University in Australia.

Xavier Nuttin has been senior Asia analyst in the Policy Unit of the Directorate General for External Relations of the European Parliament since 2005. Prior to holding this position, he was an official of the European Commission from 1993, working in the Asia Directorate and afterwards the directorate covering Russia and the Caucasus. He was successively posted at the European Commission headquarters in Brussels, at the EC delegation to Thailand and then to the EC delegation to Vietnam. He was also based in Bangkok in the late 1970s/early 1980s working on education and health programmes in several countries in Asia for UNESCO, UNICEF and the World Bank.

Juliet Pietsch is a senior lecturer at the School of Politics and International Relations, Australian National University, and her research interests lie in analysing broad patterns of social and political behaviour in Australia and East Asia. Recent publications include, with Brian Graetz and Ian McAllister, *Dimensions of Australian Society: Third Edition* (2010) and, with Ian McAllister (2010), 'Human Security in Australia: Public Interest and Political Consequences', *Australian Journal of International Affairs*, 64(2): 285–304. In spring 2010, she was a visiting scholar at the Shorenstein Asia-Pacific Research Center at Stanford University.

Clara Portela is assistant professor of political science at Singapore Management University (Singapore). She holds a PhD from the European University Institute in Florence and an MA from the Free University of Berlin. She is the author of the monograph *European Union Sanctions and Foreign Policy* (Routledge 2010) and of several articles on the foreign and security policy of the EU. She has held visiting positions with the Institute for Security Studies of the EU (France) and the Australian National University. She is the recipient of the 2011 THESEUS Award for Promising Research on European Integration.

Rachminawati is junior lecturer in the International Law Department, Faculty of Law Padjadjaran University, Bandung, Indonesia. She obtained her Master's degree in European law and policy from the University of Portsmouth, UK, in 2009. Her teaching and research interests are in EU and ASEAN with a focus on international organization and human rights law.

Lai Suet-yi is a PhD candidate at the NCRE, University of Canterbury, Christchurch, New Zealand. Her research addresses interregionalism in international relations and focuses on the Asia–Europe Meeting (ASEM) as a case study. She has also taken part in the multinational research project 'Public, Elite and Media Perceptions of the EU in Asia Pacific Region' as a researcher and a research manager of the 'mirror' perceptions project 'Asia in the Eyes of Europe'.

Anna Syngellakis is Jean Monnet principal lecturer in European studies, School of Languages and Area Studies, University of Portsmouth, UK. Her teaching interests are focused on the evolution, institutions, policies and law of the European Union. Her research interests are in international and European Community environmental law and policy.

David Treisman is adjunct research fellow of Monash University and affiliated with the Monash Asia Institute. His research interests are new political macroeconomics, international financial markets and the process of financial integration in Southeast Asia. He has consulted in the private sector and for governmental agencies on various aspects of international business and finance including emerging markets, open-economy macroeconomics and financial risk management.

Douglas Webber is a professor at INSEAD. He has worked both in the Fontainebleau campus in France and at the Asia Campus in Singapore. He has a PhD in government from the University of Essex, UK. Before joining INSEAD, he worked at several British universities and at the Max Planck Institute for the Study of Societies (Cologne). From 1995 to 1997 he was a Jean Monnet Fellow at the European University Institute (Florence). He has published numerous articles on German, European and Asian politics in journals in Britain, Germany and the USA. Most recently, with Bertrand Fort, he published an edited volume *Regional Integration in East Asia and Europe* (Routledge 2006). He works mainly on European Union politics, the Franco-German relationship, German domestic politics and foreign policy, and comparative regional political integration.

Pascaline Winand is professor and director of the Monash European and EU Centre at Monash University. She holds degrees in Germanic studies, political science, international relations and diplomatic history from the Université libre de Bruxelles, Yale University and Purdue University. She is the author of the prize-winning book *Eisenhower, Kennedy and the United States of Europe* (Macmillan/St Martin's Press/Palgrave). Previously, Pascaline Winand was professor of contemporary history at the European University Institute, Florence, and a professor at the Institut d'Etudes Européennes of the Université Libre de Bruxelles (ULB), where she directed several research groups. Pascaline Winand has held visiting positions at Carnegie Mellon University, Pittsburgh, the Institute of International Relations of Kjiv Taras Shevchenko University and Tomsk State University, Russia, among others.

Ong Keng Yong is currently Singapore's high commissioner to Malaysia. Previously, he was director of the Institute of Policy Studies (IPS) in the Lee Kuan Yew School of Public Policy at the National University of Singapore and concurrently ambassador-at-large in the Singapore Ministry of Foreign Affairs (MFA) and Singapore's non-resident ambassador to Iran. He was secretary-general of Association of Southeast Asian Nations (ASEAN) from 2003 to 2008. He was posted to the Singapore Embassies in Saudi Arabia, Malaysia and the USA. He was Singapore's ambassador to India and Nepal, and press secretary to the then prime minister of Singapore, Mr Goh Chok Tong. Mr Ong also held senior appointments in the Ministry of Information, Communications and the Arts, and the People's Association in Singapore.

Acknowledgements

The editors gratefully acknowledge the kind support of the following institutions: the Konrad Adenauer Foundation, the Monash European and EU Centre, the Monash Asia Institute.

We wish to express our deepest gratitude to Professor Pascaline Winand, director of Monash European and EU Centre, Monash University, Melbourne, Australia; Dr Wilhelm Hofmeister, director of regional programme, 'Political Dialogue with Asia', Konrad Adenauer Foundation, Singapore; as well as Professor Thomas Reuter, Professor Anja Jetschke and Mr Jan Vytopil.

Prospects for EU and ASEAN Relations in the 21st Century: Growing Closer Together or Drifting Further Apart?

Daniel Novotny and Clara Portela

In recent years, scholarly discussions on the relations between the European Union (EU) and the Association of Southeast Asian Nations (ASEAN) have been dominated by economic issues, in particular the negotiation of a planned interregional Free Trade Agreement (FTA) which has, for the time being, failed to materialize. In an attempt to escape the centrality of economic issues, this volume illuminates central aspects on the relatively unexplored theme of political – or simply 'non-economic' – relations between the two entities. We also distance ourselves from security-centred approaches, prevalent in contemporary US debate, which tend to look at the ASEAN region primarily from a geopolitical perspective. Instead, this volume explores the long-neglected EU–ASEAN political relationship. From a geopolitical point of view, the EU and ASEAN are not of central importance to each other, and this is not expected to change in the immediate future. The relationship between the two regional groupings is characterized by a stark economic imbalance, whereby the economic might of the EU remains largely unmatched by ASEAN. In contrast to the Asian financial crisis of 1997, which weakened many ASEAN members considerably, the 2008 global financial crisis has left ASEAN largely unscathed, with some states even experiencing economic growth.

This volume begins by presenting a general overview of the current state of relations: Where do we stand? In Part I, Douglas Webber compares the impact of the end of the Cold War on the integration processes in ASEAN and the EU. Surprisingly, his analysis finds that the challenges of the post-Cold War period elicited similar responses in both regions. Indeed, he discovers a stronger similarity than one would have expected. Both regional organizations faced the dilemma of choosing between 'deepening' and 'widening': either proceeding to further an ambitious integration project or extending membership to immediate neighbours. However, he also concludes that the gap between the two organizations has widened as they have become less important to each other as a result of the political transformations brought about by the end of the Cold War. As amply demonstrated by existing research, the EU is not regarded as a 'hard' security provider in Southeast Asia. Yet, one of the most notable post-Cold War phenomena has been the emergence of the notion of 'Non-Traditional Security' (NTS), a field that has been the object of intense EU–ASEAN collaboration. If the EU is not a strategic actor in the traditional sense, has NTS provided an opportunity for the EU to assert itself as a 'soft security' actor? Naila Maier-Knapp explores to what extent the EU is assisting ASEAN states in responding to various non-traditional security crises in Southeast Asia, including finance, health and environment. Cooperation in NTS offered a fabulous chance for the EU to build its image as a security actor in a region whose 'hard security' landscape is dominated by the USA and, increasingly, China. Disappointingly, she concludes that the EU's considerable effort has failed to raise its politico-security profile in Southeast Asia. Still, bilateral cooperation in NTS is likely to intensify, offering a renewed opportunity for the EU to capitalize on its assistance and boost its visibility – not least in the areas of food security or border controls, an important aspect of the fight against terrorism.

In Part II, the volume explores recent concerns about the potential of a slow-down, or possibly even a reversal of the process of regionalism and interregionalism. Marshall Clark and Juliet Pietsch analyse the changing dynamics of the Indonesian elite's attitude towards the ASEAN integration process. At the core of these dynamics is Indonesia's growing international profile, reflected in its membership of the G20 and its increasing centrality in the US security discourse. Indonesian elites are growing frustrated at ASEAN's reluctance to move towards a more institutionalized form of cooperation. Concurrently, other ASEAN members worry about the interest that extra-regional powers devote to their bilateral relations with Indonesia as opposed to ASEAN as a whole, and are concerned about its potential disengagement from ASEAN. While it is uncertain that Indonesia's 'rise' will be of the magnitude predicted in certain quarters, the preservation of the principle of ASEAN centrality largely depends on how Jakarta positions itself eventually. On the economic front, David Treisman identifies a comparable threat to interregionalism as the form of interaction favoured by the EU in its relations to Southeast Asia. His analysis finds that, from an economic and financial point of view, the EU would benefit more from engaging ASEAN members on a bilateral basis rather than as a bloc. The failure of the planned EU–ASEAN FTA, partly but not only motivated by disagreements over Myanmar's participation, is a case in point.

Despite the fact that the overall context of regional integration is very different from the EU and the obstacles to deeper Asian regionalism are well known, practitioners on both sides highly value relations with the other bloc as evidenced in this volume's last section featuring practitioners' perspectives. While the developments outlined in preceding sections do not augur well for the future of EU–ASEAN relations, as the three chapters of Part III show, the evolving perceptions of certain elites sheds a more positive light on the whole picture. In the words of Ngurah Swajaya, the Indonesian Ambassador to the ASEAN Committee of Permanent Representatives, 'there is a lot [ASEAN and the EU] can learn from each other.'[1] This indicates a growing openness towards the sharing of experiences as compared with the past decade. Symptomatically, Ambassador Swajaya even presented the transfer process as already underway: 'We are learning a lot from the EU.'[2] Also, a certain relaxation has occurred in the understanding by ASEAN elites of the principles of non-interference and national sovereignty, which had been at the core of the organization from its inception, although this is more clearly the case with the original members of ASEAN rather than the newcomers that acceded in the 1990s. While this change remains very modest in scope, it opens the way for ASEAN to become a more institutionalized entity. The signing of the ASEAN Charter confirms this tendency. Natalia Chaban, Lai Suet-yi and Karima Abidat explore the perceptions of the EU in Southeast Asia and argue that the EU's role is misunderstood and underestimated due to its own failure to communicate itself effectively. Consequently, they suggest a strategy for EU public diplomacy that emphasizes dialogue and distances itself from 'monologue' practices.

While analyses focusing on the EU as a model are routinely framed in terms of the opposition between 'networked regionalism' versus supranationalism, the contributors to this section – Part III – identify specific areas where ASEAN could usefully adopt EU practices, namely human rights protection and energy security. Rachminawati and Anna Syngellakis point to the slow learning curve that ASEAN has gone through in its attempts to integrate human rights into its law and policy. Hence, they suggest that ASEAN should use the EU learning process in the area as a model to optimize its mechanisms for human rights protection, in particular in the aftermath of the establishment of an ASEAN Human Rights Body. William Kucera then observes that ASEAN governments still adopt a traditional approach to energy security based on national self-reliance, which remains largely inefficient. His contribution explains the benefits of a potential accession of ASEAN members to the Energy Charter Treaty (ECT), a multilateral legal framework that facilitates cross-border investment, diversification of supplies and the introduction of new technology across the energy cycle. It is argued that the accession to the charter will enhance energy security by limiting political risks and encouraging private financing for energy projects. This example could provide inspiration for the EU when framing its policies towards Southeast Asia, which, as Xavier Nuttin notices, still remains underdeveloped.

While the scholarly contributions assess the state of interregional cooperation, practitioners have a central role to play in the development of political relations. Thus, a special section – Part IV – is reserved for three practitioners from both regional blocs with direct experience in the Brussels–Jakarta relationship to whom we remain indebted for their insider analyses: Ambassador Ong Keng Yong, one of the most forward-looking secretary-generals in the history of ASEAN, Mr Willem Blankert, EU special adviser to the ASEAN secretariat, and Mr Xavier Nuttin, European Parliament official in charge of Southeast Asia. The overall optimism expressed in their respective analyses augurs well for future EU–ASEAN relations.

This volume draws on the expertise of authors from different backgrounds in an effort to offer a nuanced interdisciplinary perspective on EU–ASEAN relations. An international conference on 'EU–ASEAN relations', held at Monash University in Melbourne in November 2009, organized jointly by the Monash European and EU Centre (MEEUC) and the Monash Asia Institute (MAI), brought together experts from both academic and policy circles. The contributors to this volume are practitioners and academics from different disciplines, including political science, law, economics and media studies. These experts are from Europe, Southeast Asia and Oceania, ensuring that a diversity of perspectives is integrated within the volume. Collaborative works, in particular joint authorship of chapters, were encouraged. Felicitously, the selection of authors displays a perfect gender balance.

A final word of gratitude goes to MEEUC and MAI for generously funding the international conference that served as a basis for this volume, as well as to the Konrad Adenauer Foundation and – again –MEEUC for its financial support for the publication project. Very special thanks go to Professor Pascaline Winand, the director of MEEUC at Monash University, for wholeheartedly and enthusiastically lending her support to this project.

Notes

1. Ambassador Ngurah Swajaya's intervention at the event 'Making Sense of the Asian Century: Indonesia's ASEAN Priorities', organized by Friends of Europe, Hotel Sofitel, Brussels (Belgium), 14 April 2011.
2. Idem.

Part I
ASEAN and the EU Today

1
The Context of EU–ASEAN Relations: Trials and Tribulations of Regionalism in Post-Cold War Europe and Asia

Douglas Webber

Introduction

It is a common view that the divergences between European and Asian regionalism outweigh their similarities. Compared with its Asian counterpart(s), European regionalism is much more highly institutionalized (at least in a formal-legal sense) and much more demanding in terms of the criteria that a candidate state must meet to qualify for membership. Compared with the Association of Southeast Asian Nations (ASEAN), the European Union (EU) was historically also more inclusive in as far as, prior to the end of the Cold War, it organized all the big non-Communist European powers (at least once the UK joined in 1973), while ASEAN did not integrate the economically most highly developed non-Communist Asian states, first and foremost Japan.

For all their other divergences, however, regional integration processes in Europe and Asia share common historical origins: they have their roots to a large extent in the Cold War, in the perception among the leaders of the non-Communist states (in Europe in the 1950s and in Southeast Asia as the Vietnam War raged from the mid-1960s to the mid-1970s) that they had to cooperate and to overcome their internal rivalries in the face of a common external threat to their security. During the Cold War, ASEAN and its member states also had closer diplomatic relations with the EU than with the Communist states in Asia. The ties between the two organizations go back as far as 1973. Indeed, the EU was the first and, for a long time – along with Australia, New Zealand, Canada, the USA and Japan – one of the few 'dialogue partners' of ASEAN. Regular meetings between EU and ASEAN delegations began as far back as 1980.

Given the historical origins of the EU and ASEAN, the end or winding down of the Cold War raised fundamental questions about the future of regional cooperation and integration in both Asia and Europe.[1] Naturally, not all recent developments in European and Asian regionalism are attributable to this one variable. Thus, one other important dynamic that has fostered the growth of regionalism is the growing crisis of multilateral trade liberalization negotiations, which has spawned a growing number of initiatives to liberalize trade on a bilateral, regional or even interregional basis. The analysis presented in this chapter will suggest, however, that the trajectory followed by regional integration in Europe and Southeast and East Asia over the last two decades can be largely attributed to the end, or 'thawing out', of the Cold War. In turn, this geopolitical earthquake has had important – mainly negative – consequences for the capacity of the EU and ASEAN to cooperate. First, it has made both regional organizations relatively more preoccupied with their own region and immediate neighbourhood than otherwise would have been the case – the EU with itself and post-Communist Europe and ASEAN with Southeast and the wider Asia. Second, while it has facilitated the enlargement of both organizations, it has complicated and weakened efforts to forge closer or 'deeper' political integration, thus making it politically less feasible for the two bodies to engage in genuine *interregional* cooperation.

Regional integration and the end of the Cold War in Europe and Asia

The end of the Cold War may be regarded as comprising three components or levels. At the level of ideology, it involved the effective abandonment of the project or aspiration of building a political system in which the Communist Party would exercise a monopoly of political power and an economic system based on state ownership and comprehensive economic planning. In the real political world it involved the termination of Communist one-party rule, and in the real economic world the privatization of property and the liberalization of economic activity and creation of markets.

The end of the Cold War came very swiftly and abruptly in Europe. Within a period of just over two years, all of the Communist regimes in Europe collapsed and most of the former Soviet bloc embarked on a transition to market economics and – more or less – liberal democratic politics. In Asia, the end or winding-down of the Cold War has been a longer, more gradual and more attenuated process. Ideologically and in economic-systemic terms, the Cold War is arguably over, but, in as far as the Communist one-party regimes in Asia have all survived, important political vestiges of the Cold War remain, as do two Cold-War-rooted issues – the separation of North and South Korea, and of China and Taiwan – that constitute significant actual or latent threats to regional peace and stability. The contrasting tempos at which the Cold War ended or wound down meant that this process had a more dramatic impact on the agenda of regional integration in Europe than in Asia. Nonetheless, albeit at a different pace and in somewhat different forms, the end of the Cold War has generated fundamentally similar issues which regional organizations in both Europe and Asia have been forced to confront over the last 20 years and with which they are still grappling today. These issues are basically five-fold and they relate to:

(1) changing (actual or prospective) regional distributions of power;
(2) pressures for, and in culturally plural and divided states the fallout from, democratization;
(3) economic and financial globalization;
(4) the enlargement or 'widening' and institutional reform or 'deepening' of existing regional organizations;
(5) the emergence of US-led unipolarity in international military affairs.

Changing regional distributions of power

In both regions, the end of the Cold War has involved very important shifts in the actual or prospective distribution of inter-state power. In Europe, the collapse of the Soviet bloc hugely diminished the threat posed by Soviet Communism, but it immediately raised the spectre of German reunification and the issue of whether a united Germany would be much more powerful than any other Western European state. In Asia the rapid economic growth that began to develop in China following the market-oriented reforms introduced by Deng Xiaoping raised the spectre of future Chinese domination of East Asia.

The post-World War II division of Germany had facilitated West European integration by reducing the old Federal Republic to roughly the same demographic size as the other big West European powers (France, the UK and Italy). Starting in November 1989, the extremely rapid process of German reunification raised strong fears among other EU member states as to whether the new united Germany would remain committed to the goal of closer European integration and/or aspire to becoming a hegemonic regional power. Within days of the fall of the Berlin Wall and after Chancellor Helmut Kohl announced his 10-point plan for German reunification in the German Parliament in late November 1989, French President François Mitterrand was speculating ominously about a possible 'reversal of alliances' in Europe, whereby France, the UK and Russia would form a coalition to balance and counter the power and conceivable hegemonic plans of a future united Germany (Attali, 1995; Dyson and Featherstone, 1999; Genscher, 1995; Schabert, 2002, pp. 418–422). However, Mitterrand's blandishment of this threat in his meetings with German leaders was tactical. His goal and that of most other EU governments (other than the British) was to contain German power by embedding the united Germany in a more tightly integrated Europe, in particular by accelerating the introduction of a single European currency. There was already a blueprint for this but, for domestic-political reasons, Kohl was reluctant to accept it, and a concrete timetable for its timetable had yet to be agreed. For Mitterrand, this was the project that best served the goal of tying down German power, because the Deutsche Mark was, in his view, Germany's functional equivalent to a nuclear weapon. Under intense pressure after his 10-point speech to make a concrete gesture to underline the Federal Republic's continuing commitment to the European cause, Kohl effectively signed up to the single currency at the European Council meeting in Strasbourg in December 1989. The euro may thus be seen as the product of an at least implicit Franco-German bargain whereby France consented to German reunification in exchange for Germany's agreeing to give up the Deutsche Mark. In this sense, the prospect of German reunification and the shift in the distribution of power in Europe it was thought this would produce led directly to the realization of the most significant post-Cold War project to forge closer European integration.

In the light of China's demographic preponderance in East Asia, the very rapid growth of the Chinese economy since the 1980s, especially when projected into the future, raised similar fears in East Asia concerning China's future regional role to those provoked by the prospect of German reunification in Europe. Like Germany's neighbours in Europe, China's neighbours have been confronted with the choice of whether to react to the rise of post-Mao China by trying to balance its power by coalescing against it, to 'bandwagon' with it (that is to say, to acquiesce in its domination of the region) or – as most other EU member states preferred to do – to embrace and tame it by extricating it in a dense network of regional cooperation. With varying degrees of enthusiasm, with Malaysia and Thailand under Prime Minister Thaksin Shinawatra located more towards the 'Sinophile' end of the spectrum, and Indonesia and Vietnam more towards the 'Sinophobic', most neighbouring states have pursued an embracement strategy, as witnessed by ASEAN's involvement of China in the ASEAN+3 process. At the same time, however, the ASEAN states have hedged their bets by supporting a continued strong American military presence in the region. The creation – alongside the ASEAN+3 process – of the East Asian summit, in which India as well as Australia and New Zealand participate, also points to their pursuing a strategy of balancing Chinese power by incorporating India in regional cooperation.

At the same time, since the early 1990s, Chinese foreign policy has undergone a pronounced multilateral and regionalist reorientation, in part because, through its rapid economic development, China has become much more dependent on the international economy, but also because China aims to reassure its neighbours that it is a good and trustworthy regional citizen. More than any other single factor, the reciprocal will of China and its neighbours increasingly to engage each other has shaped the path taken by East Asian cooperation over the last decade (Webber, 2010, pp. 323–324).

The rise of China has also had a major impact on the EU's Asia policy. As the Chinese economy in particular has grown, China has become an increasingly important focus of the EU's, its member states' and European firms' diplomacy in Asia, while ASEAN's relative importance to the EU has declined. Relatively more government leaders, ministers and officials, and business leaders, have beaten the path to Beijing – and relatively fewer to Jakarta, Kuala Lumpur, Singapore and Bangkok. In this sense, the end of the Cold War has served to weaken EU–ASEAN relations.

Democratization pressures and fallouts

Especially in Central and Eastern Europe, where the Soviet army had imposed Communist regimes by force, the end of the Cold War also unleashed powerful forces of political liberalization and democratization. All of the former Communist regimes in Central and Eastern Europe underwent democratic transitions during a very short period in 1989 and 1990. The relationship between regional integration and democratization is, however, complex and double-edged. Each has, in different respects, affected the other.

In as far as it comprises liberal-democratic states and served as a 'beacon' for the Central and Eastern European nations, the EU by its very existence, nature and relative success in promoting peace and prosperity in Western Europe helped to foster the demand for political liberalization and democratization. Certainly, the EU subsequently assisted the process of democratic consolidation through various programmes that provided financial and technical aid to the post-Communist states, by making these states' future accession to the EU contingent upon their fulfilling stringent political criteria and then by accepting them in 2004 as members. In this respect, the post-Communist states followed a similar path to that taken earlier by the former right-wing authoritarian Southern European states: Greece, Spain and Portugal.

The political stability of many new post-Communist democracies was menaced, however, by the mobilization of ethnic, religious or communal cleavages. Where, especially under conditions of economic hardship and dislocation, they were particularly intense and the EU's means to constrain the new popularly elected political elites were limited, notably in former Yugoslavia, where democratization fuelled escalating inter-ethnic, inter-religious or inter-communal violence and bloodshed. The wars in former Yugoslavia negatively affected European integration in two ways. First, they lengthened the time horizons in which most of the former Yugoslavian republics could aspire to join the EU and thus put the brakes on the EU's widening. Of the post-Yugoslavian states, only Slovenia had become an EU member by 2011. Second, even though none of the former Yugoslavian states was then an EU member, the EU's manifest incapacity to intervene to put an end to the bloodshed plunged it into a grave crisis of credibility. The yawning gulf between the EU's lofty ambitions and the puny resources it could mobilize to accomplish them turned the 'hour of Europe' into its humiliation.

The relationship between democratization and regional integration in Asia is a great deal more muted than in Europe. The Communist political regimes in China, Vietnam, Laos and North Korea have all withstood the shock of the end of the Cold War while undertaking, as in the case of China, radical changes or, in the case of North Korea, only very limited changes in their economic systems. As is well known, ASEAN has always upheld the doctrine of mutual non-interference in member states' domestic political affairs and never required aspiring member states to be liberal democracies. Only recently, in respect of Myanmar, where the military junta allowed free elections in 1990, but refused afterwards to accept their results and put their winner under long-term house arrest, has ASEAN ventured to try to persuade a member government to implement liberalizing or democratic reforms.

Indirectly, however, the end of the Cold War had a powerful impact on authoritarian non-Communist rule in ASEAN's biggest member state and, *primus inter pares*, Indonesia. The processes of trade and financial globalization that the end of the Cold War accelerated (see next section) contributed to Indonesia's enmeshment in the Asian financial crisis that started in Thailand in 1997. More importantly, the end of the Cold War, during which the Suharto regime had been a critical anti-Communist bulwark in Southeast Asia, made the Clinton administration in the US much more indifferent to the regime's survival. The tough conditions attached to International Monetary Fund (IMF) loans to Indonesia helped to undermine Suharto's rule and pave the way for the country's democratic transition in 1998–1999. However, Indonesian democratization took the lid off various pent-up conflicts in Indonesia that the Suharto regime had suppressed by force. To the economic crisis were added the 'haze' crisis, which symbolized the post-Suharto regime's weak law-enforcement capacity, the East Timor crisis, and violent inter-communal conflicts in numerous parts of the archipelago, including Sulawesi, the Maluku Islands and Kalimantan. The preoccupation of the post-Suharto governments with the management of these crises and conflicts immobilized Indonesia's regional diplomacy, and for several years becalmed and discredited ASEAN. In the way that they created hitherto non-existent space for the political mobilization of inter-communal or inter-ethnic cleavages in Indonesia and former Yugoslavia, democratization processes had a destabilizing impact on regional political integration in both Asia and Europe during part of the post-Cold War era.

At the level of interregional, EU–ASEAN relations, democratization issues have also played an influential role. With the end of the Cold War, the EU's widening to include such states as Sweden have led it to intensify its efforts to export Europe's liberal-democratic political norms to other regions, including Asia. Consequently, since ASEAN's enlargement, the authoritarian character of the military regime in Myanmar has formed a tenacious obstacle to any intensification of relations between the two organizations.

Accelerated trade and financial globalization

Economic globalization, defined as the growth of the volume and velocity of cross-relative to within-border exchange of goods, services and capital, did not originate with the end of the Cold War. Fuelled by technological changes that reduced transportation and communications costs, and aided by the international institutional framework set up principally by the USA after World War II, globalization had been advancing for several decades before the Cold War ended. However, with the collapse of the Communist bloc in Europe and the opening of the Chinese economy from the late 1970s onwards, economic globalization accelerated sharply. Within no more than about a decade, the international economy expanded to incorporate a large part of the globe and a large part of the world's population, which had been marginal or peripheral to it for several preceding decades.

The Cold War had divided Europe and Asia more deeply than any other of the world's regions or continents. As post-Cold War intra-regional economic interdependence has grown, so governments in both regions have come under greater – but variable – pressure from transnational business interests to reduce cross-border barriers to economic exchange. In the EU, this pressure has fostered a large number of initiatives that build on the 1992 project adopted in the late 1980s and extend the scope of the single European market. The last of these was the highly controversial 'Bolkestein directive' to liberalize the internal services market. In ASEAN, business pressures for internal trade liberalization have been considerably weaker – there has been no effective ASEAN business constituency to sponsor such projects (Severino, 2006). Stronger pressure for such measures has come instead from Japanese and American multinational companies (Severino, 2003, p. 4). ASEAN government leaders have tried to harmonize foreign direct investment rules autonomously of domestic business interests for fear that otherwise such investment would be displaced to China. They did not have the luxury of waiting for pressure from the private sector, the former Singaporean Prime Minister Lee Kuan Yew is quoted as saying: 'Unless leaders lead, events will pass ASEAN by' (Severino, 2006, p. 230). This fear may also account partially for the ASEAN states' interest in the formation of an ASEAN-China free trade zone, although on the Chinese side this project may have been more strongly motivated by expectations of geopolitical rather than material economic advantage.

International financial flows have grown more rapidly than any other form of cross-border economic exchange. With them has come a greater potential for international financial crises that can disrupt intra-regional exchange-rate parities and trade. In Europe, the European Monetary System, a system of fixed exchange rates, managed to survive two bouts of extreme turbulence in the foreign exchange markets in 1992 and 1993. Although geopolitical motives were most influential in the birth of the euro, this project was also conceived as a means of pre-empting European currency crises and providing a solid underpinning of the single market, which could otherwise unravel under their impact (Issing, 2006). A single currency could also forestall possibly disruptive consequences for European exchange-rate parities of fluctuating levels of confidence in the US dollar and thus enable the EU member states to insulate themselves better against the effects of American economic policy.

Monetary cooperation in Asia was practically non-existent prior to the 1997–1998 financial crisis. It was this event that spurred first proposals for forging closer Asian monetary and financial cooperation, particularly because there was a widely shared resentment among political and business elites as to the timing and conditions of financial aid provided to crisis-hit countries by the IMF. If Japan's initial proposal to create an Asian Monetary Fund, opposed by the USA, failed, the ASEAN+3 countries in 2001 nonetheless adopted a currency-swap agreement (the Chiang Mai Initiative) aimed at warding off new such crises. The creation of an Asian Currency Unit, which could be a precursor to the regional coordination of exchange rates, also began to be discussed. Whereas in Europe trade integration historically preceded monetary integration, in Asia the sequence, shaped by the financial crisis, has been the reverse (Dieter, 2007).

This pronounced interregional divergence in the achieved levels of integration notwithstanding, money is the sector in which the most far-reaching integration projects have been realized following the end of the Cold War. But, under the weight of the financial crisis that struck in 2008, public attitudes towards the euro have grown more critical. Although the eurozone has expanded from initially 11 to 17 member states, the adoption of the euro by several longstanding member states (the UK, Denmark and Sweden) seems as far off as ever, and the repercussions of the global financial crisis that began in 2008 raised the issue of whether some member states may be forced to abandon the euro or even whether the eurozone itself may eventually collapse. At the same time, as indicated by the result of the 2005 French referendum on the proposed constitutional treaty, the unpopularity of the original Bolkestein directive in most of the old member states, increasingly critical public attitudes to immigration and the rise in various member states of national-populist political movements, market-liberalization policies have grown increasingly unpopular in Europe.

As Asia has weathered the global financial crisis much better than Europe, attitudes to market liberalization there are correspondingly more positive. During the 1997–1998 Asian crisis, in which notably the Malaysian government imposed strict controls on capital movement, this constellation was reversed. But there was no general upsurge of protectionism in Southeast or East Asia, and during the last decade a whole plethora of trade liberalization accords linking the ASEAN members to one another, as well as to the '+3' countries (China, Japan and South Korea) and the three additional members of the East Asia summit, was agreed. The coverage and hence the impact of these accords, however, is extremely variable (Ravenhill, 2008; Webber, 2010, p. 322). The level of take-up of the ASEAN Free Trade Area (AFTA) tariff concessions by companies engaged in cross-border trade in Southeast Asia is extremely low, so that ASEAN remains far from being, or being regarded as, a single market.

Enlargement and institutional reform

Enlargement is the issue with which the end of the Cold War has most clearly and unequivocally confronted existing regional organizations. In Europe, the collapse of the Soviet Communist bloc opened the path to Brussels for more than just the former Warsaw Pact member states. It reduced the constraints on the foreign policy autonomy of several other states sharing borders with the former Communist bloc, facilitating Austrian and Finnish as well as Swedish accession to the EU in 1995. German reunification had brought former East Germany into the EU already in 1990. Very quickly, most of the other former Communist states were drawn closer to the 'old' EU through the association agreements that began to prepare them for eventual entry, which occurred for the three Baltic states (Estonia, Latvia and Lithuania), Poland, Hungary, the Czech Republic, Slovakia and Slovenia in 2004, and Bulgaria and Romania in 2007. By then the number of EU members had grown during the post-Cold War period from 12 to 27.

At the time when the enlargement process was initiated, there was a fairly broad consensus among the existing member states that despite the innovations contained in the Maastricht Treaty (1992), the EU treaties had to be revised again prior to the entry of the former Communist states to ensure that with an increasingly diverse membership the EU would still be capable of making decisions. This conviction led to the intergovernmental conferences from which the Amsterdam and Nice treaties emerged in 1997 and 2000, respectively. However, the more strongly 'pro-integrationist' governments viewed the provisions of these treaties as inadequate. The Italian and Belgian governments, along with the European Parliament, insisted that they would not approve the Central and Eastern European enlargement without more far-reaching treaty changes. At the Laeken summit of the European Council in 2001, the Belgian, French and German governments sponsored an initiative to make a fourth post-Cold War attempt to revise the EU treaties. The task of drafting a new EU 'constitution' was assigned to a 'European Convention', which produced a draft document for negotiation in a new intergovernmental conference. The Constitutional Treaty that emerged from this process was approved by a majority of member states, but defeated in popular referenda in France and the Netherlands. The rejection of the treaty in two of the original six EU member states was a big political earthquake. After the French presidential elections in May 2007, a new treaty, with much the same substantive provisions as the Constitutional Treaty, was negotiated. After initially having been rejected in a referendum in Ireland and after the objections of the presidents of two of the new member states – Poland and the Czech Republic – had been overcome, the Lisbon Treaty finally entered into force in 2009. The deepening crisis of the eurozone quickly showed, however, that the Lisbon Treaty did not mark the end point of the treaty revision process in the EU. After the British government refused in December 2011 to change the treaties to facilitate closer fiscal policy integration in the eurozone, of which the UK was not a member, it seemed increasingly likely that European integration would assume an increasingly differentiated form foreshadowed by the original agreement to adopt a single currency and the Schengen Agreement dismantling border controls.

Compared with that of the EU, ASEAN's post-Cold War enlargement process was much more straightforward. The Communist Southeast Asian states and Myanmar had no Copenhagen criteria relating to democracy, human rights and market economics to fulfil and no large existing corpus of regional law that they had to adopt and be capable of enforcing. Nor did existing ASEAN states have to make financial transfers to the prospective new member states comparable to those made by the old EU member states to the poorer new members. ASEAN's enlargement process took place correspondingly faster than the EU's, notwithstanding the fact that Cambodia's accession was delayed by two years following a semi-coup in Phnom Penh shortly before the country's scheduled entry in 1997.

As in Europe, however, the end of the Cold War and growing regional economic interdependence, which the Asian financial crisis underscored, fuelled changes in the conception of the appropriate geographical boundaries of the 'region' that was to be integrated. Starting in the early 1990s, ASEAN started to develop and intensify consultations with nearby states. This process led to the first meeting of ASEAN+3 at the ASEAN summit in Kuala Lumpur in 1997. During the subsequent decade, efforts to forge closer integration within ASEAN and between ASEAN and the '+3' have proceeded more or less in parallel. However, ASEAN is evidently concerned thereby to preserve its separate identity, not to forfeit control of the regional integration process to the economically far more powerful Northeast Asian states, and not to be merged or submerged into a larger East Asian regional entity. Moreover, the discussion about and creation of the East Asia summit exposed divergent preferences among the ASEAN+3 states as to the boundaries and identity of the region – preferences that may be a surrogate for divergent levels of fear that China would come to dominate a 'smaller' East Asian grouping.

The ASEAN enlargement process also generated concerns about the organization's future capacity for joint policy making and action and – particularly because it brought into the organization some states with highly authoritarian political regimes – conflicts about the viability or appropriateness of its traditional norm of mutual non-interference in member states' domestic affairs. This conflict ignited over the Thai government's advocacy of the concept of 'flexible engagement' that, if adopted and practised, would have weakened ASEAN's non-interference norm. In practice, this conflict was won by the advocates of the *status quo* (Haacke, 2005). The same conflict recurred in the debate over the ASEAN Charter, which, adopted in 2008, was originally intended to facilitate closer integration in Southeast Asia and make ASEAN 'more like the EU', but the meagre outcome of the negotiations again pointed to a victory for ASEAN's most conservative, mainly new, member governments (Webber, 2010, pp. 321–322). The greater diversity in terms of economic development levels in the enlarged ASEAN also raised the threshold for market liberalization within the region. This concern – shared especially by the more strongly market-oriented member states, notably Singapore and Thailand – led to the economics ministers' approval in 2002 of the formulae of '10 minus x' or 'two plus x' for ASEAN economic cooperation to facilitate more rapid integration among subsets of member states. These formulae are ASEAN's functional equivalents of differentiated or multi-speed integration in the EU. However, to circumvent the higher consensus requirements for region-wide market liberalization in Southeast and wider East Asia, pro-liberalization states, led by Singapore, have more frequently reverted to the negotiation of bilateral agreements with willing partners both inside and outside the region.

Overall, while Europe and Southeast Asia are politically somewhat more integrated regions today than they were at the end of the Cold War, in both cases the process of widening has won the upper hand over that of deepening. As widening has increased the level of diversity in both organizations (as well as increasing the level of opposition to further deepening in the EU), this outcome has raised the obstacles to adopting region-wide common policies. However, enlargement in Southeast Asia poses a more acute challenge for ASEAN's cohesion than does enlargement in Europe for that of the EU. Prior to its post-Cold War enlargement, the EU had developed a large corpus of European law (the *acquis communautaire*) as well as supranational organs, such as the European Commission and the European Court of Justice, to draft and interpret it and the administrative capacity to enforce it through the bureaucracies of the member states. This heritage bolsters the cohesion of the EU by reducing the probability that member governments will be tempted or able to cheat and 'free-ride' on the others. ASEAN and its offshoots (ASEAN+3 and the EAS) share neither a large body of existing laws or binding decisions, nor strong impartial or 'third-party' organs of dispute resolution, nor, given the weak administrative capacities of some member states, favourable conditions for ensuring the implementation of joint decisions (see Hamilton-Hart, 2003). The 'ASEAN Way' of mediating conflicts by the informal exercise of peer group pressure had an uneven record even in the old ASEAN. The likelihood that it will suffice for this purpose in a bigger and more diverse East Asian regional organization – and that member states will therefore be willing and able to bind themselves to pursue common policies – is bound to be lower. Short of the development of stronger third-party/independent organs of dispute resolution, political integration in Asia rests on rather unstable, shaky foundations.

Unipolar American leadership in international military affairs

Internationally, the end of the Cold War had two relevant consequences that have shaped the course of important aspects of regional integration in Europe and Asia. First, with the Soviet Union having collapsed, Japan in deep economic doldrums during the 1990s, and Europe economically relatively stagnant and struggling to speak with a single foreign and security policy voice, the power disparity between the USA and any other state or bloc of states, especially in terms of military power-projection capabilities, increased sharply. The international balance of power tipped decisively towards the USA. Second, several international security crises that had their roots in the decline or end of the Cold War and the old bipolar world intensified or exploded. These involved multinational states (such as former Yugoslavia) that had been held together mainly by the fear of superpower military intervention; states (such as Saddam Hussein's Iraq) that could no longer be disciplined by a superpower patron (in this case the Soviet Union); states (such as North Korea) that no longer benefited to the same extent from superpower protection and had to make their own way in what they perceived as a hostile environment; states (such as Iran) that had rebelled against their former patron (in this case, the USA) and aspired to form a new pole in international politics; or terrorist groups (such as Al Qaeda) that had been formed to combat the Soviet occupation of Afghanistan and, having contributed there to the humiliation of the Red Army, now turned against the last remaining superpower, the USA.

These two consequences of the end of the Cold War posed one fundamental question to states and regional organizations in Europe and Asia: to what extent should they develop their own collective capacities to respond to such crises or rely upon the USA to manage them? Or, in the language of (realist) international relations theory, to what extent they should try to 'balance' the USA or 'bandwagon' with it? Both regions were divided over the issue of relations with the USA. Not least for this reason, neither has yet developed a significant collective capacity for crisis intervention and management that would enable it to act autonomously of the American superpower.

In as far as the old EU states were all explicit or implicit allies of the USA and virtually all of the post-Communist candidate states were eager to join the North Atlantic Treaty Organization (NATO) as well as the EU, relations with the USA should have been a less divisive issue in Europe than in Asia, where important vestiges of the Cold War have persisted. However, the first big post-Cold War regional security crisis, the wars in former Yugoslavia, provoked strong tensions between Europe and the USA as well as within the EU itself. The Yugoslavian wars made the Europeans acutely aware of their dependence on the US for the management of such crises and of their need to develop their own collective military deployment capacity if they wanted to safeguard their interests where these diverged from those of the USA. The military intervention in Kosovo in 1999, which was conducted overwhelmingly by American forces, persuaded the main EU member states of the need to develop a European rapid reaction force that could be deployed in crises in which the USA did not wish to become involved. Especially given constraints on public spending and the unpopularity of defence spending in Europe, however, progress in actually developing such a force has been painfully slow.

This decision, taken at the EU's Cologne summit in 1999, presupposed a consensus among the 'big powers' in the EU – France, the UK and Germany – that at least for some limited purposes the EU should not rely on the USA to manage security crises that affected European interests. The 1998 Saint Malo Declaration between the UK, the USA's staunchest European ally, and France, traditionally its most critical or ambivalent one, had paved the way for this initiative. Following the decision by President George W. Bush to invade Iraq, however, deep splits opened up in 2003 between those governments that supported the invasion and those – the minority, led by France and Germany – that opposed it. Underlying the different choices made on this issue by British Prime Minister Tony Blair and French President Jacques Chirac were fundamentally different attitudes towards a US-led unipolar world: Blair accepted the US's dominant position in international affairs and sought to influence American foreign policy from the inside; Chirac did not, instead aspiring to a multipolar world in which French foreign policy would be less constrained by the USA (Gordon and Shapiro, 2004, p. 179). The gradual decline of the Iraq War as a political issue mitigated the negative effects of its divisiveness on the EU member states' capacity to cooperate on foreign and security policy. France's formal re-entry into the military structures of NATO under President Sarkozy symbolized the re-creation of more stable transatlantic security relations, while, in contrast with the Iraq War, Iran's advancing nuclear programme and Russia's invasion of Georgia in 2008 exercised a unifying impact on EU member states. Still, despite its 1999 decision to launch the European Security and Defence Policy (ESDP) and its participation meanwhile in numerous humanitarian or peacekeeping missions, the EU is not much more capable now of deploying military force independently of the USA than it was 20 years ago – as the NATO military intervention in Libya in 2011 illustrated. If it is not, or only barely, capable of dealing with 'hard' security challenges on its doorstep, it is unlikely ever to play a significant role in providing such security as far afield as Southeast Asia – which is arguably what it would have to do to be regarded by ASEAN states as an equally important partner as the USA.

Divergent attitudes among the EU's big powers over the USA's world role, strong public reservations about defence spending and overseas military deployments, the relative weakness of the EU states' military intervention capacities and Europe's consequent continuing dependence on the USA in this sphere combine to place important limits on the scope for closer military-security integration in the EU. However, along with the perception of a common security threat posed by the Soviet Union and the settlement of bilateral territorial conflicts, such as that between France and Germany over the Saarland, the strong post-World War II American military presence in Western Europe, which secured the West European states against each other as well as the region as a whole against the Soviet bloc, created a very propitious environment for European integration in other policy domains. States tend not to integrate as long as they view each other as mutual security threats and are therefore mutually distrustful (Webber, 2007). In this regard, the conditions not only for security but also for wider political integration are much less favourable in Asia than in Europe. No common perceived external threat unites East Asia, numerous territorial conflicts pitch states in the region against each other, and the American military presence, while arguably fulfilling a stabilizing role, secures some states (Japan, South Korea) against others (China, North Korea) but does not provide a reciprocal security guarantee as it does in Europe, where EU membership is almost identical with that of NATO.

In this (compared with Europe) much tenser security environment, the potential for intraregional conflict and divisions over American unipolarity and foreign policy is much greater. Moves towards closer regional security cooperation, which began with the creation of the ASEAN Regional Forum (ARF) in 1994, have remained very limited. The most striking manifestation of such cooperation has been on the issue of North Korea's nuclear weapons programme, on which the regional big powers (while differing over the more fundamental issue of the regime's existence and survival) share at least a limited common interest in restraining Pyongyang. This shared interest led to the launching in 2003 of the so-called Six Party Talks, which involved China, Japan, Russia and South Korea, as well as the USA and North Korea as the chief protagonists. But these talks did not persuade North Korea to stop developing nuclear weapons and collapsed when that country withdrew from them in 2009. It appears at least doubtful whether they will ever be transformed into a permanent forum of security cooperation in Northeast Asia, as had occasionally been mooted.

The American invasion of Iraq did not polarize East Asia to the same extent as it did Europe, thanks at least partly to the relatively low-key stance adopted on this issue by China. In general, pursued as part of a long-term strategy of 'peaceful development', Chinese diplomacy appears to have aimed to avoid any major confrontation with the USA while forging closer ties with Southeast Asian states and reassuring them as to the benign nature of China's future foreign policy intentions. It has tried to advance this agenda by offering and concluding 'strategic partnerships' with several states and pledging to settle bilateral disputes peacefully. Chinese foreign policy towards Southeast Asia, the role it has played in the conflict over North Korea's nuclear weapons programme and its concern to avoid an overt confrontation with the USA have helped to keep East Asian security on a more even keel than it otherwise would be. However, uncertain to varying degrees as to how far they can trust an increasingly powerful China, most Southeast Asian states are hedging their bets by simultaneously maintaining, reviving or forming (closer) security ties with the USA or, like Singapore, pursuing a self-avowedly 'promiscuous' foreign policy aiming to develop close ties with as many big powers as possible and ensuring that they all have a stake in regional security and stability. Moreover, owing to conflicts over attitudes to the history of bilateral relations, the shifting bilateral balance of power, ongoing maritime territorial disputes and growing competition for access to indispensable overseas natural resources, Sino-Japanese relations remain strained. Perceiving a growing Chinese military threat to its security, Japan has strengthened its security alliance with the USA. China and Japan play such a central role in international politics in Asia that no major acceleration or increase in the level of Asian political integration can occur so long as their relationship has not improved radically.

Conclusions and implications for EU–ASEAN relations

The decline and end of the Cold War has profoundly shaped the course of regional integration in Europe and Asia over the last two decades. This chapter has identified and discussed five key challenges that this geopolitical turning-point posed for pre-existing regional organizations. The EU and ASEAN have responded to these challenges by widening to incorporate new members, extending integration into new issue areas, and revising the accords on which they are based to facilitate and expedite the adoption of common policies. Overall the two organizations' record in handling these challenges has, however, been uneven. Regional stability has arguably been enhanced by embedding the united Germany more deeply and comprehensively in a more integrated EU and engaging an increasingly powerful China in regional cooperation processes in East Asia. Moves by both the EU and ASEAN to liberalize regional trade may have helped to counter protectionist pressures at a time when global multilateral trade liberalization talks have marked time, but it is less certain that closer monetary integration in Europe, and as yet untested provisions for greater monetary and financial cooperation in East Asia, have better equipped either region to better manage financial crises. Indeed, in Europe the single currency may have exacerbated them. Neither organization or region has been able to decisively enhance its collective security crisis-management capabilities or lessen its dependence on the USA as the primary provider of 'hard' security, and both suffered severe, although not permanent, blows to their credibility as a result of their incapacity to respond effectively to the crises engendered respectively by the collapse of the Suharto regime in Indonesia and the wars that broke out in former Yugoslavia.

The challenge that these organizations have best managed is that of enlargement. Under different conditions and at slightly different speeds, both the EU and ASEAN have opened their doors to neighbouring, mostly post- or, in Asia, still-Communist states. The Central and East European enlargement of the EU especially constitutes an immense achievement, which may extend the zone of democratic capitalist stability in Europe from the former inner-German border and the Berlin Wall up to the borders of post-Soviet Russia. ASEAN has not only absorbed the Indo-Chinese states (Vietnam, Cambodia and Laos) but also piloted the extension of regional cooperation first northwards towards China, Japan and South Korea, none of which participated in Cold War-era Asian integration, and then, more hesitantly, westwards towards India and southwards towards Australia and New Zealand as well.

Hitherto, the post-Cold War enlargements have not come at the cost of the 'depth' of integration in either region. In particular, in Europe the reunification of Germany actually precipitated a deepening of European integration by facilitating and accelerating the introduction of the euro, which is now the currency of 17 of the 27 EU member states. By and large, however, in both regions the enlargement process has outpaced that of the reform of pre-existing decision-making procedures and norms. The probability that in the long term the member states of the enlarged regional organizations will be able to adopt effective common policies under existing norms and procedures, or alternatively to reach a consensus to reform decision-making norms so that such policies could be adopted, or even implemented, has declined with enlargement. This is especially the case in Asia, where the levels of socio-economic and political diversity, and therefore also potential divergences of interest between states, are higher than in Europe and the capacity of regional organizations to ensure the compliance of member states with common policies or decisions, where it has been possible for them to be adopted, is lower.

In the EU, growing decision-making deadlock as a consequence of the priority that enlargement has effectively enjoyed over institutional reform would exacerbate an already existing imbalance between 'negative integration' (the abolition of barriers to cross-border exchange) and 'positive integration' (the development of common policies that intervene in and correct the workings of the market) (Scharpf, 1999, pp. 43–83). By making the adoption of common policies more difficult, enlargement without corresponding institutional reform militates against further 'positive integration'. But it leaves the scope for greater 'negative' (i.e. market-liberalizing) integration largely intact because, under the EU treaties, the European Commission and the European Court of Justice (ECJ) have significant powers to liberalize markets without having to seek approval from the Council or the European Parliament.[2] If more and more citizens of the EU member states should come to believe that European integration serves as a kind of Trojan horse for market liberalization at the expense of values of equality and social justice, as the debate in France in particular over the Constitutional Treaty suggested (European Commission, 2005), this could jeopardize prospects for further and closer European integration or even the maintenance of the *status quo*. Poorer, less well-educated citizens of EU member states already view the integration process much more sceptically than others (Fligstein, 2008).

The challenges generated by the end of the Cold War and the way in which the EU and ASEAN have tried to deal with them have had important implications for the two organizations' relationship. First, as a consequence of these challenges, each has become more preoccupied with 'home' and/or its immediate neighbourhood. In other words, they have become more self-absorbed and introspective. In relative terms, the (human, financial and other) resources available to them to develop and expand their bilateral relationship have diminished. Second, the failure of the two organizations to strengthen their decision-making capabilities at the same pace as they have expanded and become more diverse has made it more difficult for them to agree on and pursue a common policy towards each other. Neither does the EU have a common ASEAN or Southeast Asia policy, except in trade, nor, less still, does ASEAN have a common EU or European policy. Moreover, to the extent that the new member states of both organizations are less world-market-oriented than the old ones and have a commensurately weaker stake in the promotion of economic links with the other region, enlargement has tended to reduce the importance that each side attaches to the bilateral relationship. However, the fact that, unlike ASEAN, the EU has a common external trade policy does mean that when EU–ASEAN trade liberalization talks failed in 2009, the EU was able to shift its strategy from negotiating with ASEAN as a whole to negotiating with individual ASEAN member states, starting with the one with the most open economy – namely Singapore. No similar option existed *vis-à-vis* the EU for ASEAN. Third, the meteoric rise of China has prompted not only ASEAN but also the EU and its member states to deploy a relatively larger share of their diplomatic resources to engaging and developing ties with Beijing – increasingly, and at ASEAN's expense, the EU's Asia policy has tended to become its China policy (or policies), and vice versa. As ASEAN's combined output is not much greater than that of South Korea alone and makes up little more than one-tenth of the East Asian economy, it is scarcely surprising that the EU's economic diplomacy has become increasingly focused on Northeast Asia as opposed to Southeast Asia. In the long term the ASEAN states are likely to be able to deal with the EU on more equal terms only by linking up their economies and cooperating more closely with their economically far larger northern – Chinese, Japanese and South Korean – neighbours. This process began with the creation of ASEAN+3 after the Asian financial crisis (Webber, 2010). However, it did not get very far in the ensuing decade, and the obstacles to the development of an East Asian free trade zone or customs union – not to mention a politically much more integrated East Asia – remain very daunting indeed.

The foregoing analysis suggests that in assessing EU–ASEAN relations and their difficulties, it is critical not to overlook the wood for the trees. The obstacles to their intensification and improvement lies less in contingent, conjunctural issues (such as the character of the political regime in Myanmar) than in more fundamental, structural factors (such as, in particular, the ways in which the end or winding-down of the Cold War has transformed the relationship of both organizations with the states in their respective neighbourhoods and made them relatively less important to each other).

Notes

1. The terms 'cooperation' and 'integration' are used interchangeably in this chapter.
2. Symptomatic of the ECJ's predisposition to attach greater importance to market freedoms over social rights was its judgment in the Laval labour dispute in Sweden in 2008, when it declared illegal a trade union blockade of a building site employing Latvian workers at wage rates below those stipulated in the relevant Swedish collective agreement. This ruling threatened to undermine the Swedish system of free collective wage bargaining that had been explicitly safeguarded in a protocol to Sweden's EU accession treaty. The European Central Bank is equally politically unaccountable in its conduct of monetary policy in the eurozone.

Bibliography

Attali J. (1995) *Verbatim III 1988–1991* (Paris: Fayard).
Dieter H. (2007) 'The future of monetary regionalism in Asia', in H. Dieter (ed.), *The Evolution of Regionalism in Asia: Economic and Security Issues* (Abingdon and New York: Routledge), 123–142.
Dyson K. and Featherstone K. (1999) *The Road to Maastricht: Negotiating Economic and Monetary Union* (Oxford: Oxford University Press).
European Commission (2005) *The European Constitution: Post-referendum Survey in France* (Brussels: European Commission).
Fligstein N. (2008) *Euro-Clash: The EU, European Identity, and the Future of Europe* (Oxford: Oxford University Press).
Genscher H.-D. (1995) *Erinnerungen* (Berlin: Siedler).

Gordon P.H. and Shapiro J. (2004) *Allies at War: America, Europe, and the Crisis over Iraq* (Washington, DC: Brookings Institution).
Haacke J. (2005) 'The development of ASEAN's diplomatic and security culture: Not beyond "flexible engagement"' in B. Fort and D. Webber (eds.), *Regional Integration in East Asia and Europe: Convergence or Divergence?* (London and New York: Routledge), 150–171.
Hamilton-Hart N. (2003) 'Asia's new regionalism: Government capacity and cooperation in the Western Pacific', *Review of International Political Economy*, 10, 2, 222–245.
Issing O. (2006) 'Monetary missionary: Interview', *Financial Times*, 28–29 October.
Ravenhill J. (2008) 'Fighting irrelevance: An economic community "with ASEAN characteristics"', *The Pacific Review*, 21, 3, 469–488.
Schabert T. (2002) *Wie Weltgeschichte gemacht wird: Frankreich und die deutsche Einheit* (Stuttgart: Klett-Cotta).
Scharpf F.W. (1999) *Governing in Europe: Effective and Democratic?* (Oxford/New York: Oxford University Press).
Severino R. (2003) 'The future of ASEAN economic integration', unpublished paper presented to a conference, *Regional Integration in Europe and Asia: Pasts, Presents and Futures*, organized by INSEAD and the Asia Europe Foundation, Singapore, 7 July.
Severino R. (2006) *Southeast Asia in Search of an ASEAN Community* (Singapore: Institute of Southeast Asian Studies).
Webber D. (2007) 'Trade and Security in East Asia: Political (non-?) integration in an insecure region' in Heribert D. (ed.), *The Evolution of Regionalism in Asia: Economic and Security Issues* (Abingdon and New York: Routledge), 145–159.
Webber D. (2010) 'The regional integration that didn't happen: Cooperation without integration in early twenty-first century East Asia', *The Pacific Review*, 23, 3, 313–334.

2
The EU and Non-Traditional Security in Southeast Asia

Naila Maier-Knapp

Introduction

To the states of Southeast Asia, national security has always been a game played within two arenas. The internal security dimension has been the prerogative of the state, and the external security dimension has been subject to the involvement of external powers and the institutional peace emergent from the creation of the Association of Southeast Asian Nations (ASEAN) in 1967. In both arenas, military power has been an important variable for ordering the political realm and securing stability. The Asian financial crisis of 1997/1998 slightly shifted the state- and military-centric view, and altered the threat perceptions and the responsive and cooperative understandings of the states in the region. First, the crisis demonstrated Southeast Asia's dependency on external actors and the need to create intraregional structures to supplement the international institutions. Second, the crisis accounted for the fall of the Indonesian and Thai governments and, hence, questioned the utility of the traditional concept of security along the lines of military power for state survival.[1]

Security threats from within were no longer considered to be emanating from ethno-nationalist insurgent groups nor confined to national boundaries. The late 1990s marked a time in the region when old and new aspects of security came together, and the conceptual upheaval paralleled the growing international discourse on human security[2] and humanitarian intervention. However, Southeast Asian states remained apparently unaffected by the shift in the security referent that this discourse implied (Evans, 2004) – that is, the shift away from the state as the security referent, and the military as the only security provider. Instead, the international debate appeared to be an opportunity for the military in many Southeast Asian countries to cement itself as the prime and sometimes sole security provider for the nation-state as a whole (Emmers, 2004). Amitav Acharya has argued that this development has also been a result of the state limiting the political space for civil society to develop into an alternative non-state security provider supplementing state responsibilities (Acharya, 2006, p. 248).

While Japan and Thailand have been receptive to the concept of human security and its normative implications (Evans, 2009), most Southeast Asian and East Asian states, in particular China, have been reluctant to adopt this concept. From a Western perspective, the concept connotes the centralization of human rights and the aversion to the state as the centre-point of security. Alternatively, East Asian states endorsed the notion of non-traditional security (NTS) that comprises the evolution and expansion of security threats in the post-Cold War era. On the regional level, this trend is manifest within the various East Asian fora, such as the ASEAN summit or the ASEAN Regional Forum (ARF), where NTS has become a respectable and viable concept to classify a broad range of regional stability and security concerns that are sometimes located in the socio-economic realm. Despite its controversial status within East Asia, in recent years, human security has become more relevant in the aforementioned fora, but is neither explicitly mainstreamed in the output of these fora nor implemented in a people-inclusive manner on the domestic level in the Southeast Asian states who are members of these fora.

Non-traditional security in Southeast Asia and the European Union

NTS is a vague concept that primarily possesses the utility to distinguish between traditional security threats, that is, state-versus-state threats, and new forms of security threats that have been increasingly unveiled after the Cold War. However, it does not offer any further differentiation. It does not exclude traditional security means and does not compel the usage of non-robust and non-military measures. It considers threats to be from both within and outside a state (Capie and Evans, 2007, p. 174).

NTS is a broad concept that is used in the various multilateral fora of the East Asian region, because it represents a concept that many of the participating states can relate to and agree on. The notion appeals to Southeast Asia because of its utility as an umbrella concept to address a broad range of challenges to the region. Furthermore, it manages to incorporate both the state and the individual in society as the security referents. It is a concept that, due to its extensiveness, prevents weaknesses that might enable non-state actors to attack the states' activities. In turn, it is this comprehensiveness which questions the people-oriented as well as analytical value of it. Furthermore, it does not offer safeguards for securitization *à la* Copenhagen School[3] and, for instance, may be utilized for state survival of non-democratic regimes. Ralf Emmers has raised the concern that, despite the concept's theoretical inclusion of non-state actors, Southeast Asian states seem to have instrumentalized the concept of securitizing and reaffirming the state's central role in providing security and being the final referent of security (Emmers, 2004).

This possibility of undemocratic and illiberal abuse of the concept is the core explanation behind the European Union's (EU) scepticism towards NTS. This concept of threats may counteract the EU's principled dialogue and cooperation with and within Southeast Asia. As a political entity based on liberal-democratic principles and human rights, the EU ardently projects these core norms and values onto the international level.

> The EU's action on the international scene is guided by the principles that inspired its own creation, development and enlargement, and which it seeks to advance in the wider world: democracy, the rule of law, the universality and indivisibility of human rights and fundamental freedoms, respect for human dignity, the principles of equality and solidarity, and respect for the principles of the United Nations Charter and international law. The EU seeks to develop relations and build partnerships with third-countries, and international, regional or global organizations that share the principles referred to in the first subparagraph. It promotes multilateral solutions to common problems, in particular within the framework of the United Nations.
> (European Union, 2007: Title V, Chapter 1, Art. 10a)

Simultaneously, the EU has to realize that in spite of the controversy behind this concept, NTS has opened a window of opportunity for the EU to establish an image of a political and security actor, as well as a normative influence in the region. First, by the potential to securitize, EU engagement in securitized sectors could be theoretically perceived to be a form of security actorness by the counterpart. Second, when the socio-economic sector becomes a security priority, this generally presupposes a crisis or an abundance of vulnerabilities in the sector. When domestic capabilities are insufficient for an effective response to achieve human and state security, external assistance may be needed. In these cases, the prospect of jeopardizing state survival by crises or vulnerabilities may outweigh concerns about the corrosive effects of external influence to the local normative context. External assistance is more acceptable and visible against the backdrop of crises. Building on this logic, the empirical analysis will revolve around instances of crises in Southeast Asia and sketch the European response to them. Third, the broad spectrum of NTS threats compels adaptation on the side of the military forces to remain relevant. Consequently, external actors with advanced technologies and professional militaries, such as those in some of the EU member states, are welcome assistants for security sector reform. From a Western perspective, such reforms are intrinsically tied to democratization and, thus, cementing the military's security relevance may hypothetically lead to a creeping power minimization of the militaries in political life. Mark Beeson and Alex Bellamy have observed that within the Philippines, Thailand and Indonesia, these reforms have so far revealed merely an embryonic and rhetorical retrenchment of the military from political power (Beeson and Bellamy, 2008).

These deliberations suggest that the EU's chance of increasing visibility and normative impact depends on the successful ideational internalization by the counterpart. This seems to be most efficient if internalization is not only sector-specific, but also embedded in a dual-levelled approach addressing the Southeast Asian nation-state as a whole. This approach is understood as a two-pronged elitist-societal cognitive process. The EU, which consists of the Commission and the member states as external actors, has in the last two decades pursued a multi-sectoral and multi-levelled approach with East Asia (as evidenced for example by the Asia-Europe Meeting (ASEM), new strategy for Southeast Asia in 2003 or current Partnership and Cooperation Agreements, among others). The EU constitutes one of the most credible external partners in conveying norms, because it actually lives them. That is, it practises and promotes them internally, given its make-up as a mini-international sphere. In addition, the EU has adopted the concepts of comprehensive[4] and human security and has rhetorically committed itself to the linkage of security and development, whereupon reforms and political will are still lagging behind the security-development nexus[5] rhetoric (Youngs, 2008).

As a regional organization of developed and democratic countries, NTS categories in other parts of the world do not necessarily conflate with the EU's understanding of security. Christoph Schuck has compared the Human Development Index and the degree of political freedom and participation, substantiated by data from Freedom House, between the ASEAN and EU member states to clarify the diverging indicators entailing the difference in security understanding (Schuck, 2009). Therefore, EU engagement in a crisis-affected sector with security implications for a Southeast Asian country may be considered by both the EU and its counterpart as development assistance, whereupon, hypothetically, such actorness should be perceived as NTS actorness by the counterpart. It appears that NTS may have risen in prominence as a security concept in East Asia, but that its official use is still very vague, patchy and confined to its limited analytical value as an umbrella concept for a variety of issues.

The following paragraphs will elucidate the reality of the EU's NTS engagement and impact in three very different policy sectors. These are the financial, environmental and health sectors that have undergone phases of crises in some Southeast Asian countries and stimulated various regional integrative dynamics and debates in the multilateral fora of the region. Gauging the effectiveness of the EU as an actor with regard to material input-output and comparing its actions with the contributions of ASEAN and other external powers proves to be partially feasible and marginally meaningful, given the variety of sectors and the units of measurement. Therefore, to establish an understanding of effectiveness, the following paragraphs will address image building and norm internalization, whereupon the material dimension is also taken into account as the chapter presumes the material and ideational spheres to be mutually constitutive. The analysis will draw on social-constructivism to evaluate EU actorness, that is, actorness as a collective, from an elitist and public perspective, against the backdrop of NTS.

Analytical framework

The vast literature on the EU's cooperation and dialogue with East Asian states shows the prevalence of the international political economy (IPE) approach to understanding and analysing the relationship (Dent, 1999; Robles 2004). IPE possesses immense power to explain the overall relationship between East Asian states and the EU. However, in cases of sector-specific crises within Southeast Asia, where the analytical objective is to assess EU actorness on NTS from a Southeast Asian perspective, there is an opportunity for idealist approaches. In this connection, social-constructivism provides a deeper grasp of this kind of actorness and assumes that crises and potentially securitized sectors are subject to social and interpretive micro-processes.

This chapter presumes that the EU, as an international actor, is 'an entity that is capable of formulating purposes and making decisions, and thus engaging in some form of purposive action' (Bretherton and Vogler, 2006, p. 17). Following Charlotte Bretherton and John Vogler's definition, the EU is understood to be 'identifiable [and to be able to] aggregate interests, formulate goals and policies, make and implement decisions' (Rüland, 2002, p. 10). Arising out of Rüland's definition is the problem of identification and, thus, perceived actorness. This chapter acknowledges the efforts of individual EU member states in Southeast Asia, but concentrates on actorness based on one EU collective identity on behalf of the member states. This could be, for instance, in the form of the Commission or ESDP external activities. This simplification circumvents the complex discussion of the EU's internal multi-headed decision-making process, which has been discussed in detail elsewhere (Hix, 1999; Richardson, 2006), and simplifies the EU as a black box with a presumed specific consensus-based pacifist security culture and mixed toolkit (Maier-Knapp, 2007). This will allow a focus on the guiding objective, which is to assess EU's actorness in the three specified sectors within ASEAN from a social-constructivist perspective. From this theoretical view, the criterion of actorness in international relations remains conceptually docile and irrelevant if it is not identifiable or perceived by the sociological other, but is based only on one's own perception of actions.

Actorness becomes meaningful and verified if there are perceptions by both sides. These perceptions do not have to be consistent. In fact, diverging perceptions may crystallize and pinpoint the major problems within and between the actors that could be improved.

The methodology is twofold and follows a scheme that first describes the crisis and regional reaction in Southeast Asia, and then examines the EU's response and assistance provision. Subsequently, EU cooperative efforts in the respective sectors will be illustrated. These actions will thereby be filled with meaning by the perceptions of the Southeast Asian political elite and public. The latter represents the primary victim of the NTS threats, but identifying public perception is more complicated than establishing the elite's perception. The problems are the lapse of time of the crises and the lack of information of the crisis-affected Southeast Asian societies. Compared with Western societies, Southeast Asian societies have overall less access to the media and, thus, information about EU activities in the region – should coverage be provided – unless they are directly targeted by the projects. For a representative interpretation of the public's perception of the EU, the problem of time and accessibility compel a methodological mixture of document and media analysis during and after the crisis periods, as well as communication with the public to get a general feeling of what could be an overall perception tendency.

EU actorness in Southeast Asia

In light of Southeast Asia's adoption of a broad view on security implying the employment of NTS and state centrality, the EU, in theory, should be perceived as a type of security actor in the region. The following cases will outline the Southeast Asian regional responses to contextualize and identify the limitations of EU actorness, and then elucidate the different aspects and limited utility of NTS in Southeast Asia for the EU after the specific crises.

Financial sector: Asian financial crisis

As previously mentioned, the Asian financial crisis of 1997/1998 was the watershed for revisiting Southeast Asian security thinking. It proved to be a catalyst for regional integration in the field of finance. Before the crisis, regionalism was confined to amendments of the Memorandum of Understanding on the ASEAN Swap Arrangements adopted by ASEAN member states at the ASEAN summit on 5 August 1977 in Kuala Lumpur. Alongside the International Monetary Fund's (IMF) involvement, the crisis stimulated responses at the national and regional levels. Within the ASEAN framework, the ASEAN Surveillance Process was launched to complement the IMF's global surveillance and maintain the regional and integrative dynamic of recovery. At the ASEAN Plus Three (APT) meeting in Chiang Mai in 2000, the

APT members agreed to the Chiang Mai Initiative (CMI) to monitor capital flows and initiate and strengthen regional surveillance, and swap networks and training personnel within East Asia. The CMI became the point of reference for enhanced East Asian financial cooperation. It expanded the previous ASEAN swap arrangements by allowing member states to withdraw double the amount they contributed and extend the time period. Despite the impact of the crisis having accelerated integration in comparison with many other policy sectors, the regional integrative dynamic within the field of finance did not lead to spillover effects into high politics. Furthermore, it remained intergovernmental and did not progress to any form of supranationalism.

EU Asian financial crisis actorness

From the outset, the sensitivity of this field confined regional integrative dynamics and external assistance. Nevertheless, there have been EU short- and long-term activities pursuant to the crisis. In the first few years post-crisis, beyond channelling a significant amount of financial assistance to the IMF (Brittan, 1999, p. 492) and declaring solidarity, the EU collaborated with Southeast Asia within the ASEM framework and initiated the ASEM Asia Financial Crisis Response Trust Fund, the European Financial Expertise Network, the trade and investment pledge, ASEM Public Debt Management Forum, the Kobe Research Project, the Bali Initiative, the symposium on combating underground banking and supervising alternate remittance systems, and the Tianjin Initiative on Closer Economic and Financial Cooperation. In spite of these collaborative efforts, the substantial financial contribution ranking the EU among the top five donors, and the continuous European investment and openness towards imports from Southeast Asia, it was not perceived as a major player contributing to the recovery either by the political elite or by the public.

The IMF is the pre-eminent external institution associated with the crisis and its recovery, albeit with a rather negative connotation. Some representatives of Southeast Asian political elites have been aware of the ASEM initiatives, but, generally, in their eyes, it seems that the EU remained invisible during and after the crisis (Interview with ASEAN member state official, 31 May 2010). EU activities related to the financial sector, such as cooperation on anti-money laundering or workshops on sharing best practices within the ASEM framework, present a minimalist EU influence. The sensitivities of this sector impede EU engagement. Current cooperative efforts in the finance sector are to be seen as an element of an international socialization process. They build on information exchange and confidence building, rather than on tangible collaborative efforts, to create an environment conducive to mutual understanding, and enhanced cooperation and harmonization, which may lead to tangible outcomes in global fora.

Before the euro crisis, ASEAN member states have always unhesitatingly marvelled at and aspired to learn from the EU Monetary Union. Despite some attractiveness of the European financial system, it has not replaced American influence in this sector in Southeast Asia. The EU is not regarded as an alternative partner to or ally against the USA in the international financial system, although there may be areas where the EU and Asia share more similarities with each other than with the USA (Interview with EU official, 18 November 2008). The EU's impact on the sector is less of a direct influence or actorness, but rather is considered as a monetary and financial model worth emulating occasionally.

Environmental sector: haze

The forest and land fires and the resulting smoke blanket over Indonesia and its neighbouring countries, referred to as the haze, is a common, annually recurring phenomenon in Southeast Asia. The fires' intensity and spread depends on the interplay of climatic variables (El Niño Southern Oscillation), and socio-economic and institutional factors associated with the agricultural and timber industry. Over the years, the haze from the fires in Indonesia has had considerable negative impact on the health, transport and economic sectors of Indonesia and its neighbouring countries.

ASEAN regional cooperation on transboundary pollution was initiated in the 1990s, with a direct reference to the haze since 1992. Subsequent years saw the creation of the Haze Technical Task Force (HTTF), and the adoption of the Regional Haze Action Plan (RHAP) in 1997 to strengthen regional capabilities and support the national level after the severe haze that year. In 1999, the HTTF approved the Operational RHAP (ORHAP), widening ASEAN's scope of action. On 25 November 2003, the ASEAN Agreement on Transboundary Haze was endorsed to provide a legal framework for regional cooperation, but as of 2011, it has still not been ratified by all ASEAN states. Indonesia, the main culprit of the haze issue, opposed binding itself to the agreement and, instead, initiated the Sub-Regional Ministerial Steering Committee on Transboundary Haze Pollution that invoked Indonesia's national counter-haze strategy.

Similar to the previous case of the Asian financial crisis, this transnational problem depicts the reluctance of young sovereign states to share sovereignty and legally allow external interference. Despite increased institution-building since the Vientiane Action Programme in 2004 envisaged the ASEAN Security Community, ASEAN Economic Community and ASEAN Socio-Cultural Community, ASEAN member states continue rejecting deep and hard institutions. State sovereignty, understood as state authority and control, is the underlying essence of this rationale. The difference in institutionalization does not necessarily delimit the EU's scope of haze actorness in the region, but it shows the EU's limited normative impact with regard to the Southeast Asian way of institution-building so far. This is not to paint the future black since, indeed, fora such as the ARF or ASEM, which are founded on the ASEAN way of soft institutionalization, are aiming for greater tangible output, which may require stronger institutions.

EU haze actorness

Before the 1997 haze crisis, the EU had already been aware of the forest fire issue in Indonesia. From 26 June until 3 July 1992, the Commission sent a Forestry Mission to set up fire protection mechanisms. In 1995, as part of the EU's Forestry Programme for Indonesia, the EU Fire Response Group and Ministry of Forestry launched a Forest Fire Prevention and Control Project with an initial budget of US$ 4,879,759 for a seven-year period (Dennis, 1998). Development projects with the EU have generally been approved by Indonesia while they do not undermine the political interests of Indonesia's governing elite. The Forest Fire Prevention and Control Project linked EU activities with the local community level in South Sumatra. It consisted of training, satellite monitoring, early warning and fire danger rating, and related activities in conjunction with the Indonesian side. The objectives were both short-term (giving information and advice on alternative land clearing techniques, along with warning letters from the government on punitive action and organizing public awareness campaigns) and long-term (creating job opportunities and raising the economic standard in rural areas) (Dennis, 1998). The project was followed by the five-year South Sumatra Forest Fire Management Project in 2003. While the Forest Fire Prevention and Control Project was a long-term pre-emptive collaborative effort, the EU Fire Response Group (EUFREG) was a direct response to the haze crisis of 1997 and lasted from October 1997 until May 1998. EUFREG was an assessment mission of the EU Directorate General for Agriculture in cooperation with the Indonesian Ministry of Forestry and Estate Crops that would, *inter alia*, act as a focal point for EU member states' activities and indicate the form of EU aid to be provided to the affected provinces. A handful of EU-funded projects implemented by non-state actors such as the *Deutsche Gesellschaft für Technische Zusammenarbeit* (GTZ)[6] were also visible on site.

Six years after the 1997 haze crisis, the EU initiated a worldwide programme that indirectly and pre-emptively addresses the haze. This is the Forest Law Enforcement, Governance and Trade (FLEGT) Action Plan of 2003, which is still in its nascent stage. FLEGT seeks to use the EU's economic leverage to tackle illegal logging, and to associate sustainable forestry management with good governance and the harmonization and reform of existing legislation in third countries. It is a legal verification and certification scheme that offers better access to the European market only to those timber-exporting countries that have signed a FLEGT voluntary partnership agreement (VPA) with the EU. FLEGT indirectly impacts the Indonesian forest fires by targeting the issue of forest governance. Both the EC on behalf of the EU and Indonesia consented to the FLEGT VPA in January 2007. While both sides are still negotiating the FLEGT VPA, local forestry information centres have been established in the West Kalimantan and Jambi regions, providing information transparency on forest governance. The bilateral negotiations with Malaysia and Indonesia are at an advanced stage and on 25 January 2010, the EU created the European Forest Institute in Kuala Lumpur as the regional headquarters for FLEGT. Other ASEAN member states have expressed their interest in FLEGT, with particular interest in the FLEGT licence that would legitimize and facilitate timber trade with the EU. This licence acts as the main economic incentive driving FLEGT and pushing states into accepting the normative conditionality that comes with it. Corruption is the central problem within the Southeast Asian timber industry. FLEGT minimizes this issue in the context of illegal logging within national territories. Environmental protection and conservation of biodiversity may also be achieved through FLEGT; however, the general problem of trading illegal timber from non-FLEGT VPA states, concerned with the labelling of modified wood products of third country origin, persists. FLEGT offers a motivation to trade legitimately, but guarantees neither the exclusion of illegal products nor the elimination of traditional structures of cronyism and corruption within the forestry sector.

The example of the haze shows the EU's global awareness and interest in tackling vulnerabilities and preventively defusing crises in remote parts of the world. Over time, the EU and its member states have shifted their focus from short-term to long-term projects to tackle the haze problem. Given the lack of current EU projects on the haze, it appears that the EU is currently more focused on addressing the underlying causes of the haze and assisting Indonesia in reforming the forestry sector. The projects may be limited, but haze-related EU actorness and influence on site commensurate to other external players should not be underestimated (Dennis, 1999, pp. 26–46). EU haze actorness is perceived by the Indonesian side as a form of comprehensive development assistance including a normative dimension. In Indonesia, beyond the assistance-receiving communities of the South Sumatra Forest Fire Management Project or political elite and timber industry interested in the FLEGT licence, the EU's direct and indirect actorness on the haze appears virtually invisible. EU haze activities have not contributed to the EU's political and security role in the region. This is not to suggest that the EU as a whole or the EU individual member states are not perceived to be environmental or developmental actors. It is rather that using the NTS frame in relation to the haze issue in Southeast Asia does not yield any significantly new insights into the EU's perceived actorness, whereas the concept of NTS in relation to the overall role of the EU as an environmental actor may provide more substance.

Environmental actor EU

Among the Southeast Asian political elite, there is a general normative implication when contemplating EU actorness in Southeast Asia. In particular, in recent years, parallel to the EU's fervent promotion of climate change onto the international security agenda, this perception is increasingly encompassing environmental standards. This image is relatively young and still in an emerging phase. It is less contingent on the EU's environmental activities with ASEAN, but rather dependent on the global developments and the EU's international engagement and identity in this field. Southeast Asian central decision makers seem more open to the European promotion of these environmental norms than to the EU's democracy and human rights agenda, whereby the environmental norms may imply an indirect diffusion of the EU's liberal-democratic principles.

The majority of ASEAN member states regard themselves as environmental victims of the West. Consequently, adaptation according to the EU style, eventually implying a compromise that may effectively undermine economic growth, is already facing resentment within East Asian economies. The EU's environmental impact will increase if the developing ASEAN member states manage to synthesize economic growth with sustainable development. The ASEAN Secretariat supports the greening of its member states but remains powerless in influencing the national policy strategies in this field. Here again, the EU may aspire to be a useful model, but it lacks convincing incentives for the political and business leaders of particularly less developed ASEAN member states to change their mindset.

FLEGT seems to be able to capture the ASEAN zeitgeist of what these states deem as adequate engagement in the environmental sector. It combines the economic and cost-benefit rationales of Southeast Asian leaders as 'chief executive officers' of their country with an ideational agenda. The latter is acceptable, given the economic benefits. Generally speaking, as long as the economy develops and the state profits, normative concessions appear to be to some extent tolerable, for instance, as was displayed in the signing of the EU-Indonesia Partnership and Cooperation Agreement of September 2009, or the EU-Philippine Partnership and Cooperation Agreement of June 2010.

Health sector: avian influenza

In the 1990s, Southeast Asian leaders had not been alarmed by individual cases of avian influenza reported in East Asia. The large-scale outbreak of the virus in the winter of 2003 generated national and regional efforts, of which the ones on the regional and wider regional scale were within the multilateral frameworks of ASEAN, APT and the East Asian Summit (EAS). At the 10th ASEAN summit from 29 to 30 November 2004, ASEAN leaders regarded this virus as one of the top threats and, in the following years,

ASEAN member states established the ASEAN Outbreak Response Teams, the Highly Pathogenic Avian Influenza (HPAI) Task Force, an ASEAN Expert Group on Communicable Diseases, a Regional Framework for Control and Eradication of HPAI and an ASEAN Animal Health Trust Fund. ASEAN member states committed to regional coordination, information sharing and collaboration to be implemented under the aegis of the ASEAN Health Ministers' Meeting and the ASEAN Ministers' Meeting on Agriculture and Forestry. The avian influenza has triggered East Asian institution-building that appears to lack the political support of the participants to be an effective regional level alongside the national responses (Maier-Knapp, 2011).

EU avian influenza actorness

The EU has been a substantial financial contributor to international organizations allocating funds to affected Southeast Asian countries (FAO, 2008). It supported the immediate national response plans of affected countries by channelling funds through the Avian and Human Influenza Facility (AHIF) of the World Bank, and is still continuing financial long-term assistance on avian influenza in the region. Bilateral EU activities with the region have been scarce, and the majority of European help mainly went through international institutions addressing the global dimension of the threat. Consequently, while this underlined the EU's preferred multilateral actorness, there have also been a number of avian influenza development assistance projects on the state-to-state level. International institutions administering the EU's funds impede the EU's actorness visibility and aid effectiveness, while simultaneously alleviating the EU's administrative burden.

Although this chapter has focused on the regional actorness level and considered the EU as a black box, it is noteworthy that the EU's limited actorness visibility also stems from the internal complexities, which could be in the form of conflicts over competences and competing member state presence parallel to the EU's presence in a third country. For instance, in connection with the avian influenza, it was expressed that there was room for improvement with regard to the Commission and the EU member states' coordination and information exchange with each other on their avian influenza external development assistance (Interview with EU official, 4 November 2009).

Within the AEMM and ASEAN-EU JCC or ASEM, interaction remained predominantly declaratory. At the 6th ASEM Foreign Ministers' Meeting (FMM) from 17 to 18 April 2004, the ministers decided on an ASEM Seminar on the Management of Public Health Emergencies 'and tasked ASEM SOM and coordinators to define concrete initiatives in this regard, including an expert meeting on controlling international epidemics' (ASEM Foreign Ministers, 2004, pp. 5–6). From 12 to 14 November 2007, China hosted the Workshop on Avian Influenza Control and, at the 7th ASEM in Beijing from 24 to 25 October 2008, Japan committed to finance an issue-based leadership initiative of Japan, the UK and China on the Rapid Containment of Pandemic Influenza. It was launched on the occasion of the 9th ASEM FMM in Hanoi from 25 to 26 May 2009, with Japan sponsoring a stockpile of 500,000 Tamiflu doses. The avian influenza response under the umbrella of ASEM shows that EU and ASEAN member states have moved beyond the declaratory level. The forum has progressed from launching an initiative concerned with information sharing to a tangible, pre-emptive security initiative.

The EU has been involved in both the fire-fighting and long-term responses (associated with technical and development assistance both at the supranational and bilateral country-to-country levels). The EU as a single international actor has been relatively invisible. EU presence among the affected public appeared to be, for instance, associated with implementing agencies or individual EU member state staff sharing their Western expertise and impacting the behavioural and normative changes in the region's poultry industry. Thus, while the EU as the financer becomes indirectly a promoter of behavioural standards and an important element in the chain of norm diffusion, it lacks visibility when compared with its member states.

Summary

This chapter has initially posited that NTS should hypothetically facilitate the creation of a type of EU politico-security image among the political elite and general public in Southeast Asia. In particular, this should happen in sectors of heightened sensitization caused by crises endangering state and human security. The case studies have illustrated the broad spectrum of pre-emptive and responsive as well as long-term and short-term EU collaborative action and verbal action with regard to the crises and respective sectors of governance. In reference to the social-constructivist perspective presented in this chapter, the case studies have demonstrated the semi-utility of sector-specific NTS cooperation and declarations in influencing ASEAN member states and EU image building beyond the economic dimension. Influence via actorness appears possible if economic growth remains uninterrupted and Southeast Asian states can yield benefits in comparison to the *status quo*.

Additionally, the case studies have highlighted the regional developments and some activities of other external actors and, hence, to some extent also contextualized EU actorness. At the beginning of this chapter, concerns were expressed about the military cementing its pivotal role through NTS. The described regional dynamics could not confirm this, but have indicated that NTS threats have strengthened the central role of the state in providing security. Furthermore, regional integrative dynamics in the sectors fell short of the people-dimension that the ASEAN Secretariat aims for. It seems that only in instances when the EU insisted on the discussion of this dimension did the Southeast Asian side officially acknowledge the people-dimension. Regional and interregional cooperative efforts on NTS seem to serve the strengthening of the governing elites.

Despite the remote geography and the relatively minor security importance of Southeast Asia to the EU, European presence and activities during the crises and in their aftermath have supported national responses and regional integrative dynamics and been commensurate to activities and assistance provided by other major Western development and humanitarian actors in the region, such as Australia, Canada and the USA. While the EU contributed in all cases and with very large sums involved, it frequently lacked on-site presence, and its actorness or perceived visibility was minimal in proportion to its efforts.

The chapter has demonstrated that perceptions of EU actorness and effectiveness have ultimately been a matter of interpretation by the political elite of ASEAN member states, and not the public. The general public in Southeast Asia is familiar with traditional state and security concepts. It is not accustomed to a political supranational creature such as the EU. The parallel engagement of EU member states and other external actors on site blurred the EU's visibility. The public particularly relates the concept of Europe to former European colonial powers in the region. It should also be understood that the financial crisis and the haze pre-date and, in fact, triggered the academic debate of NTS in Southeast Asia. Hence, elite perceptions of these crises (as documented in secondary and primary sources) should be considered as a snapshot which lacks the NTS debate and, therefore, is suggestive of the EU being a humanitarian actor or development donor rather than a NTS actor.

Finally, it does not appear that the EU or the Southeast Asian states themselves regard and apply the concept of NTS in connection with the management of NTS crises. It seems that NTS is used only to describe the type of threat or crisis rather than the response to these problems. The EU acknowledges the vulnerability of Southeast Asia to NTS threats and is fostering the security-development nexus and, therefore, pursuing approaches to assisting Southeast Asia in a comprehensive manner. Yet, since the EU only occasionally and patchily views Southeast Asia through a security lens, it does not see itself as a security actor in the region and regards NTS rather in relation to developmental and humanitarian actorness. The EU's self-perception is interrelated with the projection of its identity. In the light of Southeast Asia's volatile security environment, it is important for the EU and its member states to develop their security ambition in the region. They need to think more strategically about Southeast Asia in order for Southeast Asia to appreciate them as security actors. That is, the EU member states need to continue expanding their strategic capabilities and integrate these in a narrative that allows them to take part in Asia's security.

Concluding remarks

This chapter has shown that from a social-constructivist perspective, the NTS frame has failed to deliver any substance to the EU's politico-security actorness in Southeast Asia. The lack of official employment and altercation of the concept within and between the two sides suggests NTS to be limited analytically fruitful to describe specific EU security actorness. Nevertheless, the case studies indicate that the EU's sector-specific engagement is incremental and that, for instance, once the Partnership and Cooperation Agreements have been signed with some ASEAN member states to provide a legal and cooperative basis for joint committees, the likelihood of reciprocal influence on NTS may be increased.

However, one must be warned that even the successful conduct of the Aceh Monitoring Mission did not alter the low politico-security profile of the EU. After the mission, the EU was seen as a crisis manager and peace-implementer, but not as a security actor *per se*. Thus, one must be careful with one's ambitions. On the one hand, designing projects that accommodate the needs of the governing elites may putatively enhance one's profile and accelerate the 'aid bureaucracy'. On the other hand, it may strengthen certain power and normative structures that counter the EU's normative agenda in its external relations and, thus, call into question the EU's identity and actorness on NTS challenges.

Despite the challenges, the first visit of the chairman of the European Union Military Committee to the ASEAN Secretariat in October 2009, and his offer to share EU expertise in the fields of maritime security, disaster relief and peace support operations, should be seen as a positive signal to ASEAN and its member states. It shows that the EU as a collective actor is interested in establishing some form of security relationship and is keen to delve into the opportunity that certain NTS niches provide. It may also serve as the starting point for a deeper conceptual discussion of NTS and a process that can make Southeast Asia take the EU more seriously as a politico-security actor in the region.

Notes

1. By traditional security this article means the conventional way that states address security threats, that is, via the military.
2. When defining the concept of human security, the bulk of scholarly literature refers to the UNDP Report of 1994. The article adopts the definition of this document and conceptualizes human security as the ideal state of security of an individual. This implies the guarantee of well-being in the following spheres, for example economic, political, environmental, food security and so on.
3. Arguing in accordance with the social-constructivist approach of this article, the concept of securitization is understood as a speech act whereupon threat

perceptions are created inter-subjectively as defined by Barry Buzan, Jaap de Wilde and Ole Waever in 1998.
4. Comprehensive security is a post-Cold War security concept that addresses the multi- and cross-sectoral nature of security threats.
5. This article understands that the security-development nexus is strongly linked to the concept of human security. It perceives this concept in the sense that national and state security are intrinsically connected with poverty reduction and the provision of human security.
6. It is noteworthy that the GTZ and other EU non-state actors, as well as EU member states themselves, have been involved in assisting the combat of the fire and haze issue in Indonesia since the severe case of the forest fires in 1982/1983.

Bibliography

Acharya A. (2006) 'Securitisation in Asia: Functional and normative implications' in A. Acharya, M.C. Anthony and R. Emmers (eds.), *Non-traditional Security in Asia: Dilemmas in Securitisation* (Aldershot: Ashgate), 247–250.
ASEM Foreign Ministers (2004) *Chairman's Statement*. Paper presented at the ASEM Foreign Ministers' Meeting, www.aseminfoboard.org/content/documents/FMM6_ ChairStatement.pdf, accessed 18 November 2010.
Beeson M. and Bellamy A. (2008) *Securing Southeast Asia: The Politics of Security Sector Reform*, 6th edn (London: Routledge).
Bretherton C. and Vogler J. (2006) 'Conceptualising actors and actorness' in C. Bretherton and J. Vogler (eds.), *The European Union as a Global Actor* (New York: Routledge), 12–36.
Brittan S.L. (1999) 'Europe/Asia relations', *The Pacific Review*, 12, 3.
Capie D. and Evans P. (2007) 'Non-traditional security' in D. Capie and P. Evans (eds.), *The Asia-Pacific Security Lexicon*, 2nd edn (Singapore: Institute for Southeast Asian Studies), 173–178.
Dennis R. (1998) '*EU-Forest Fire Prevention and Control Project*'. Paper from University of Freiburg, www.fire.uni-freiburg.de/se_asia/projects/eu.html, accessed 10 March 2010.
Dennis R. (1999) *A Review of Fire Projects in Indonesia (1982–1998)* (Bogor: Centre for International Forestry Research).
Dent C. (1999) *The European Union and East Asia: An Economic Relationship* (London: Routledge).
Emmers R. (2004) *Non-Traditional Security in the Asia-Pacific: The Dynamics of Securitisation* (Singapore: Marshall Cavendish).
European Union Member States (2007) *Treaty of Lisbon*, www.bookshop.europa.eu/ eubookshop/ download.action?fileName=FXAC07306ENC_002.pdf&eubphfUid= 534817&catalogNbr=FX-AC-07-306-EN-C, accessed 12 April 2009.
Evans P. (2004) 'Human security and East Asia: In the beginning', *Journal of East Asian Studies*, 4, 2, 263–284.
Evans P. (2009) 'Human security in extremis' in S. Peou (ed.), *Human Security in East Asia: Challenges for Collaborative Action* (Abingdon: Routledge), 79–93.
Food and Agriculture Organisation (2008) *Funding and Donor Contributions*, www.fao. org/avianflu/ en/donors.html, accessed 5 March 2010.
Hix S. (1999) *Political System of the European Union* (New York: St. Martin's Press).

Maier-Knapp N. (2007) *Prospect of the European Union to become a Military Community: Analysis of the Major Nation-State Actors' Perspectives on the European Security and Defence Policy* (Christchurch: University of Canterbury).

Maier-Knapp N. (2011) 'Regional and interregional integrative dynamics of ASEAN and EU in response to the Avian Influenza', *Asia Europe Journal*, 8, 4, 541–554.

Richardson, J. (ed.) (2006) *European Union: Power and Policy-Making*, 3rd edn (Abingdon: Routledge).

Robles A., Jr. (2004) *The Political Economy of Interregional Relations: ASEAN and the EU* (Aldershot: Ashgate).

Rüland J. (2002) *Interregionalism in International Relations: Conference Summary*. Paper presented at the Conference on Interregionalism in International Relations.

Schuck C. (2009) 'Non-traditional security aspects compared: The European Union and ASEAN' in J.L. de Sales Marques, R. Seidelmann and A. Vasilache (eds.), *Asia and Europe: Dynamics of Inter- and Intra-Regional Dialogues*, 5th edn (Baden-Baden: Nomos), 335–350.

Youngs R. (2008) 'Fusing security and development: Just another Euro-platitude?', *Journal of European Integration*, 30, 3, 419–437.

Part II
(Inter)Regionalism in Danger?

3
Democratisation and Indonesia's Changing Perceptions of ASEAN and its Alternatives

Marshall Clark and Juliet Pietsch

Introduction

In many ways, Indonesia is regarded as one of the most important members of the Association of Southeast Asian Nations (ASEAN). It is for this reason that Indonesia's embrace of democratization, as well as the West's enthusiastic embrace of the world's third-largest democracy, has led to raised eyebrows in the region. Calls within Indonesia for the development of a 'post-ASEAN' regional strategy are also causing disquiet within the region. What will become of ASEAN and all it stands for, Indonesia's neighbours are apparently asking, if Indonesia's increasing dissatisfaction with ASEAN leads to more aggressive overtures to the West and other non-ASEAN members such as China and Japan?

Indonesia's neighbours do not need to be overly concerned with Indonesia's future foreign policy direction. We will argue that Indonesia is not yet fully committed to embracing a 'post-ASEAN' foreign policy. For instance, recent non-ASEAN initiatives to strengthen regional integration – such as the Asia-Pacific Community (APC) and the East Asia Community – have been politely, but not enthusiastically, received in Indonesia. Despite the attraction of a new regional gathering in the Asia-Pacific region, Indonesian elite opinion – the opinion of academe and the media in particular – towards regionalism remains focused on the important role of ASEAN. This is despite the fact that ASEAN, as well as its expanded regional arrangements such as the ASEAN Regional Forum (ARF) and ASEAN+3 (ASEAN plus China, South Korea and Japan) grouping, is widely regarded as an example of 'soft' or 'weak' institutionalism that compares unfavourably against the 'strong' institutionalism of other, more successful regional organizations, such as the EU. Consequently, within Indonesia the EU is seen as a better model for the enhancement of East Asian regional integration (see, for example, Prabowo, 2009). This does not mean, however, that Indonesia is pushing for a more 'EU-style' ASEAN. Rather, we would suggest that increasingly negative comparisons between ASEAN and the EU are symptomatic of post-New Order Indonesia's 'awakening' as a major regional and even global power, which is closely related to Indonesia's ongoing democratization process.

The primary aim of this chapter is to examine why there is a perception within Indonesia that the EU model is superior to the present framework of Southeast Asian regionalism. Important factors to be considered include: (1) the fact that Indonesian analysts and media commentators have become increasingly frustrated with ASEAN's organizational limitations; and (2) the attraction of the 'strong' institutionalism of alternative regional organizations such as the EU, which is regarded as being far more effective and 'people-centred' than ASEAN, with 'deeper' trade and security cooperation. In terms of participative regionalism, with more effective trade negotiations and security arrangements, there are already strong indications that Indonesia's foreign policy elite are increasingly prepared to look beyond the ASEAN framework (Rüland, 2009). Overall, this chapter will examine to what extent Indonesia's increasing dissatisfaction with ASEAN and concomitant interest in a so-called 'post-ASEAN' regional strategy is closely related to Indonesia's rapid and generally successful democratic consolidation. In examining this question, this chapter will take into account academic scholarship on the connection between democratization and regionalism.

Indonesia driving, and outgrowing, ASEAN

In a new policy initiative explicitly based on the lessons from Indonesia's previous 'confrontation' (*konfrontasi*) with Malaysia under President Sukarno, the Indonesian government under Suharto (1966–1998) wholeheartedly endorsed the formation of ASEAN. Consequently, during Suharto's New Order era Indonesia was heavily involved in the business of regionalism and ASEAN was treated as the legitimate exponent and embodiment of official regionalism in Southeast Asia. Besides being one of the original founding members, from the outset Indonesia has taken an active role in fostering ASEAN and developing its charters and precepts. Indonesian think-tanks such as the Jakarta-based Centre for Strategic and International Studies (CSIS) have provided a great deal of scholarly and policy input for the Indonesian government, greatly assisting it with its dealings with ASEAN (Hadiwinata, 2009, p. 66). CSIS also played an active role in establishing the ASEAN 'Track II' forum in 1988. Known as the ASEAN Institutes of Strategic and International Studies (ASEAN-ISIS), the members of this new forum have served as 'policy recommenders' to their respective countries for the advancement of ASEAN (Caballero-Anthony, 2005, p. 161).[1] This Track II forum has experienced a great deal of success in contributing towards various discourses on security in ASEAN, including the establishment of the ARF as the association's security flagship.

Indonesia was an active driver of ASEAN and its associated regional groupings for many of the same reasons as its neighbours in the region. In the first instance, Indonesia's endorsement of the formation of ASEAN was based on the widespread fear in the region and among Indonesian military leaders in particular of the possible threat of Communism to the stability of the region, which might in turn threaten national integrity (Hadiwinata, 2009, pp. 60–61). In reality, ASEAN primarily allowed the postcolonial nation-states of the Southeast Asian region to focus on the consolidation and protection of national sovereignty, as well as the fostering of political stability and economic development. In an effort to ensure that ASEAN became a regional ally to fight against the spread of Communism in the region, Indonesia attempted to impose its nationalist doctrines onto ASEAN (Hadiwinata, 2009, p. 61). For example, Indonesia ensured that concepts such as consensus decision-making (*musyawarah* and *mufakat*) and non-interference (*anti-intervensi asing*) became underlying principles of ASEAN and its operational style, the so-called 'ASEAN Way'. ASEAN's 'non-interference' policy effectively allowed Suharto's authoritarian New Order regime to remain firmly ensconced in power for decades, without significant intraregional censure or criticism.

In time, the political success of ASEAN began to contribute to its economic advance, which in turn presented an image to the world of a region not in turmoil but rather of one of development. According to Tarling (2006, p. 187), the stability that had been cultivated within the region, as well as the policies its leaders pursued, and the changing nature of international finance, was conducive to increasing investment in the region, no longer through government aid but from the private sector. However, ASEAN was faced with a new economic situation with the onset of the 1997 economic crisis, when talk of one or two of ASEAN's members joining the economic tigers of East Asia changed to talk of corruption and crony capitalism. Moreover, during the crisis, rather than working together, ASEAN leaders engaged in unseemly mutual recriminations: 'The Association itself stood impotent in the face of both financial meltdown and the growing internal political discord in its member states that accompanied it' (Jones and Smith, 2007, p. 168).

The absence of a coordinated regional response, according to Jones and Smith (2007), should have destroyed the credibility of the 'ASEAN Way' and its Southeast Asian application, let alone its application in the wider East Asian context, as in the ASEAN+3 grouping. This was not the case. The evidence of political and economic failure, not to mention the collective humiliation by essentially 'Western' organizations such as the IMF and World Bank, was reinterpreted in such a way that a call for greater regional solidarity emerged.

Indonesia, which was particularly humiliated by the disastrous socio-economic consequences of the financial crisis, was driven to take on a greater leadership role in the region. It spearheaded a democracy drive in ASEAN, including the 2003 recommendation that the ASEAN Security Community (ASC) should concern itself with 'political development'. According to Rüland, this democracy-driven claim to regional leadership was 'the expression of a deeply felt sense of entitlement severely frustrated during and in the aftermath of the Asian financial crisis' (Rüland, 2009, p. 397). In response, Indonesia was further humiliated by its neighbours. The post-1998 leadership vacuum in ASEAN was increasingly filled by Malaysia, Singapore and, until the 2006 coup, Thailand. Moreover, Indonesia was blamed for non-compliance with regional agreements such as the ASEAN Haze Pollution Agreement. Deepening Indonesia's feelings of inferiority, the International Court of Justice ruled against Indonesia in the territorial dispute with Malaysia over two islands off the coast of East Kalimantan (Sipadan and Ligatan). It is in this context that in recent years a growing number of criticisms of ASEAN have emerged. In the eyes of its harshest detractors, ASEAN has turned out to be 'a futile venture in useless regionalism' (Sukma, 2008, p. 135) and many have observed that ASEAN hasn't actually achieved a great deal. Yet to many of its supporters, 'the Association is the most successful instance of regional cooperation outside the European Union' (Sukma, 2008, p. 135).

Indonesia's push for regional change

Rizal Sukma of the Jakarta-based CSIS suggests that in the last ten years or so, any Indonesian critiques of ASEAN, and official calls for the spirit, if not the letter, of a 'democracy agenda' must be viewed in terms of Indonesia's own political transformation (Sukma, 2008). Since the resignation of President Suharto in 1998 and the demise of his authoritarian regime, ASEAN's largest member has been undergoing its own political development, that is, democratization. In this respect, in calling for democracy in Southeast Asia, Indonesia is projecting its own experience onto the region (Sukma, 2008). Certainly Indonesian perceptions of ASEAN, especially in the last ten years or so, need to be analysed in terms of Indonesia's own experiences of democracy. But despite the common-sense nature of this assertion, such an approach is actually quite innovative. According to Dosch (2008, p. 70), domestic politics are often completely neglected in the explanatory study of regionalism in Southeast Asia.

To cite one of Dosch's arguments (2008, p. 69), the most obvious impact of the wave of democratization within the politics of Southeast Asia 'has been the broadening of institutional settings for political decision-making', which has increased the accountability of governments 'and that has in turn allowed for the direct participation of a growing number of actors outside government, or inside the government but outside its executive branch'.

In the academic literature on the connection between democratization and regionalism, this style of regionalism has been termed as 'participatory regionalism'. Yet scholars have also noted that the realization of a more 'participatory regionalism' in Southeast Asia, one that engages civil society and pushes for regional conflict management, a greater transparency and rule-based interactions, faces considerable barriers (Acharya, 2003).

According to Acharya (2003, p. 376), there are a number of possible consequences of democratization for regionalism. First, democratization necessarily alters the domestic political climate on which regional interactions are based (as we have seen with the weakly consolidated democracies of Indonesia, the Philippines and, before the 2006 coup, Thailand). Second, civil society groups may have become irrevocably hostile towards regional institutions such as ASEAN, which have hitherto backed regimes that have excluded their participation (such as the authoritarian regime in Myanmar). Third, it is possible that regional institutions with authoritarian styles of leadership (such as ASEAN) could lose legitimacy and support from within the population of those member states that have experienced greater domestic political openness (such as Indonesia, the Philippines and, to a lesser extent, Thailand, Malaysia and Singapore). What is beyond doubt is that no longer can democratic transitions in Southeast Asia be ignored by an elite-centred and politically illiberal form of regional institutionalism.

In Indonesia, where the notion of democracy since the fall of the New Order regime has been, to a large extent, based on indigenous principles of harmony and consensus, no longer does the foreign ministry ignore the interests or criticisms of domestic actors. Indonesian calls for reform in ASEAN, therefore, must be viewed in terms of Indonesia's political liberalization. Nevertheless, as this chapter argues, in analysing post-authoritarian Indonesian perceptions of ASEAN, we must also be mindful of the historical specificity of Indonesia's experiences of security and regionalism. We must also be aware of the local impact of global trends and circumstances, such as the end of the Cold War and accelerating globalization.

Leading Indonesian academic commentators couch their analysis of ASEAN in a similar historical vein. For example, although Imran Cotan of Indonesia's Department of Foreign Affairs argues that ASEAN is Indonesia's most important regional organizational involvement, Rizal Sukma contests this view. According to Sukma (2009), it is not in Indonesia's best interests to put all its diplomatic eggs in the one regional basket. This is in large part due to ASEAN's sluggish response to the many great changes in recent decades, including new threats to state and human security, the wave of democratization throughout the region, and new and alternative models of regionalism. Indonesia's foreign policy initiatives in recent years – such as the Bali Democracy Forum (BDF), the G20 and strategic defence and trade agreements with non-ASEAN countries such as Australia, China and

India – indicate that in many ways Indonesia has already begun to formulate a more globally oriented foreign policy (Rüland, 2009).

Yusuf Wanandi, also from the CSIS, supports Sukma's critique. Wanandi is similarly frustrated by ASEAN's organizational intransigence, and he has long questioned whether ASEAN constitutes the right arena for Indonesia's supposedly 'neutralist' foreign policy. According to this view, to borrow Rüland's words, 'ASEAN membership has done Indonesia more harm than good and, in fact, stifled Indonesia's age-honored "free and active" (*bebas dan aktif*) doctrine' (Rüland, 2009, p. 384). Wanandi has also bemoaned the fact that Indonesia, smothered under the regional umbrella of ASEAN, cannot directly respond to new regional challenges such as China's surging economic growth, nor establish itself as the instigator (*pelopor*) or driving force of broader East Asian regional cooperation (Seminar 'Kaji ulang ASEAN sebagai sokoguru politik luar negeri Indonesia', 2008).

Over the last decade Jakarta has unsuccessfully initiated various proposals to take on a much more substantive role within Southeast Asia. We have already mentioned Indonesia's failed push for democratic reform earlier in the decade. Other thwarted proposals include the 2003 idea of an ASEAN contingent for peacekeeping, as well as a comprehensive plan for Southeast Asian security, the ASEAN Security Community (ASC). According to Dosch (2008, p. 74), the latter proposal was to include provisions to improve legal cooperation and to establish a commission for human rights that would address potential violations in the fight against terrorism. Since then, Indonesia has become much more determined to push the other members in ASEAN in the direction of human rights reform, especially in relation to the ruling regime of Myanmar. For the thriving democracy of Indonesia, Myanmar's unremitting political and civil rights violations are an 'insufferable embarrassment' (Suryodiningrat, 2009). Moreover, the snail's pace at which ASEAN member governments are proceeding with the implementation of the rules of the recently ratified 2008 ASEAN Charter and its associated human rights body does little to assuage the scepticism of Indonesia's ASEAN critics (Rüland, 2009, p. 386).

Both Wanandi and Sukma have been outspoken in conveying Indonesia's dissatisfaction with the recent formulation of key ASEAN documents such as the 2008 Charter and the terms of reference for the human rights body. Indonesia, they argue, struggled hard to convince fellow ASEAN members on the importance of having a credible ASEAN human rights body, especially during the ongoing debate on its terms of reference. 'Yet Indonesia's views', according to Sukma (2009), 'seem to have fallen on deaf ears'. The terms of reference were so watered down from their original intent that 'they became an aesthetic fig leaf to cover inaction' (Suryodiningrat, 2009). As Suryodiningrat (2009) suggests, by continuing to ignore the human rights issue, ASEAN's underlying government-to-government basis is seeping to the surface.

Perhaps there is also the gradual realization among the civil society in many other fellow members that eventually nothing can change ASEAN in its human rights outlook if the association does not reinvent itself. After all, how much can one expect from an organization that was constructed to serve the convenience of its leaders and not the values of its citizens?

Indeed, Wanandi (Seminar 'Kaji ulang ASEAN sebagai sokoguru politik luar negeri Indonesia' 2008) has highlighted the fact that ASEAN is not yet in a position to incorporate the potential input of non-state or unofficial actors. This is despite the fact that as part of a newly democratizing nation, Indonesian citizens are becoming increasingly well informed about Indonesia's regional engagement. Indonesian citizens and NGO actors, frustrated by being continuously locked out of the elite 'talk-fests' (*omongan saja*) of ASEAN's summit diplomacy, are also becoming increasingly articulate in expressing their desire to be involved in intraregional political participation. Leading by example, Wanandi claims that his think-tank, CSIS, has often involved both political figures and NGOs in Track II discussions relating to regionalism as well as practical endeavours, such as the provision of disaster relief in Myanmar in the aftermath of Cyclone Nargis in 2008. Acharya has also examined the amenability of NGO groups to work with governments as well as participate in the ASEAN People's Assembly, first held in November 2000 in Indonesia, immediately following an ASEAN summit in Singapore (Acharya, 2003, p. 386). There is still some resistance to engaging domestic and regional civil society, however, as demonstrated by opposition to the People's Assembly from the governments of Myanmar, Laos and Vietnam. Moreover, the Track II elite are not always as open to NGO or Track III input as they imagine. For instance, the unadvertised $US1,400 registration fee for the premier ASEAN 'talk-fest' of 2010 – the Asia-Pacific Roundtable (APR)[2] held in Kuala Lumpur in June – certainly gives the impression, perhaps mistakenly so, that the input of non-state or unofficial actors is of little purport. For many outside observers, the Track II fora are far too exclusive, limited to elite communities such as government officials, a small number of senior academics, business people and the media (Hadiwinata, 2009, p. 67).

Comparisons with the EU's 'people-centred' regionalism

The frustration of Indonesian academe, media and NGOs has been shared by other NGOs in Southeast Asia. Consider the disappointing experience of Solidarity for Asian People's Advocacy (SAPA), a transnational network of civil society groups who were fortunate enough to be invited to provide Track III input into what the ASEAN Charter should say: 'The Charter is a disappointment. [It] falls short of what is needed to establish a "people-centered" and "people-empowered" ASEAN. It succeeds in codifying past

ASEAN agreements, and consolidating the legal framework that would define the Association. However, it fails to put people at the center, much less empower them' (Dosch, 2008, p. 79). The charter, which was ultimately drafted and ratified by Track I political leaders, fell considerably short of the 'people-centred' hopes of SAPA, among other Track III NGOs involved. Part of the disappointment and frustration associated with the process and outcome of the ASEAN Charter is no doubt inspired by the growing understanding that other regional organizations, such as the EU, are far more rigorous in ensuring that human rights issues are integral to regional integration.

The Indonesian media has added to the criticism of ASEAN's lack of non-government or non-official engagement by making negative comparisons with the EU. For example, Meidyatama Suryadiningrat of *The Jakarta Post* suggests that ASEAN can take a few tips from the EU. Suryadiningrat regards the democratic impulse of EU referenda as a useful framework:

> Learning from ASEAN's very own 'model' (*soko guru*), the European Union, Indonesia can see how several (European) nations were forced to organize a referendum to legitimize the proposed Charter. The idea we can take away from this is the notion of how an EU Charter is hand-balled to the citizenry (*rakyat*) through a referendum. If there were to be a referendum in Indonesia, then the government would need to take notice of the protests of the people. It is no longer acceptable that simply because of the need to maintain ASEAN neighborliness Indonesia needs to ratify the latest ASEAN Charter.
> (Seminar 'Kaji ulang ASEAN sebagai sokoguru politik luar negeri Indonesia', 2008)

As Emmerson describes, soon after the ASEAN Charter was signed in 2008, an unnamed commentator in Jakarta described it as 'garbage', because it lacked strong provisions for human rights (2008, p. 35). Another unnamed observer characterized the charter's content 'as a victory for some of the least democratic states in the region' (2008, pp. 35–36).

The ratification of the ASEAN Charter illustrates the tensions and disappointments that can arise when the suggestions of Track III actors are ignored, or given mere lip-service, before the actual signing by Track I actors, the relatively illiberal ASEAN governments. Nevertheless, the experience of the rejected EU Constitution of 2005, and then the rejected EU Treaty of Lisbon of 2008, demonstrates the tensions and disappointments that can also occur when regionalist projects are transferred in the opposite direction: from Track I to Track III. As Emmerson explains, the initial EU Constitution was unable to be ratified, as it was rejected in referenda held for that purpose by absolute majorities in France and the Netherlands. In 2008 a less ambitious version, the Treaty of Lisbon, was in most cases submitted to member parliaments for approval. France, the Netherlands and 16 other states ratified the text, none of them by referendum. The Irish government, however, did consult the voters, who rejected the treaty by 53 to 47 per cent.

Evidently, an EU-style 'people-centred' ASEAN described by the Indonesian media commentators above is, in Emmerson's words, 'easier to advocate than to implement' (2008, p. 51). Indonesia, of course, might be more inclined to advocate participatory regionalism than other ASEAN member states. This is because, following Amitav Acharya's (2003) definition of participatory regionalism, there is a growing expectation that a democratically elected government should become 'more responsive to the demands of civil society', and thereby allow a 'wider range of transnational issues' to be addressed. Other ASEAN members, however, may not be so keen. As Emmerson (2008, p. 51) points out, 'democracy is not a key that fits all locks.'

Sukma (2009), meanwhile, suggests that Indonesia should no longer blindly praise ASEAN, considering its many well-documented shortcomings: 'We should stand tall and proclaim that enough is enough. It is enough for Indonesia to imprison itself in the "golden cage" of ASEAN for more than 40 years.' Besides the factors already discussed, there are a number of other important reasons for Indonesian dissatisfaction with ASEAN. For instance, ASEAN has not been as successful in fostering peace in the region as it would like. Colbert (1986), and later Narine (1998), argued that the continued existence of intraregional territory disputes – the Philippines continues to dispute Malaysia's sovereignty over Sabah, and Malaysia's relations with Thailand are also frequently strained due to border disputes – disqualified Southeast Asia from being a security community. Divisions between member states have continued to undermine ASEAN's supposed unity (Sukma, 2009). For example, as is often reported in the Indonesian media, Indonesia and Malaysia have long held differences of opinion over many issues, including the ill-treatment of Indonesian citizens in Malaysia (see, for example, Santoso, 2008). The maritime border between Indonesia and Malaysia and the land border between Thailand and Cambodia have also become ongoing sources of conflict. These border conflicts are often reported in Indonesian newspapers (see 'Isu Kamboja-Thailand Belum Terselesaikan', 2008; Myanmar dan Sengketa Kamboja-Thailand Jadi Topik Bahasan', 2008; Sukarjaputra, 2009). The government and mass media of maritime Southeast Asian countries such as Indonesia and the Philippines are far less tolerant of the military junta in Myanmar than mainland ASEAN members. As mentioned earlier, this hard-line stance, borne out of frustration with ASEAN's good-neighbourly attempts to pressure the ruling regime, is causing some disquiet. Meanwhile, at the ASEAN summit in October 2009, the host nation Thailand and neighbouring Cambodia remained at loggerheads over the fate of former fugitive Thai leader Thaksin Shinawatra, after Cambodian premier Hun Sen offered him a job as an economic adviser.

Sukma (2009) argues that ASEAN's policy of non-interference has in fact facilitated the various bitter divisions and border disputes in the region, not to mention domestic violations. Emmerson (2008, p. 23) describes the situation well: 'ASEAN's aversion to interference sustained a reciprocal kind of impunity: Each member regime could do what it wished behind its own borders, provided it gave the same leeway to other member regimes. In an abusively ruled country such as Myanmar, the arrangement fostered tolerance of repression – the region turning a blind eye.'

The criticisms of academic elites directed at ASEAN are also being echoed by the Indonesian mass media. In 2008 and 2009 there were several articles comparing ASEAN unfavourably against the EU. For example, in an article appearing in *Kompas* (2009), Handono Eko Prabowo, a lecturer at Yogyakarta's Sanata Dharma University, explains that the diversity of ASEAN and lack of integration among its member states reinforces the notion that the EU is successfully integrated and is, therefore, a model framework of regionalism. The EU's other attractive features include its stability, peacefulness and prosperity, as well as its ability to allow people, goods and services to move unencumbered across national borders. An EU-style single currency is also a bonus. Perhaps the most alluring aspect of the EU is its 'democratic' consultation with voters via referenda, allowing citizens to vote down draft constitutions, for example. Prabowo is referring to the ill-fated efforts by European leaders to establish a constitution for the EU between 2005 and 2008 – efforts, as we have discussed above, ultimately scuttled by referenda where majorities voted the document down. Prabowo concludes that in comparison to the EU, ASEAN is a long way from transforming itself into a fully integrated community, mainly due to long-standing economic disparities, political differences and cultural diversity. Perhaps, he suggests, real integration can only occur when ASEAN's resources are combined with the extra nations of ASEAN+3. Such a move, he imagines, will allow the members of ASEAN to not only survive in the present global context, but also to strengthen politically and prosper economically.

In contrast, Jones and Smith (2007) belittle the formation of ASEAN+3 and the promises and proposals for further East Asian regional integration. What benefit is there for strong powers such as China and Japan, they ask, to associate themselves with ASEAN's flawed Southeast Asian project? Furthermore, as this chapter has revealed, Indonesian commentators in academe and the media have become increasingly frustrated with ASEAN's organizational intransigency, especially when compared to the paragon of regionalism, the EU. Suryadiningrat (2009), for instance, warns that if it does not respond to EU-style innovations, then ASEAN is destined to suffer from 'an ongoing malaise'. Indonesian political leaders and policy makers, meanwhile, already overwhelmed with numerous regional fora, committees, meetings and acronyms, are demonstrating a degree of regionalism fatigue. This may partly explain the political elite's lack of enthusiasm for the Rudd and Hatoyama proposals – and constantly reiterated support for ASEAN – which will be discussed below.

Indonesia's 'post-ASEAN' alternatives

The more Indonesian political leaders attest to the efficacy of ASEAN and Indonesia's ongoing willingness to be fully committed to its success, the more the other ASEAN countries raise their eyebrows. Worse than this, there are arguments to suggest that the inclusion through democratization of more non-governmental actors in Indonesia has weakened the cooperative identity of the ASEAN grouping (Emmerson, 2005). Rüland, for instance, argues that Indonesia's democratization, together with a strengthening nationalism, is having the unintended effect of eroding ASEAN's cohesion (Rüland, 2009). Indeed, there have been growing criticisms of Indonesia's recent tendency to include more bottom-up input, not to mention Indonesia's new-found delusions of regional grandeur. When asked by *The Bangkok Post* whether Indonesia might become 'so obsessed with its grand agenda', including greater involvement in the G20, that 'ASEAN could be belittled', Indonesia's new Foreign Minister Marty Natalegawa responded: 'We don't see it as a zero-sum game. Our diplomacy is able enough to do these multipronged efforts. For us, ASEAN is not an option, it's a fact of life' (Callick, 2009). The seditious nature of the *Bangkok Post*'s questioning is just as revealing as Natalegawa's diplomatic answer.

Together with its push for the democratization of ASEAN and its apparently more globally oriented foreign policy, Indonesia's increasing impatience with ASEAN may inadvertently increase Indonesia's isolation in ASEAN and an attrition of the trust of its partners (Rüland, 2009). It certainly does not inspire a sense of commitment to greater regional integration. Singapore, for instance, is increasingly uncomfortable with Indonesia's growing stature on the world stage, seemingly at the cost of an ASEAN focus. For Singapore, an ASEAN without Indonesia would be a major calamity, as ASEAN has served Singapore's business and security interests well, as well as allowing Singapore to play a major strategic role in the region. Myanmar, in contrast, is unimpressed by Indonesia's increasingly blatant criticism of its poor human rights record. Thailand for its part must remain silent in the face of Indonesia's outspokenness, as it shares important cross-border trade links with Myanmar and its allies such as Laos. The soft-authoritarian Malaysia, meanwhile, has long grown accustomed to patronizing its much larger and noisier neighbour, and the occasional barbed comment is thrown in Indonesia's direction regarding the 'haphazard' nature of Indonesia's democratic consolidation. Indeed, many Malaysians are sceptical of the true extent of Indonesia's democratic transformation. In general, there are broad questions in the region regarding Indonesia becoming 'too big for its boots', especially as Indonesia – as the world's third-largest democracy and biggest regional power in Southeast Asia – has been invited to represent the region in the G20, as well as act as the Southeast Asian host for the 2010 visit of US President Barack Obama to the region.

Given regional disquiet, should Indonesia, riding the crest of the wave of democratic euphoria, seriously consider recent calls to develop a 'post-ASEAN' regional strategy (see, for example, Sukma, 2009)? Among other things, Sukma (2008, 2009) is keen to warn Indonesian policy makers that as a regional power Indonesia needs to respond in a timely fashion to the growing need for new and more productive regional arrangements in East Asia. ASEAN, with its fair share of regionalism recalcitrants and democratic backsliders, has a lot of room for improvement in this regard. Sukma fears that ASEAN is widely regarded by other nations in the East Asia region of being incapable of responding to new challenges, such as the emerging influence of China and, to a lesser extent, India. As a result, by holding fast with the ASEAN 'old grouping', Indonesia is in danger of being left by the wayside in relation to new regional frameworks being developed and proposed by the so-called 'middle power' regional powers, such as Australia and Japan. Sukma specifically mentions former Prime Minister Rudd's 'APC' proposal, and he warns Indonesian policy makers that it would be irresponsible if Indonesia did not play an active role in forging closer regional relations with the 'new' regional powers such as Australia.

In terms of purpose and structure, Rudd's APC was to be modelled on the EU. The aim was to create an APC by 2020, a single pan-regional body that brings together the USA, China, India, Indonesia, Japan and the other countries of the region with a broad agenda to deal with political, economic and security challenges. However, Rudd's proposal was not widely greeted with open arms in the region. In Jakarta, veteran MP and foreign policy watchdog Theo Sambuaga supported Rudd's efforts to encourage debate on a broad regional forum, but he warned that Asia was very different to Europe, and any new body should emerge gradually from the existing ASEAN forum: 'ASEAN countries are largely different than the EU. Economic growth is very different between each country as well as the political system, social background and ethnicity. We don't need a new bloc yet. Let the existing blocs evolve naturally as they have been' (Colebatch et al., 2008).

Indonesian defence minister, Juwono Sudarsono, dismissed Rudd's push for an all-encompassing regional body. Sudarsono asserted the government's default position that Indonesia prefers to work through fora already in place, such as ASEAN. 'Our view in Indonesia is we have to work out problems region by region. Australia will lead the southern flank. ASEAN will tackle the Southeast Asian cluster, and we have to see what happens between China and Japan, and Korea, in North-East Asia. That we feel is more realistic, regionally' (Flitton, 2009). Similarly, Indonesia's foreign minister, Marty Natalegawa, made it clear that Indonesia remained underwhelmed by Rudd's APC proposal: 'So far the Indonesian government is not quite convinced of the benefits to the country,' Natalegawa mentioned in Indonesia's *Tempo* news magazine. 'What benefit would there be by forming a new forum, having more meetings, more acronyms, with addressing challenges like climate change and poverty?' (Gartrell, 2009). Despite winning some support for the plan in the 18 months since it was first raised, Natalegawa said that Indonesia did not see the need for it, or for Japan's rival plan for a narrower East Asian Community. 'Indonesia is not turning down the options, but our approach must be one step at a time' (Gartrell, 2009). Many other reports in a similar vein, including several from Indonesia, suggested that most countries in the region would have preferred to stay with existing institutions rather than set up a new body (see 'ASEAN Tertarik pada Usulan Rudd, 2008; Rudd Dorong Integrasi ASEAN', 2008).

Japan's proposal for the idea of a new regional body was also modelled on the EU, and received a similarly lukewarm reception. The former Japanese prime minister, Yukio Hatoyama's East Asian Community proposal – which was envisaged to broaden the ASEAN+3 framework to embrace countries like Australia and New Zealand and a wider free trade area – was primarily intended to address and overcome regional differences. This included deep-seated Sino-Japanese cultural, economic and territorial rivalry, most recently manifested in the territorial dispute between China and Japan over oil and gas fields under the East China Sea. Wanting to make the region 'a sea of fraternity instead of a sea of disputes', Hatoyama ruffled a few feathers as it pointedly excluded the USA (Hartcher, 2009). Rather than creating a new forum for the USA to throw its weight around, as it were, Hatoyama's project was designed to create an alternative: 'The financial crisis has suggested to many that the era of US unilateralism may come to an end. It has also raised doubts about the permanence of the dollar as the key global currency' (Hartcher, 2009). As an alternative to the hegemony of the US dollar, Hatoyama's plan included a EU-style common currency.

Washington was deeply unhappy about the Hatoyama regional proposal. This is because the USA, which was distracted by wars in Afghanistan and Iraq, had only recently re-engaged with the region, particularly in Southeast Asia. Within Asia itself opinion was divided on the issue. According to the Malaysian prime minister, Najib Razak, any future Asia-wide community 'must' engage with the USA (Hartcher, 2009). Singapore's prime minister used his first bilateral meeting with the new Japanese prime minister to emphasize the need for the USA to be included in any strategic-level regional body. 'Some countries want the United States to be part of a future regional framework as a counterbalance to China's influence', in the words of an unnamed diplomat (Hartcher, 2009). Chaiwat Khamchoo, an analyst at Bangkok's Chulalongkorn University, said 'Whether we like it or not, I think we could not avoid a US role because the US is a big country which has powers both in economic and security matters.' Furthermore, 'some countries in the region are suspicious of each other so they want the US to play a role' (Hartcher, 2009).

Jones and Smith (2007) assert the contrary, but dubious, thesis emerging from certain quarters of Southeast Asian academe, that for several years now it has been the US hegemon that has threatened the construction of a new and purposeful East Asian regional identity. In the past, outside China it was only Malaysia's former prime minister, Mahathir Mohamad (1995), in conjunction with the occasional Japanese ultra-nationalist who was seriously associated with promoting anti-Americanism as a basis for pan-Asian identity. More realistically, it is possible to interpret the latest Japanese proposal – not unlike earlier proposals for an East Asian community – as an attempt by Japan to position itself as a potential counterweight to American influence in the region, simultaneously improving its image in Asia by diluting the impression that it is a US dependent in the Pacific (Jones and Smith, 2007, p. 182).

With or without US involvement, the Hatoyama proposal gathered a modest amount of momentum, garnering the support of Indonesia, South Korea and the acquiescence of China and Australia. According to Richard Woolcott, the Rudd government's special envoy for the proposed APC, 'we're not unhappy about the Japanese idea because it's helped stimulate discussion. It's good that both the Rudd and Hatoyama governments are considering how regional co-operation can best be advanced' (Hartcher, 2009).

Ultimately, in Indonesia the reception of the Rudd and Hatoyama proposals had been lukewarm and did not receive an enthusiastic embrace. Indonesia's interest, modest as it was, appeared to be not so much sparked by the Rudd and Hatoyama rhetoric in particular but rather by the prospect of increasing regionalization with states outside the ASEAN region. Inspired by the 'hard' institutionalism of the EU, it could well be that Indonesia is more interested in developing a regional institution, or rather a revamped model of ASEAN, that is far more effective and 'bottom-up' or 'people-centred' than ASEAN as it stands, with 'deeper' trade and security cooperation (see Oratmangun, 2009). There are already indications that other East Asian nations share Indonesia's desire for more effective cooperation. Ravenhill, for instance, points out that the majority of preferential trade agreements that East Asian countries have negotiated or are negotiating are with states outside the region: 'East Asian countries typically have signed on to agreements with extra-regional partners that are "deeper" and contain more WTO Plus provisions than those negotiated with other countries within East Asia' (Ravenhill, 2009, p. 231). Indeed, in 2008–2009 there were several reports appearing in the Indonesian media detailing Indonesia's efforts to expand its trade links with non-traditional markets, including South Korea, Russia, Eastern Europe, Africa and Latin America (see Aulia, 2009; Hendram, 2009).

Conclusion

The discussion above has described the underwhelming responses of Indonesian political figures towards the Rudd and Hatoyama proposals for a new regional body. This chapter has also outlined the enthusiasm that Suharto-era ministers – and indeed some post-Suharto ministers – have shown for ASEAN and the common interests, norms and identity that have contributed to the inter-state peace among the states of Southeast Asia. However, there are serious questions being asked about whether ASEAN will be able to put its modest rhetorical commitment to encouraging reform and democracy into actual practice. Based on its history of non-interference, as well as the lack and even fear of democracy on the part of some of its members, there are doubts about whether ASEAN can practise what it is preaching.

The democratization of Indonesia, this chapter has argued, is the crucial factor in the growing criticism of ASEAN in recent years. It is the democracy agenda in Indonesia that has led to the broader desire to engage in 'deeper' and more 'people-centred' regional cooperation, as modelled by the 'hard' institutionalism of the EU. With these attitudes in mind, we echo Jones and Smith's (2007) recommendation that we need to look beyond the recent academic trend of upholding the notion of East Asian regionalism as an attractively multilateral, norm-governed enterprise. Instead, as Jones and Smith suggest, we need to consider an empirical assessment of the reality of East Asian regionalism, which is, as we have shown, often quite negative. This chapter's brief overview of the history of Indonesia's regional involvement, as well as Indonesian perceptions of the various models of regional integration on offer, is a modest step in this direction.

Our final conclusion is ambivalent. On the one hand, given the ongoing criticism of ASEAN by Indonesian academe and media, it appears that Indonesia has 'outgrown' ASEAN. Elite opinion suggests that perhaps it is time for Indonesia to downgrade ASEAN's significance for Indonesian foreign policy and develop a foreign policy that is more global, or 'post-ASEAN' in its orientation. Rüland (2009) argues that this is the very same conclusion that has already been reached at the highest levels of Indonesia's legislature, notwithstanding foreign ministry expressions of ongoing commitment to ASEAN. On the other hand, with no indication that Indonesia's foreign ministry is prepared to abandon ASEAN just yet, Indonesia's importance to the region suggests that an Indonesia-led push for democratic reform in ASEAN is not completely out of the question. Indonesia might not be as isolated in the region as it feels. After all, there are progressive democratic elements in other ASEAN countries, such as the Philippines, Thailand, Cambodia, Malaysia and Singapore. Ultimately, given the awareness of most ASEAN member governments that making some accommodations towards a more participatory style of regionalism will improve their interactions with

Western countries and Western aid donors (Acharya, 2003, p. 399), the latter conclusion would be of the greatest benefit to both Indonesia and ASEAN. This would also allow Indonesia to work simultaneously within a regional and global foreign policy orientation.

Notes

1. The initial members of ASEAN-ISIS included the CSIS in Jakarta, the Institute of Strategic and International Studies (ISIS) in Kuala Lumpur, the Institute for Strategic and Development Studies (ISDS) in Manila, the Singapore Institute of International Affairs (SIIA) in Singapore, and the Institute for Security and International Studies (ISIS) in Bangkok. Consequently three other members have joined the grouping, including the Institute of International Relations (IIR) in Hanoi, the Institute of Foreign Affairs (IFA) in Vientiane and the Brunei Darussalam Institute of Policy and Strategic Studies (BDIPSS) in Bandar Sri Begawan.
2. The APR is an annual Track II conference organized by the Institute of Strategic and International Studies (ISIS) in Kuala Lumpur on behalf of ASEAN-ISIS, a network of Southeast Asia's leading think-tanks.

Bibliography

Acharya A. (2003) 'Democratisation and the prospects for participatory regionalism in Southeast Asia', *Third World Quarterly*, 24, 375–390.
'ASEAN Tertarik pada Usulan Rudd' (2008) *Kompas*, 14 June 2008.
Aulia L. (2009) 'ASEAN-KORSEL: Membuka Era Baru yang Serba Hijau', *Kompas*, 1 June 2009.
Caballero-Anthony M. (2005) *Regional Security in Southeast Asia: Beyond the ASEAN Way* (Singapore: Institute of Southeast Asian Studies (ISEAS)).
Callick R. (2009) 'A consummate master of diplomacy', *The Australian*, 19 November 2009.
Colbert E. (1986) 'ASEAN as a regional organization: Economics, politics and security' in K.D. Jackson, S. Paribatra and J.S. Djiwandono (eds.), *ASEAN in a Regional and Global Context* (Berkeley, CA: Institute of East Asian Studies), 194–210.
Colebatch T., Forbes M. and Toy M.-A. (2008) 'Keating blast for Rudd's Asia union', *The Age*, 6 June 2008.
Dosch J. (2008) 'Sovereignty rules: Human security, civil society, and the limits of liberal reform' in D.K. Emmerson (ed.), *Hard Choices: Security, Democracy and Regionalism in Southeast Asia* (Stanford, CA: The Walter H. Shorenstein Asia-Pacific Research Center), 59–90.
Emmerson D.K. (2005) 'Security, community and democracy in Southeast Asia: Analyzing ASEAN', *Japanese Journal of Political Science*, 6, 165–185.
Emmerson D.K. (2008) 'Critical terms: Security, Democracy, and Regionalism in Southeast Asia' in D.K. Emmerson (ed.), *Hard Choices: Security, Democracy and Regionalism in Southeast Asia* (Stanford, CA: The Walter H. Shorenstein Asia-Pacific Research Center), 3–56.
Flitton D. (2009) 'Indonesia rejects Rudd's Asia plan', *The Age*, 27 May 2009.
Gartrell A. (2009) 'Indonesia pours cold water on Rudd plan', *The Age*, 18 November 2009.

Hadiwinata B.S. (2009) 'International relations in Indonesia: Historical legacy, political intrusion, and commercialization', *International Relations of the Asia-Pacific*, 9, 55–81.
Hartcher P. (2009) 'Big-picture man with a yen to bond passes the bucks of Uncle Sam', *The Age*, 20 October 2009.
Hendram A. (2009) 'Diplomasi Indonesia Fokus ke ASEAN', *Seputar Indonesia*, 7 January 2009.
'Isu Kamboja-Thailand Belum Terselesaikan' (2008) *Kompas*, 25 July 2008.
Jones D.M. and Smith M.L.R. (2007) 'Constructing communities: The curious case of East Asian regionalism', *Review of International Studies*, 33, 165–186.
Mohamad M. and Yoshihara S. (1995) *The Voice of Asia* (Tokyo: Kodansha).
'Myanmar dan Sengketa Kamboja-Thailand Jadi Topik Bahasan' (2008) *Kompas*, 22 July 2008.
Narine S. (1998) 'ASEAN and the management of regional security', *Pacific Affairs*, 71, 2, 195–214.
Prabowo T.H.E. (2009) 'Model Integrasi Eropa Untuk ASEAN', *Kompas*, 20 May 2009.
Ravenhill J. (2009) 'East Asian regionalism: Much ado about nothing?', *Review of International Studies*, 35, 215–235.
'Rudd Dorong Integrasi ASEAN' (2008) *Seputar Indonesia*, 14 June 2008.
üRüland J. (2009) 'Deepening ASEAN cooperation through democratization? The Indonesian legislature and foreign policymaking', *International Relations of the Asia-Pacific*, 9, 373–402.
Santoso F. (2008) 'Semangat ASEAN: Kompetisi Global dan Peradaban Serumpun', *Kompas*, 4 April 2008.
Seminar 'Kaji ulang ASEAN sebagai sokoguru politik luar negeri Indonesia' (2008) (Jakarta: Centre for Strategic and International Studies (CSIS)).
Sukarjaputra R. (2009) 'Potensi Konflik karena Masalah Perbatasan', *Kompas*, 22 March 2009.
Sukma R. (2008) 'Political development: A democracy agenda for ASEAN?' in D. Emmerson (ed.), *Hard Choices: Security, Democracy, and Regionalism in South-east Asia* (Stanford, CA: The Walter H. Shorenstein Asia-Pacific Research Centre), 135–149.
Sukma R. (2009) 'Indonesia needs a post-ASEAN foreign policy', *The Jakarta Post*, 30 June 2009.
Suryodiningrat M. (2009) 'Southeast Asian Nations Risk Dissension by Ignoring Human Rights', *YaleGlobal Online*. http://yaleglobal.yale.edu/content/southeast-asian-nations-risk-dissension-ignoring-human-rights, accessed 19 November 2009.
Tarling N. (2006) *Regionalism in Southeast Asia: To Foster the Political Will* (London: Routledge).

4
The EU's Asia Strategy in Trade and Investment: Externalities, Interdependencies and the Prospects for Coordination with ASEAN

David Treisman

Introduction

During the last decade, greater cooperation and coordination with Asia has loomed large on the European Union's (EU's) political agenda. Central to this agenda has been the strengthening of mutual trade and investment flows with the region and the formation of strategic alliances in Asia. In 2001, the EU updated its Asia strategy and outlined a strategic framework in which six key priority areas were identified: security, economics, development, law, environmental concerns and social awareness (EU, 2001).

In the area of economics, the EU called for the further strengthening of mutual trade and investment flows with the Asian region through bilateral economic relations, economic cooperation and policy dialogues on economic and financial issues including market access for poor developing countries, transport and energy. In particular, the EU stressed the importance of economic cooperation with regional groupings and emphasized the role that the Association of Southeast Asian Nations (ASEAN) could play as an ally and as a 'force for liberalisation and progress on trade and investment issues' (EU, 2001, p. 16).

ASEAN was established in 1967 as a regional grouping with an emphasis on mitigating the then current security concerns of the Southeast Asian region. Since the end of the Cold War, ASEAN's focus has shifted towards emphasizing the economic integration of its members. ASEAN, reminiscent of but not on par with the EU, is recognized more as a regional economic area or grouping than as an integrated area or community with a common/shared defence, foreign, fiscal and monetary policy. As with regional economic groupings, it would be expected that the EU and ASEAN would share several policy synergies and that ASEAN could play a significant role as the EU's core strategic economic/financial ally in Asia.

Much of the literature on EU–Asian relations has focused on interregionalism (the interaction of one region with another) and has produced mixed findings as to the role played by the EU or ASEAN in the Asian region. Gilson (2005) investigated the emergence of interregionalism between the EU and East Asia and noted that ASEAN is regarded by the EU as being a key economic and political ally but that, on the whole, despite the numerous documents and pledges, the EU maintains little interest in Asia. A similar argument is put forth by Moeller's (2007) study into the obstacles and opportunities of the EU–ASEAN relationship, in which it is highlighted that although the two groupings have a shared general political and economic outlook, their relationship has not moved from being consultative to substantive. Boisseau du Rocher (2006, p. 247) analyses the EU's potential role in ASEAN's relationship with its Northeast Asian partners (China, Japan and South Korea) and purports that the EU can play a significant role in ensuring stability within ASEAN and the broader East Asian region but cautions EU policy makers not to regard Southeast Asia as a 'mere periphery' of China. Diametrically opposed views are offered by Rüland (2001), who in analysing the interregional relationship between the EU and ASEAN concludes that, due to the increasing economic stratification of Asia and the shift of EU interests to East Asia (especially China), ASEAN will struggle to maintain a central position in the EU's relations with Asia. This is a message echoed by Van der Geest's (2006) findings from a survey of Asian specialists exploring likely scenarios for the future of EU–East Asia relations, in which it was concluded that further integration of ASEAN is likely but China's domestic political economy is the most important factor shaping the Asian region.

This paper contributes to the debate of EU–ASEAN relations (within the context of the broader Asian region) by critically appraising whether it is in the EU's best interests to regard ASEAN as a core strategic economic/financial ally in Asia (a notion explained in the next section) and whether further engagement with ASEAN members should occur on a bilateral (regional grouping to state) or interregional (regional grouping to regional grouping) basis. This appraisal focuses on the economic/financial dimensions of interdependency from an EU perspective and occurs in two stages. First, an analysis of the existent economic and financial interdependencies between the EU and Asia is undertaken utilizing a rational choice approach. Second, analysis into the decision-making process of ASEAN and of the findings of a recently completed advanced time series model is undertaken to assess ASEAN's capacity as a strategic ally and whether the EU should engage ASEAN on a interregional basis. The findings of this paper indicated that in economic/financial terms, China is a more suitable candidate as the EU's core strategic ally in Asia, and that the EU's benefit will be equal to or greater through bilateral engagement of individual ASEAN member states.

The remainder of the paper proceeds as follows: in the next section the rationale for international policy coordination as a basis for a strategic alliance is explored. The paper then analyses several quantitative indicators of interdependency that define capability in the economic/financial context, the decision-making mechanism of ASEAN and its capacity as a strategic ally.

International policy coordination: the basis for strategic alliance

The rationale for international policy coordination lies in the interdependence of economies. Within an international context, economic exchange occurs in an anarchical international system in which states have magnified influence over the functioning of markets. Under these circumstances, the accepted notion of atomistic competition no longer holds true, as a linear relationship exists between the size of a state and their influence over markets. Concomitantly, the implementation of national economic policies creates externalities or spillovers (actions of an individual or group that influence the well-being of others without their consent – see Gwartney et al. (2000) for a readable introduction) that, in turn, are transmitted through the interdependency of markets: characteristics of what is commonly referred to as the modern, globalized international system.

It is at the confluence of state influence, externalities and interdependency that international policy coordination has potential utility. Much criticism and debate exists over the actual utility of international policy coordination – see Feldstein (1988). When viewed as a dynamic system, the logic behind the utility of international policy coordination remains sound: governments wish to meet their own national economic objectives for which they make policy; economic stability (viewed as a public good) is desired as it improves the likelihood of meeting national economic objectives; national economic policies create externalities; interdependence of markets acts as a conduit for the transmission of externalities and thereby disrupting stability; similarly interdependence of markets allows for feedback as it acts as a conduit for exerting state influence; policy makers will thus utilize this interrelationship (between influence, externalities and interdependence) by cooperating with other state representatives in order to internalize any externalities (the use of either market mechanism, government regulation, self-governing institutions or a mix of these institutions to diminish externalities – see Gupta and Prakash (1993) for a general introduction), thus culminating in the meeting of the original national economic objectives (Frenkel et al. 1990).

This logic is based on a rational actor assumption. In the practice of international relations, the elegant logic provided by the rational actor assumption is less clear-cut as states do not have homogenous policy preferences, structures or markets. This naturally distorts the expected from the actual outcome of international policy coordination and has provided the basis for debate over its utility. Despite the debate as to the merits of international policy coordination, many critics, including Feldstein (1988), Frenkel et al. (1990) and Bagwell and Staiger (2004), recognize that international economic coordination occurs when the parties concerned view the process as being in their mutual self-interests. It is on this basis that Willett (1999) calls for the analysis of international policy coordination to include political economy considerations.

International policy coordination thus requires shared goals and objectives that meet the self-interests of the independent parties and in which each party's ability to further its own self-interests depends on how other parties behave: a strategic alliance (Lake and Powell, 1999). However, as size is the key determinant of influence, international policy coordination is best sought with states that possess internal markets sizeable enough to give them leverage in setting standards – referred to by Drezner (2001, p. 21) as 'core states'. Therefore, a core party may be engaged with more than one other core party on a bilateral or interregional basis in the same policy space at the same time. Similarly, in the absence of core-to-core engagement, all other factors being equal, the core party is anticipated to hold a comparative advantage over smaller parties. This argument can be likened in many respects to that of an oligopoly.

Strategic alliances are inextricably linked to strategic decision making. Within the context of this paper, strategic decision making pertains to the externalities arising from and influence between states and their markets, and thus falls within the guise of the strategic-choice approach of international relations which, due to its common theoretical basis (rational choice), is synergistic with the economic rationale for international policy coordination. With this synergy, a joint theoretical approach is utilized to address the focus of this paper. Strategic alliances, by tradition, are multidimensional, and the importance of the other pillars of international relations (social and military) is fundamental for a complete analysis of EU–ASEAN relations. Although these other pillars fall outside of the scope of the paper, the common feature of all dimensions of a strategic alliance is the capability and capacity of the actors to engage in such alliances. In the political economic context, capability and capacity arises through the interdependency of the parties and consists of two critical components: in generating externalities and in influencing markets.

With these two critical components in mind, ASEAN's capability and capacity is investigated in two stages consisting of four key dimensions of the broader EU–Asia political economy:

1. Trade: the export of goods and service originating in the EU and Asia;
2. Foreign direct investment: the flows of foreign direct investment (debt and equity) from the EU and Asia;

3. Money and finance: international portfolio investment flows from the EU and Asia.
4. The decision-making mechanism of ASEAN: ASEAN's capacity to engage in and influence strategic interactions.

Dimensions one to three jointly address Asian nations' potential/capability to generate externalities for the EU by analysing the existent economic and financial interdependencies between the EU and Asia. Dimensions one to three should ideally include identification and quantification of externalities generated from markets within the Asian region. However, as noted by Swann (1999), externalities, although highly relevant, are notoriously difficult to isolate and quantify. Instead, Swann (1999) suggests analysing the underlying basis for externalities: interdependence of markets (a quantifiable indicator of the potential to generate externalities). The analysis proceeds in this regard by investigating the capability of nations/groupings to generate externalities on the basis that as the size of states and their markets matters, the greater their interdependencies, the greater the potential for externalities and influence and thus the more important the potential ally.

Dimension four focuses on the decision-making process of the grouping, and assesses ASEAN's capacity to influence markets and thus its ability to fulfil the role of a strategic ally, and whether the EU should engage ASEAN on an interregional basis.

These dimensions have been selected specifically to provide insights into the political-economic relationship between the EU and Asia while being in accordance with the economic/financial priority areas as outlined in the European Commission's 2001 Strategic Framework. This paper's analysis is undertaken from an EU standpoint and assumes, while remaining theoretically consistent and without loss of generality, that as institutions the EU and ASEAN possess homogeneity among their members' policy preferences and assumes awareness by EU decision makers as to policy and ally alternatives available within the Asian region. Models/indicators applied in the analysis are outlined in the respective sub-sections below.

ASEAN's capability to generate externalities: the interdependence of the EU and Asia

Trade

To assess the interdependency of EU and Asia in terms of the trade in goods and services, the export/import share of goods and services between the EU and major economies in the Asian region in any given year were determined by:

$$X_{SHARE} = \frac{\sum_{sd} X_{sd}}{\sum_{sw} X_{sw}} \times 100 \tag{1}$$

where s is the set of countries in the source, d is the set of countries in the destination, w is the set of countries in the world and X is the bilateral total export/import flow. Thus sd and sw indicate exports to/imports from the source to the destination and the world respectively. *XSHARE* is the export/import share as a percentage of total exports/imports.

Equation (1) is referred to by Petri (2006) as the relative measure of trade intensity and is argued to be an appropriate measure/indicator of interdependency when the objective is to assess the importance of trading partners to each other. Exports and imports (collectively net exports) impact upon the gross domestic product of a nation (size in economic terms). Thus, as size matters, higher values indicate greater interdependence with and importance of the selected trading ally (Mikic and Gilbert, 2007). Data used to determine the export/import share of the EU and major economies in the Asian region were drawn from the International Monetary Fund's *Direction of Trade Statistics* and are compared with those produced for the Eurostat database for the period 2004–2008. The 2004–2008 time period was selected due to the availability of comparable data. The resultant export and import shares for the period are presented in Figures 4.1 and 4.2/Tables 4.1 and 4.2 respectively. In both cases, alternative Asian nations/partners to that of ASEAN are presented. Figure 4.1 and Table 4.1 places the EU at the source with the Asian economies at the destination, revealing the relative importance of particular Asian economies for EU exports. Figure 4.2 and Table 4.2 reverses the source-destination relationship of Figure 4.1 and Table 4.1,

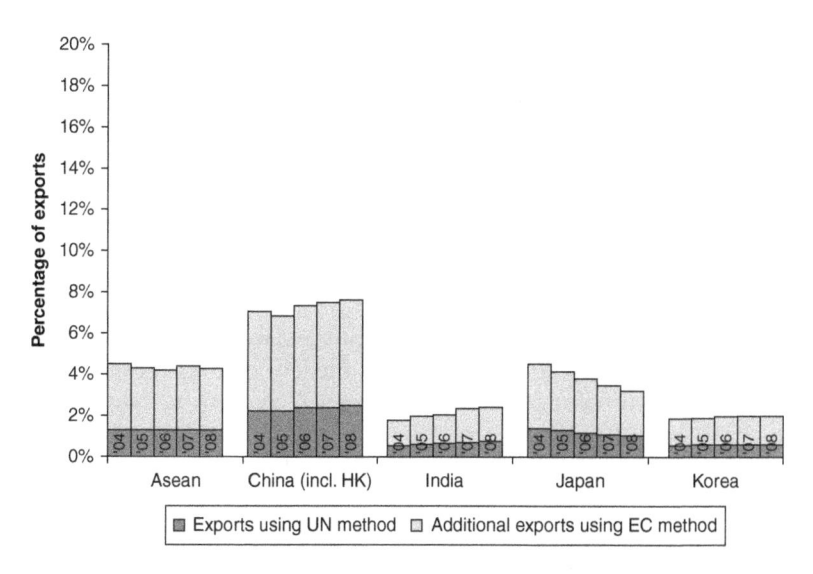

Figure 4.1 Percentage EU-27 exports to major Asian economies: 2004–2008.
Source: IMF (2009) and author's calculation.

68 *(Inter)Regionalism in Danger?*

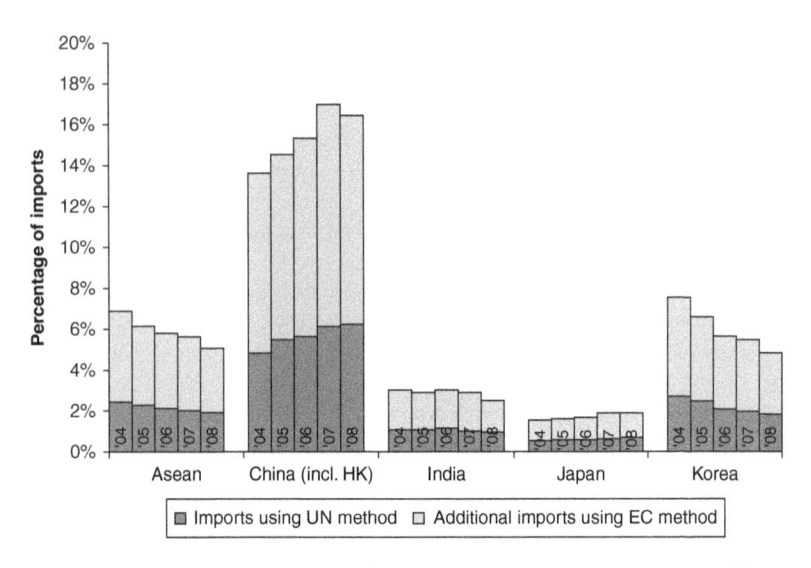

Figure 4.2 Percentage EU-27 imports from major Asian economies: 2004–2008.
Source: IMF (2009) and author's calculation.

thereby revealing the relative importance of imports from Asian economies to the EU.

Two methods have been deployed in determining relative exports/imports: the method proposed by the United Nations (UN method) and the method utilized by the European Commission (EC method) in its Eurostat database. The underlying formula of both methods remains the same. The key distinction exists in that the EC method excludes all intra-EU exports and imports in its calculations, whereas the UN method does not. It is debatable as to which method is more appropriate, and becomes more complex when intra-EU exports and imports are included. For the 2004–2008 period, intra-EU exports accounted for between 67 and 68 per cent of its total world exports and intra-EU imports accounted for between 6 and 65 per cent of its total world imports, creating significant differences between the findings from using the UN and EC methods in which resultant trade figures can appear over- or underestimated by approximately three times their actual size. Thus, for purposes of clarity, both the UN and EC methods are presented in Figures 4.1 and 4.2/Tables 4.1 and 4.2 – the UN method being the figures' lower bar in the stacked column and the EC method being the combined stack of the lower and upper bars. However, the following analysis of Figures 4.1 and 4.2/Tables 4.1 and 4.2 was undertaken using the UN method on the basis that the EU on the whole is not yet fully integrated.

Figure 4.1/Table 4.1 reveals that collectively the major Asian economies account for approximately 6 per cent of total EU exports. The condition of

Table 4.1 Comparison of UN and EC methods of calculating percentage EU-27 exports to major Asian economies: 2004–2008

Year	ASEAN UN (%)	ASEAN EC (%)	China (incl. HK) UN (%)	China (incl. HK) EC (%)	India UN (%)	India EC (%)	Japan UN (%)	Japan EC (%)	Korea UN (%)	Korea EC (%)
2004	1.4	4.5	2.2	7.0	0.6	1.8	1.4	4.5	0.6	1.9
2005	1.4	4.3	2.2	6.8	0.7	2.0	1.3	4.1	0.6	1.9
2006	1.3	4.2	2.4	7.3	0.7	2.1	1.2	3.8	0.6	1.9
2007	1.4	4.4	2.4	7.4	0.8	2.4	1.1	3.5	0.6	2.0
2008	1.4	4.2	2.5	7.6	0.8	2.4	1.1	3.2	0.6	2.0

Source: IMF (2009) and author's calculations.

Table 4.2 Comparison of UN and EC methods of calculating percentage EU-27 imports from major Asian economies: 2004–2008

Year	ASEAN UN (%)	ASEAN EC (%)	China (incl. HK) UN (%)	China (incl. HK) EC (%)	India UN (%)	India EC (%)	Japan UN (%)	Japan EC (%)	Korea UN (%)	Korea EC (%)
2004	2.4	6.9	4.8	13.5	1.0	3.0	0.6	1.6	2.7	7.5
2005	2.3	6.1	5.4	14.5	1.1	2.8	0.6	1.6	2.4	6.5
2006	2.1	5.8	5.6	15.3	1.1	3.0	0.6	1.7	2.1	5.6
2007	2.0	5.6	6.1	16.9	1.0	2.9	0.7	1.8	1.9	5.4
2008	1.9	5.0	6.1	16.4	0.9	2.5	0.7	1.9	1.8	4.8

Source: IMF (2009) and author's calculations.

relative exports to the major Asian economies was stable over the period under consideration.

Figure 4.1/Table 4.1 also reveals the relative importance of ASEAN as an Asian destination for EU exports. EU exports to ASEAN have been relatively stable over the 2004–2008 period, averaging 1.4 per cent of total exports. A similar stability but lower percentage of total EU exports is shared by Korea at 0.6 per cent. This is in contrast with declining exports to Japan over the period averaging 1.2 per cent of total EU exports. Total EU exports to China increased over the period, averaging 2.3 per cent – approximately 1.6 times more than ASEAN, whereas, total EU exports to India over the period increased and averaged 0.7 per cent. Thus, over the period under analysis, ASEAN ranked second, lagging notably behind China in terms of relative importance as an Asian destination for EU exports.

Figure 4.2/Table 4.2 reveals that collectively the major Asian economies contributed approximately 11–12 per cent of total EU imports. The condition of relative imports from major Asian economies was stable over the period under consideration.

Figure 4.2/Table 4.2 also indicates that the relative importance of EU imports from ASEAN has been declining over the period with average total imports of 2.1 per cent. Total EU imports from India and Korea followed a similar trend over the period, averaging 1 and 2.2 per cent, respectively. EU imports from China rose and averaged 5.6 per cent (approximately 2.6 times more goods and services than imported from ASEAN), as did EU imports from Japan, averaging 0.6 per cent. Thus, over the period under analysis, ASEAN ranked third, lagging notably behind China and narrowly behind Korea in terms of relative importance as an Asian source for EU imports.

Foreign direct investment

Foreign direct investment (FDI) flows between the EU and major Asian economies in any given year were determined by:

$$\text{FDIPC}_d = \frac{\text{FDI}_{sd}}{\text{POPULATION}_d} \quad (2)$$

where s is the set of countries in the source, d is the set of countries in the destination and FDI is the bilateral FDI flow. Thus sd is the flow from the source to the destination and FDIPC_d the FDI flow per capita (in euros) in the destination country. Thus, equation (2) is an indicator of the relative size of FDI flows.

FDI is a common feature of the globalized international system, and is considered to be international investment where the objective of the investor is obtaining a lasting interest in an enterprise resident in another economy (Patterson et al., 2004). For these reasons, FDI flows and stocks give rise to significant interdependency. FDI is generally dependent on several linked factors associated with enhanced growth performance in, stage of development and size of destination economies. Thus, in order to have a meaningful comparison of FDI flows across destinations, per capita measures were implemented (Hunya et al., 2007).

The data utilized in determining this indicator cover the period 2004–2006 and were drawn from Eurostat's *European Union Foreign Direct Investment Yearbook 2008*. Once again, the period of 2004–2006 was chosen on the basis of availability of consistent data. Analysis of both FDI stocks and flows would have been preferred. However, due to the limited availability of geographical FDI stock and flow data, the analysis concentrated on FDI inflows to and outflows from the EU. Recording of FDI outflows/inflows to the EU should, on a theoretical basis, be measurably equivalent to FDI inflows/outflows from an Asian perspective.

Figures 4.3, 4.4, 4.5 and 4.6 include per capita measures from/to the EU to/from the world, acting as a global average and thus a benchmark indicator for assessing flows to/from Asian destinations/sources. Using this benchmark, within Asian destination/sources comparisons demonstrate the relative importance of the Asian economies under investigation. Comparisons to the benchmark indicator do not provide any direct evidence as to the relative importance of the Asian region. However, due to the selection of major Asian economies, it is likely that the findings from the comparisons extend to the region as a whole.

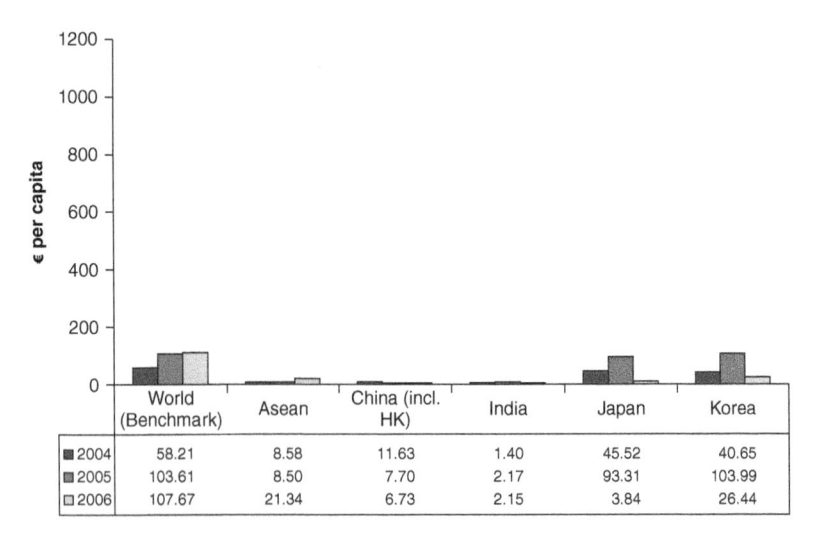

	World (Benchmark)	Asean	China (incl. HK)	India	Japan	Korea
2004	58.21	8.58	11.63	1.40	45.52	40.65
2005	103.61	8.50	7.70	2.17	93.31	103.99
2006	107.67	21.34	6.73	2.15	3.84	26.44

Figure 4.3 Per capita FDI outflow from the EU: 2004–2006 (euros).
Source: EU (2008) and author's calculation.

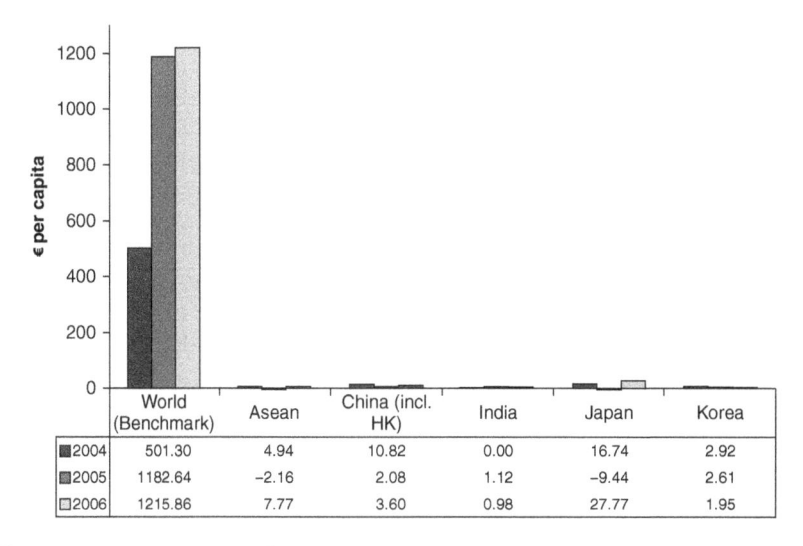

	World (Benchmark)	Asean	China (incl. HK)	India	Japan	Korea
2004	501.30	4.94	10.82	0.00	16.74	2.92
2005	1182.64	-2.16	2.08	1.12	-9.44	2.61
2006	1215.86	7.77	3.60	0.98	27.77	1.95

Figure 4.4 Per capita FDI inflows to the EU: 2004–2006 (euros).
Source: EU (2008) and author's calculation.

Figure 4.3 outlines the resultant FDI per capita outflows from the EU to the major Asian economies for the period 2004–2006. With the exception of Korea in 2005, all the Asian economies over the period under consideration fell below the benchmark indicator, which itself trended upwards over the period. This implies that the major Asian economies as destinations have a lower than average importance to the EU.

Within Asian destination comparisons (see Figure 4.3), ASEAN received more EU FDI per capita outflows than India over the entire period and more than China for 2005–2006 and Japan for 2006. EU FDI per capita outflows to Japan and Korea were considerably greater than ASEAN for 2004–2005 and 2004–2006 respectively. Trends in EU FDI per capita outflows to ASEAN tended to be stable in the earlier stages of the period with a marked increase in 2006. Japan and Korea shared a similar trend with EU FDI per capita outflows peaking in 2005 and declining rapidly in 2006. India's trend increased and stabilized towards the end of the period. China experienced declining EU FDI per capita outflows over the entire period. Thus, over the period under analysis, ASEAN ranked third in importance, lagging notably behind Korea and Japan as an Asian destination for EU FDI outflows.

Figure 4.4 outlines FDI per capita inflows to the EU from major Asian economies for the period 2004–2006. All the Asian economies fell well below the benchmark indicator over the period, while the benchmark indicator trended upwards. This implies that the major Asian economies as sources for EU FDI inflows have a lower than average importance to the EU.

Within Asian source comparisons (see Figure 4.4), ASEAN was a greater source for EU FDI per capita inflows than India and Korea in 2004 and 2006, Japan in 2005 and China in 2006. Per capita inflows from ASEAN were sizeably less than Japan in 2004 and 2006 and notably less than China, India and Korea in 2005. Trends in FDI per capita inflows from ASEAN, as with Japan, fluctuated over the period. Per capita inflows from China followed a similar trend but remained positive over the entire period. Per capita inflows from India followed an opposite trend, peaking in 2005, while per capita inflows from Korea declined over the entire period. Thus, over the period under analysis, ASEAN ranked third in importance, lagging notably behind Japan and less so behind China as an Asian source of FDI inflows to the EU.

Money and finance
Total international portfolio investment (PI) flows between the EU and major Asian economies in any given year were determined by:

$$PIPC_d = \frac{PI_{sd}}{POPULATION_d} \qquad (3)$$

where s is the set of countries in the source, d is the set of countries in the destination and PI is the bilateral PI flow. Thus sd is the flow from the source to the destination and $PIPC_d$ the PI flow per capita (in US dollars) in the destination country. Thus, equation (3) is an indicator of the relative size of PI flows.

PI is also a common feature of the globalized international system, and is considered to be international investment where the objective is short-term gains through investment in equity securities, debt securities (including bonds, notes, money market instruments) and financial derivatives in another economy (IMF, 1993). For these reasons, PI flows and stocks give rise to significant interdependency. Total PI includes all securities classified as equity, debt or derivative – see IMF (1993) for further details. PI is generally dependent on several linked factors associated with risks and returns in destination economies. Thus, per capita measures were implemented in order to have a meaningful comparison of PI flows across destinations.

The data utilized in determining this indicator are flow measures covering the period 2004–2006 and were drawn from the International Monetary Fund's *Consolidated Portfolio Investment Surveys*. The flow measures and time period were selected due to availability of data for selected sources/destinations of interest, but certain irregularities exist: data available for ASEAN as a source of PI includes only five of its ten member nations (Indonesia, Malaysia, the Philippines, Singapore and Thailand: collectively known as ASEAN-5), but still covers the bulk of the investable market of ASEAN. Likewise, complete data are lacking or no reporting is made in the surveys for PI originating in Latvia, Lithuania and Slovenia. China as a

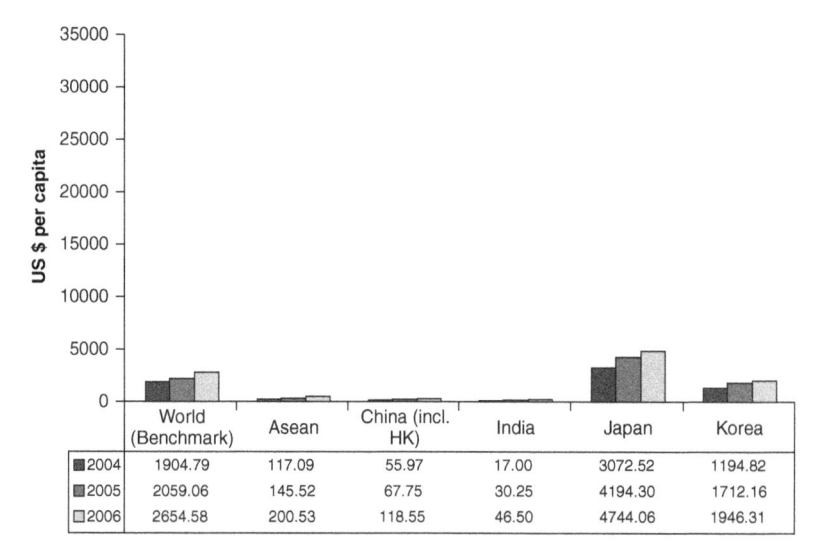

	World (Benchmark)	Asean	China (incl. HK)	India	Japan	Korea
2004	1904.79	117.09	55.97	17.00	3072.52	1194.82
2005	2059.06	145.52	67.75	30.25	4194.30	1712.16
2006	2654.58	200.53	118.55	46.50	4744.06	1946.31

Figure 4.5 Per capita total portfolio investment outflows from the EU-27: 2004–2006 (US$).
Source: IMF (2004, 2005, 2006) and author's calculation.

source of PI is also not reported, but Hong Kong, which in its own right is a financial centre, is expected to provide the bulk of what is jointly considered to be EU inflows originating from China (sum of mainland China and Hong Kong). All destination countries were included in the International Monetary Fund's *Consolidated Portfolio Investment Surveys*.

Figure 4.5 outlines the resultant PI per capita outflows from the EU to the major Asian economies for the period 2004–2006. When comparing EU PI per capita outflows to the major Asian economies with the benchmark indicator (which trended upwards), it is evident that Japan well exceeded the benchmark over the period under investigation. Korea fell short of the benchmark indicator, while ASEAN, China and India fell sizeably below the benchmark for the period. This implies that apart from Japan, Asia as a destination for PI has a below average importance to the EU.

Within Asian destination comparisons (see Figure 4.5), ASEAN received substantially less EU PI per capita outflows than either Japan or Korea over the period. Levels of EU PI per capita to ASEAN were significantly higher than EU PI per capita outflows to China or India for each year under investigation. Trends in EU PI per capita outflows to all major Asian economies were positive over the time period, with the greatest year on year variations arising through Japan and Korea. Thus, over the period under analysis, ASEAN ranked third in importance, lagging notably behind Japan and Korea as an Asian destination for EU PI per capita outflows.

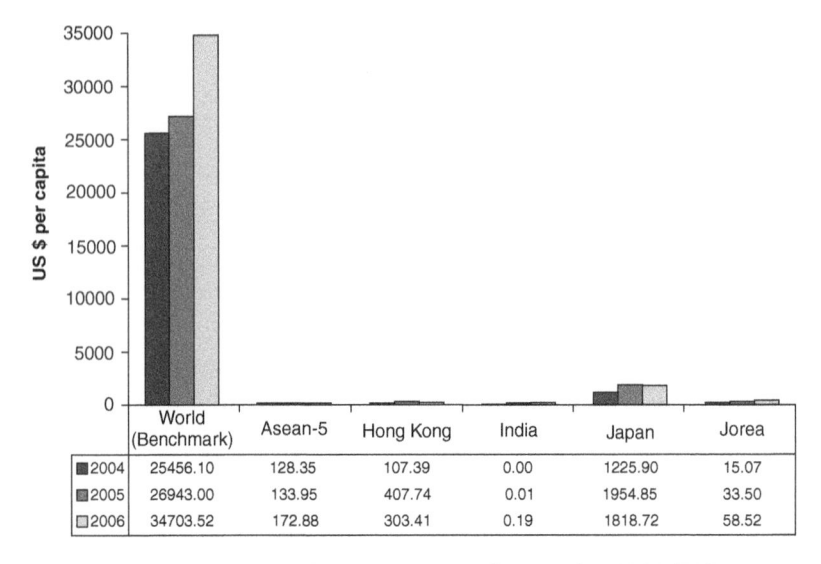

	World (Benchmark)	Asean-5	Hong Kong	India	Japan	Jorea
2004	25456.10	128.35	107.39	0.00	1225.90	15.07
2005	26943.00	133.95	407.74	0.01	1954.85	33.50
2006	34703.52	172.88	303.41	0.19	1818.72	58.52

Figure 4.6 Per capita total portfolio investment inflows to the EU-27 (US$).
Source: IMF (2004, 2005, 2006) and author's calculation.

Figure 4.6 outlines the resultant PI per capita inflows to the EU from major Asian economies for the period 2004–2006. The benchmark indicator trended upwards over the period. When comparing EU PI per capita inflows from the major Asian economies with the benchmark indicator, it is clear that all the major Asian economies fall grossly below the benchmark for the period. This indicates that the major Asian economies are not significant sources of PI per capita inflows to the EU and have little importance in this regard.

Within Asian source comparisons (see Figure 4.6), ASEAN (in this case ASEAN-5) was a greater source of EU PI per capita inflows then either India or Korea over the period. ASEAN was responsible for more EU PI per capita inflows than China (in this case Hong Kong) in 2004. Japan as a source for EU PI per capita inflows significantly exceeded ASEAN levels over the period, as did China to a lesser degree in 2005 and 2006. Trends in EU PI per capita inflows from all major Asian economies, barring China and Japan in 2005 and 2006, were positive over the time period. Thus, over the period under analysis, ASEAN ranked third in importance, lagging notably behind Japan as an Asian source for EU PI per capita inflows.

Existent EU–Asia economic and financial relations: policy implications for the EU

Consistent with the above evidence and on the basis that size matters, current EU–Asia economic and financial relations were viewed within three key dimensions (trade, FDI and money and finance/PI) revealing several insights into the EU's interdependence with and relative importance of the Asian region and within Asian sources/destinations. On an interregional basis and in terms of trade in goods and services, albeit that the exports to and imports from Asia have been relatively stable over the period under analysis, their magnitude (approximately 6 and 11–12 per cent respectively) has remained relatively low in comparison to intra-EU trade. This finding is based on the UN method of determining relative exports/imports. The appropriateness of the UN method was argued on the basis that the EU as a whole is not fully integrated.

The differences between the UN and EC's methods (approximately three times the magnitude) indicate a disharmony in the EU's political economy: policy makers view interregional trade using the EU method, while the market uses the UN method. This means there will be little EU market-based pressure arising in the policy-making process to encourage intensification of relations with ASEAN or the Asian region. The discrepancy between the two methods also explains Moeller's (2007, p. 480) insight that although the two groupings have a shared general political and economic outlook, their relationship has not moved from being consultative to substantive. Thus, the EU is its own most important zone of trade, and the Asian region's capability to generate externalities remains subordinated in size and status to that of the EU.

In terms of FDI per capita and PI per capita, it was demonstrated that, barring FDI outflows to Korea and PI outflows to Japan, the Asian region fell below the benchmark indicator. This implies that, with some notable exceptions, the Asian region's capacity to generate externalities in terms of FDI, money and finance is below average.

On a within Asian sources/destination basis, the evidence revealed the relative importance of ASEAN in generating externalities. With the exception of EU exports of goods and services in which ASEAN ranked second, ASEAN consistently ranked third in all other categories – see summary provided by Table 4.3. In terms of trade (using the UN method), ASEAN only accounts for approximately 1.4 per cent of the EU's total exports and 2.1 per cent of the EU's total imports. When viewing EU FDI flows for the period, ASEAN only accounted for between €8.6 and €21.3 per capita in FDI outflows and between €–2.2 and €7.8 per capita FDI inflows. On the basis of PI flows for the period, ASEAN contributed between US\$117.1 and US\$200.5 per capita outflows and between US\$128.4 and US\$172.8 per capita inflows.

When compared with the other major Asian economies under investigation, the findings implied that ASEAN is not the principal potential generator of externalities in the Asian region and thus lacks the capability to be considered a core strategic ally. The principal potential generators are split between China holding the ranking of first in terms of trade (both exports

Table 4.3 Summary of relative importance rankings for ASEAN and other major Asian economies from an EU perspective

Grouping/state	Trade		FDI		PI	
	Exports	Imports	Outflows	Inflows	Outflows	Inflows
ASEAN	2	3	3	3	3	3
China (incl. HK)	1	1	4	2	4	2
India	4	4	5	5	5	5
Japan	3	5	2	1	1	1
Korea	5	2	1	4	2	4

Source: Author's calculations, refer to text for commentary and explanation

and imports), Japan in terms of FDI inflows and PI (outflows and inflows) and Korea in terms of FDI outflows. In addressing which of the three alternatives (China, Japan and Korea) should hold the status as the EU's core Asian economic/financial strategic ally, size remains the key determinant. Currently this means Japan and China, the latter of which the EU (itself) predicts will be the second-largest economic power in the world by the year 2025 (EU, 2009a, p. 10).

ASEAN's capacity as a strategic ally: decision-making and influence

Central to the notion of a core strategic alliance is the interaction of the parties which, in turn, is a function of the parties' capacity and capability. The analysis of the capability of ASEAN to generate externalities in economic and financial terms was addressed above. The analysis now turns to investigating ASEAN's capacity to influence markets. For, as Gourevitch (1999) demonstrates, a strategic actor's varying capacity determines its influence and ability to engage in strategic interactions, or in this case its ability to internalize externalities. Fundamental to this argument is ASEAN's capacity to make decisions and ensure that they, in turn, influence markets. Thus, to assess ASEAN's capacity, greater analysis into how ASEAN makes decisions (decision-making process) and how it affects its markets (influence) is needed.

Decision making in ASEAN has developed in accordance with its central ethos: consensus-based decision making. This has, under ASEAN's informal institutional framework, prevented the domination of any single member in the decision-making process and has, concomitantly, made any key ASEAN institutional features inextricably linked to the decision-making processes among its member states. ASEAN's consensus-based decision making is conducted via the members' heads of state/leaders or their ministers. Ambassadorial or equivalent representation at a regional/ASEAN level was only fully constituted in 2010 and possesses limited/subordinated decision-making capacity. This means that major ASEAN decisions and policies continue to be negotiated between the members' governments prior to their proclamation through the ASEAN framework: traditionally at the heads of state/leaders' summits. The policy and decision making executed through the ASEAN framework is made at the ministerial level, and currently consists of three permanent annual ministerial meetings/groupings (ASEAN, 2004, 2010; Chesterman, 2008; ISEAS, 2009; Tan, 2003; Thambipillai and Saravanamuttu, 1985).

With this decision-making regime in mind, Treisman (2010) analysed ASEAN's influence on markets. Treisman (2010) undertook this analysis by evaluating ASEAN's claimed successes towards supranational integration among Southeast Asia's financial markets by locating and estimating multiple structural breaks in two equity market-based indicators. Once this was achieved, a method could be applied to examine the effects of the ASEAN decision-making regime on variations in Southeast Asian equity prices. Treisman's (2010) evaluation specifically investigated the decision-making regime represented by the ASEAN Finance Ministers Meetings (one of ASEAN's mainstay ministerial level meetings) and their relationship with points of long-term change in the overall structure (structural breaks) of the region's equity markets. In elementary terms, the evaluation undertaken by Treisman (2010) is analogous to taking two parallel time lines and comparing how well the dates on which their intercept shifts/breaks overlap, thereby quantifying the influence of ASEAN politics on its markets.

The main findings of Treisman's (2010) paper was that the influence of ASEAN politics has been greater in recent years, but the magnitude of influence has remained minor and did not significantly vary from one break to the next. Together, these findings provide strong evidence that the politics of ASEAN has, in fact, had little bearing on the development of financial integration among Southeast Asia's financial markets (Treisman, 2010).

ASEAN's capacity as a strategic ally: policy implications for the EU

The investigation of ASEAN's decision-making process revealed several interesting features, the most notable of which are ASEAN's consensus-based decision making and its informal institutional framework. These characteristics have historically served ASEAN well, in so far as providing its members with a non-controversial or non-adversarial forum within which to engage in regional politics. However, consensus-based decision making is associative of decision making undertaken on a lowest common denominator basis. This, coupled with the informal institutional framework, which maintains non-domination by members and subordinates all decisions and policy processes to the heads of state/leaders' summits and ministerial meetings, ensures that ASEAN's decisions will not take a form or scope that may impede the individual members' national self interests. This does not bode well for the EU should their intended relations with ASEAN extend to mechanisms (such as those aimed to achieve structural change or freer markets) that require ASEAN members to incur immediate individual losses for future collective gains.

The evidence as to the influence of ASEAN on its markets produced by Treisman (2010) naturally has significant implications as to ASEAN's capacity to engage in strategic interactions which are intended to internalize externalities. The peculiarities of the ASEAN decision-making process, the use of a core ministerial meeting and traditionally sensitive indicators (equity markets) in Treisman's (2010) analysis imply that his findings extend beyond ASEAN's influence over financial markets alone and to ASEAN's influence in all other aspects of the economy. These conclusions suggest that ASEAN's capacity to influence markets with the intention of internalizing externalities is minor.

Thus, it is submitted that ASEAN lacks the capacity to influence and engage in strategic interactions. The above analysis indicates that the EU is in a stark position, in which it must consider the genuine credibility of ASEAN as a core strategic ally and whether it should be engaged on an interregional basis. Although countries' capacities to internalize externalities vary, their execution of political will is assumed absolute. However, as noted by Gourevitch (1999), such execution/interactions involve deployment of party capabilities towards each other. This, in light of the findings as to ASEAN's capacity, means that the EU could engage ASEAN member states individually/bilaterally (grouping to state), thereby exploiting its comparative advantage in capability to achieve an outcome equal to or greater than that of engaging ASEAN interregionally. The finding's validity has subsequently been demonstrated through the EU's suspension of negotiating a free trade agreement (FTA) with ASEAN in favour of bilateral FTA negotiations with several Southeast Asian nations, most notably Singapore, Vietnam and Malaysia. However, the EU affirms that its ultimate objective remains an agreement with the ASEAN region (EU, 2009b, 2010a, 2010b).

Conclusion

This paper critically appraised whether it is in the EU's best interests to regard ASEAN as a core strategic economic/financial ally in Asia and whether further engagement with ASEAN members should occur on an interregional basis. In undertaking this appraisal, the paper relied upon a joint application of the rationale for international policy coordination and the strategic-choice approach of international relations. This permitted an analysis of the economic/financial dimensions of the topic from an EU perspective through the investigation into the capability of nations/groupings to generate externalities and their concomitant capacity to influence markets.

The paper addressed the topic in two stages. First, an analysis of the existent economic and financial relationships between the EU and Asia was undertaken. To this end, the paper investigated three key dimensions: trade, FDI and money and finance/PI. The analysis indicated that, with some notable exceptions, the Asian region's capability to generate externalities for the EU in terms of FDI, money and finance was below average. On a within Asia basis, compared with the other major Asian economies under investigation, ASEAN was found not to be a principal potential generator of externalities for the EU in the Asian region. Instead, the principal potential generators were split between China holding the ranking of first in terms of trade (both exports and imports), Japan in terms of FDI inflows and PI (outflows and inflows), and Korea in terms of FDI outflows. Thus, at present and in terms of economics/finance, ASEAN lacks the capability to be a strategic ally for the EU. Instead, a more suitable candidate exists in the form of China.

Second, the paper analysed the decision-making process/regime of ASEAN and the findings of a recently completed advanced time series model in order to assess ASEAN's capacity, as a strategic ally and whether the EU should engage ASEAN on a interregional basis. It was demonstrated that ASEAN currently lacks the capacity to influence and engage in strategic interactions, and that the EU, using its comparative advantage in capability, could engage ASEAN member states bilaterally in order to achieve a benefit equal to or greater than that of engaging ASEAN interregionally.

As mentioned above, this paper is limited by focusing on the economic/financial pillars of relations between the EU and ASEAN in the broader Asian context and by the time period used in the analysis. Examination of other pillars will surely reveal further insights into the grand strategic interactions between the two regions, as would a greater time frame. Investigation of the EU's capacity to influence markets would also shed more light on its own status as a core strategic ally. Similarly, additional analysis into the notion of a core strategic ally is needed: its defining components are themselves dynamic in the temporal dimension, and although the rationale for international coordination is clear, the system in which states operate, both practically and theoretically, is anarchical and thus fundamentally presumes and often leads to non-cooperation among states. However, at this stage, based on the above analysis and findings, it would not be in the EU's best interests to regard ASEAN as a core financial/economic strategic ally, and the EU is expected to continue to seek further engagement with individual ASEAN members on a bilateral basis.

Bibliography

ASEAN (2004) ASEAN Secretariat, 'Organisational structure of ASEAN', www.aseansec. org/13103.htm, date accessed 6 November 2008.

ASEAN (2010) ASEAN Secretariat, 'Full complement of the Committee of Permanent Representatives to ASEAN', http://www.aseansec.org/24427.htm, date accessed 10 January 2011.
Boisseau Du Rocher S. (2006) 'ASEAN and Northeast Asia: Stakes and implications for the European Union – ASEAN partnership', *Asia Europe Journal*, 4, 2, 229–249.
Bagwell K. and Staiger R.W. (2004) 'National sovereignty in an interdependent world', *NBER Working Paper Series*, no. 10249.
Chesterman S. (2008) 'Does ASEAN exist? The Association of Southeast Asian Nations as an international legal person', *Singapore Yearbook of International Law*, 12, 199–211.
Drezner D. (2001) 'State power and the structure of global governance'. Presented at the annual meeting of the American Political Sciences Association, San Francisco, CA.
EU (2001) Commission of the European communities, *Europe and Asia: A strategic framework for enhanced partnerships*, 4 September.
EU (2008) Commission of the European communities, *Eurostat pocket books: European Union foreign direct investment yearbook 2008* (Luxembourg: European Communities).
EU (2009a) Commission of the European communities, *The world in 2025: Rising Asia and socio-ecological transition*, DG Research Socio-economic Sciences and Humanities.
EU (2009b) Commission of the European communities, *EU to launch FTA negotiations with individual ASEAN countries, beginning with Singapore*, http://trade.ec.europa.eu/doclib/html/145651.htm, date accessed 11 January 2011.
EU (2010a) Commission of the European communities, *EU and Vietnam to launch free trade negotiations*, http://europa.eu/rapid/pressReleasesAction.do?reference=IP/10/219&format=HTML&aged=1&language=EN&guiLanguage=en, date accessed 11 January 2011.
EU (2010b) Commission of the European communities, *EU and Malaysia launch negotiations for free trade agreement*, http://trade.ec.europa.eu/doclib/press/index.cfm?id=625, date accessed 11 January 2011.
Feldstein M.S. (1988) 'Distinguished lecture on economics in government: Thinking about international economic coordination', *The Journal of Economic Perspectives*, 2, 2, 3–13.
Frenkel J., Goldstein M. and Masson P. (1990) 'The rationale for, and effects of, international economic policy coordination' in W.H. Branson, J. Frenkel, and M. Goldstein (eds.), *International Policy Coordination and Exchange Rate Fluctuations* (Chicago, IL: University of Chicago Press), 9–62.
Gilson J. (2005) 'New interregionalism? The EU and East Asia', *Journal of European Integration*, 27, 3, 307–326.
Gourevitch P.A. (1999) 'The governance problem in international relations', in D.A. Lake and R. Powell (eds.), *Strategic Choice and International Relations* (Princeton, NJ: Princeton University Press), 137–164.
Gupta A. and Prakash A. (1993) 'On Internalization of Externalities', *Indian Institute of Management Working Papers*, no. 1126.
Gwartney J., Stroup R. and Sobel R. (2000) *Economics: Private and Public Choice* (Orlando, FL: The Dryden Press).
Hunya G., Holzner M. and Wörz J. (2007) *How to Assess the Impact of FDI on an Economy* (Wien, Austria: Vienna Institute for International Economic Studies).
IMF (1993) International Monetary Fund, *Balance of Payments Manual* (Washington, DC: International Monetary Fund).

IMF (2004) International Monetary Fund, *Coordinated Portfolio Investment Survey, Year-End 2004* (Washington, DC: International Monetary Fund).
IMF (2005) International Monetary Fund, *Coordinated Portfolio Investment Survey, Year-End 2005* (Washington, DC: International Monetary Fund).
IMF (2006) International Monetary Fund, *Coordinated Portfolio Investment Survey, Year-End 2006* (Washington, DC: International Monetary Fund).
IMF (2009) International Monetary Fund, *Direction of Trade Statistics* (Washington, DC: International Monetary Fund).
ISEAS (2009) ASEAN Studies Centre, *Life After the Charter* (Institute of Southeast Asian Studies (Singapore: Institute of Southeast Asian Studies).
Lake D.A. and Powell R. (1999) 'International relations: A strategic choice approach' in D.A. Lake and R. Powell (eds.), *Strategic Choice and International Relations* (Princeton, NJ: Princeton University Press), 3–38.
Mikic M. and Gilbert J. (2007) *Trade Statistics in Policymaking – A Handbook of Commonly Used Trade Indices and Indicators* (Bangkok: United Nations Economic and social commission for Asia and the Pacific).
Moeller J.O. (2007) 'ASEAN's relations with the European Union: Obstacles and opportunities', *Contemporary Southeast Asia*, 29, 3, 465–482.
Patterson N., Montanjees M., Motala J. and Cardillo C. (2004) *Foreign Direct Investment: Trends, Data Availability, Concepts, and Recording Practices* (Washington, DC: International Monetary Fund).
Petri P.A. (2006) 'Is East Asia becoming more interdependent?', *Journal of Asian Economics*, 17, 3, 381–394.
Rüland J. (2001), 'ASEAN and the European Union: A bumpy interregional relationship', *Rheinische Friedrich Wilhelms-Universität Bonn Center for European Integration Studies Discussion Papers*, no. 95.
Swann G.M.P. (1999) 'The economics of measurement', *Report for the National Measurement Survey Review*, UK Department for Business, Innovation & Skills, London.
Tan G. (2003) *ASEAN: Economic Development and Cooperation* (Singapore: Eastern Universities Press).
Thambipillai P. and Saravanamuttu J. (1985) *ASEAN Negotiations: Two Insights* (Singapore: Institute of Southeast Asian Studies).
Treisman D. (2010), 'Multiple Regime Shifts: The Influence of ASEAN Politics on Financial Integration within South-East Asia', *Monash University Department of Economics Discussion Papers*, no. 31.
Van der Geest W. (2006) 'Shaping factors of EU – East Asia relations', *Asia Europe Journal*, 4, 2, 131–149.
Willett T.D. (1999) 'Developments in the political economy of policy coordination', *Open Economies Review*, 10, 2, 221–253.

Part III

Shifting Perceptions:
Can the EU be a Model for ASEAN?

5
The EU in Southeast Asian Public Opinion: Public Diplomacy Case

Natalia Chaban, Lai Suet-yi and Karima Abidat

Listening and hearing: conceptualizing the role of public opinion survey in EU public diplomacy practices

Globalization and changing global architecture (i.e. the emergence of new players, new 'soft' roles for traditional 'hard' powers, and the ever-increasing popularity of a 'soft' power (Elgström, 2010: online)) are giving international relations and diplomacy worldwide a more intense focus on public diplomacy (PD). Successful PD, defined as 'an international actor's attempt to advance the ends of policy by engaging with foreign publics' (Cowan and Cull, 2008, p. 6), masters five elements in its practice: listening, advocacy, cultural diplomacy, exchange and international broadcasting (Cull, 2008, pp. 31–32). One particular element of this taxonomy– listening –is given a priority over the other four. Identified as an 'actors' attempt to manage the international environment by collecting and collating data about public and their opinions overseas and using that data to redirect its policy or its wider public diplomacy approach accordingly' (Ibid., p. 32), it is an integral part of the other four PD practices. Yet, despite its importance, systematic listening to international publics is typically overlooked by the makers of foreign policy.

Importantly, listening is the key practice for a successful transition from a monologue mode of PD (a necessary, but limited 'one-way communication to advocate foreign policy strategies' (Cowan and Arsenault, 2008, p. 13)) to dialogue and collaboration modes. These respectively 'provide an opportunity to listen or allow for feedback or critical responses from the audience' (Ibid., p. 16) and 'participate in a project together' (Ibid., p. 21), thus prioritizing relationship building. Cowan and Arsenault stressed that the 'need to be heard represents an almost universal human characteristic' (Ibid., p. 19), and cited Martin Buber's (1958) vision of a 'true dialogue, in which participants willingly and openly engage in true relationship-building exchanges in which feeling of control and dominance are minimised' (Cowan and

Arsenault, 2008, p. 18). Predictably, the lack of listening skills and a heavy reliance on monologue (especially by economically and socially advanced international powers, including former metropoles) could be treated 'with suspicion' (Leonard, 2002, pp. 6–7) by weaker counterparts and former colonies.

'Research into foreign perceptions and attitudes' was listed by Lynch (2005, p. 15) as one of the three areas supporting the European Union (EU) PD efforts on par with 'communication and information strategies (...) and cultural and educational actions' (Ibid.). However, there has been little effort to systematically assess how the EU's message is received internationally (not least due to overlooked and underbudgeted EU PD status (see Korski, 2008; Gouveia and Plumridge, 2005; Hendrikson, 2006; Ociepka and Ryniejska, 2005)). In parallel, there is an underdeveloped scholarly effort to evaluate the views on the EU among the general public in the third countries,[1] mainly due to the sheer cost and cumbersome logistics of administering large-scale public surveys. Existing public survey studies[2] do not exclusively focus on the EU and do not take into consideration a regional perspective.

To address the problem, this study explores how listening practices could enhance post-Lisbon EU PD monologue, dialogue and collaboration modes. In particular, we examine general public opinion on the EU in selected Southeast Asian countries (Thailand, Singapore, Vietnam, Indonesia, the Philippines and Malaysia) and discuss how public opinion surveys may contribute to EU PD in one particular geopolitical region. This analysis uses the data generated by a pioneering transnational comparative research project 'The EU in the Eyes of Asia-Pacific' (Chaban and Holland, 2008; Chaban et al., 2009; Holland et al., 2007; Holland and Chaban, 2010). This project is surveying news media coverage of the EU, as well as public and national stakeholders' opinions on the EU, in 20 Asia-Pacific locations between 2002 and 2012, including six Southeast Asian ones (Thailand and Singapore (study conducted in 2006–2007), Vietnam, Indonesia and the Philippines (2008–2009) and Malaysia (2009–2010)). Uniquely, the project conducted a national public opinion survey in each location, sampling 400 citizens per location[3] (margin of error for the sample in each country is ±4.9 per cent). While the surveys took place in different years, this study has comparative value because identical questionnaires were used in each location and delivered by a professional social research company in the native languages.[4]

EU–Southeast Asia: dialogue between the regions

The study assumes that systematic region-focused comparative public opinion studies are a necessary political tool within the EU's post-Lisbon foreign policy: as a regional entity itself, the EU promotes region-to-region dialogue, thus, informed insights into what unites and divides members of a region in their views on the EU is a useful asset to the incumbent European External

Action Service (EEAS). From a pragmatic point of view, a more nuanced knowledge of regional contexts could increase the efficiency of the EU's official and public diplomacy efforts in both a third country and the region it belongs to. It is assumed the general public in Southeast Asia should possess heightened awareness of pronounced attitudes towards and visible connections to the EU as a significant local, regional and global player. This is due to Europe's colonial links to the region in the past, post 9/11 cultural/civilizational tensions between the West (of which the EU is a part) and the Islamic World (which is present in Southeast Asia), the EU's bilateral trade, developmental aid and preferential trade arrangements, as well as the ongoing EU–ASEAN (Association of the Southeast Asian Nations) interregional dialogue.

This study's general focus on EU PD (and international public opinion in particular) is new to the scholarship of EU–Southeast Asia relations. Numerous studies on EU–Southeast Asia interactions have mainly focused on the EU's political and economic relations with the region on bilateral and/or interregional levels. Typically, these studies highlight conflict (especially when it comes to the issues of human rights, democracy and Myanmar/Burma) (e.g. Balme and Bridges, 2008; Bridges, 1999; Camroux, 2008; Haacke, 2010; Jones, 2008; Manea, 2008; Murray and Rees, 2010; Oerstroem, 2007; Peterson, 2006; Rüland, 2001; Yeo, 2007). In contrast, studies that explore people-to-people links and prioritize points of concord (rather than discord) are rare. This analysis addresses this double deficit, recognizing Fort's idea (2008) that misconceptions grounded in a lack of empathy and understanding are major obstacles to a more open and effective dialogue between Europe and Asia. According to a commentator from Southeast Asia (Duong, 2008), 'the considerable differences in respect of culture, opinions, politics as well as misperception and ill-informed views of each other's role in the international arena have unfortunately constituted a real challenge for a comprehensive cooperation between the two continents.' Respectively, this analysis considers the results of the public opinion surveys with regard to that which will unite nations and people. This question stems from Depkat's observation (2004, p. 176) that '[t]he study of international relations... has shifted away from state-centred forms of analyses towards retracing the informal social and cultural interactions among nations and peoples.'

Inevitably, historical colonial links as well as current economic, political and humanitarian ties (on bilateral and interregional levels) guide the modern-day imagery of the EU in Southeast Asian societies. Even though the 50-year-old political entity of the EU has never been a colonial ruler, the EU's identity in the region reflects the legacy of former colonial powers/current EU member states. Specifically for the countries in this study, British colonial rule was experienced in Singapore, Malaysia and Indonesia; French authority was established in Vietnam; the Spanish ruled in the Philippines; and the Portuguese and the Dutch in Indonesia. In contrast, Thailand is a special case in this analysis as well as in the history of Europe's presence in Southeast Asia. It was never colonized, but was significantly influenced by two European powers ruling in neighbouring territories, namely the British (who colonized Myanmar/Burma) and the French (who colonized Laos, Vietnam and Cambodia). Undeniably, different European colonial legacies pervaded everyday life in these Southeast Asian states, influencing, according to Copland (1990 as cited in Bridges, 1999, p. 17), 'administrative and national boundaries, transport networks, parliamentary institutions, language and literature, science and technology and even sports and popular culture'. With 'Europe' frequently used in the region as a synonym for 'the EU', Europe's colonial alter ego is likely a key consideration in raising the EU's profile in Southeast Asia, both cognitively and emotionally.

The six Southeast Asian countries in this analysis belong to the so-called 'dynamic Asian economies' (Bridges, 1999, p. 49) characterized by steadily growing wealth and standards of living. While Singapore (in a view of the CIA Factbook, 2010b: online) is a 'highly developed and successful free-market economy', Indonesia, Malaysia and Thailand have been recently described by Islam (2010) as 'Asia's middle income countries and emerging economies'. In comparison, the Philippines and Vietnam are weaker economies. The European Commission (2009a, online) recognizes Southeast Asia's 'current economic strengths and its great longer-term potential' and views the region as an attractive market and investment opportunity for EU economic operators. Yet, a certain asymmetry pervades current economic and trading ties between the EU and the six Southeast Asian economies in this study – while the EU is a significant trading partner to every country in the sample, these locations are relatively insignificant to the EU.[5]

The EU has special trading arrangements with each of these countries. Singapore and Malaysia are negotiating a FTA with the EU, while Thailand, Indonesia, Vietnam, the Philippines and Malaysia benefit from the Generalized System of Preferences (GSP) in their trade with the EU (the scheme is designed to promote economic growth in the developing world by providing preferential duty-free entry for targeted products). In addition to the GSP (classified by European Commission (online) as a development tool), the EU administers Official Development Aid (ODA) packages to Vietnam, Indonesia, Thailand and the Philippines.[6] Aiming to 'eradicate poverty and help enhance human development' (ECD to Vietnam, online), the ODA is tailored by the EU to respond to the needs of partner countries in the region. Sectors benefiting from ODA in these countries include education, health, population, water and sanitation, governance and civil society, programme assistance, economic infrastructure and services, and debt and emergency assistance (EU Donor Atlas, 2008).

Much of the economic bilateral dialogue between the EU and the six countries in this study occurs within the framework of ASEAN, a regional grouping in Southeast Asia to which the six nations belong. The EU and ASEAN have been engaged in an active interregional dialogue since the early 1970s, with the relation being intensified since the mid-1990s (ASEAN Secretariat, online). Almost four decades of interaction resulted in fruitful commercial and economic ties, yet political dialogue remains contentious (De Fleur, 2010, online). The tension between the two regions originates from their different perspectives on human rights, the East Timor conflict and the 'thorny' question of Myanmar/Burma, and may negatively impact the EU's local imagery. EU–ASEAN dialogue is assumed here to be yet another critical factor in raising the EU's public profile in the region: the presence of an intraregional formation in Southeast Asia should facilitate the general public's understanding of the EU, a complex political and economic intraregional entity on a different continent.

The sensitivity of relations between modern Europe and Southeast Asia has also been triggered by global post-9/11 tensions between the so-called 'Western' world and its Islamic counterpart. Importantly for our study, Indonesia and Malaysia are among the largest Muslim countries in the world, and Singapore, Thailand and the Philippines have sizable Muslim communities. Arguably, anti-Islamic sentiment in Europe (including the scandal regarding the offensive cartoons of Prophet Mohammad published by a newspaper in one EU member state, Denmark) may add to a mistrust of the EU on the part of the ASEAN nations.

The EU through the eyes of Southeast Asian public

Twigg (2005, p. vi) pointed out that for the EU 'to prosper it must project a positive image of itself to opinion formers and to the "man in the street" both within and beyond its borders'. Respectively, this study focused on the assessment of how positively the EU is perceived by the public in Southeast Asia. Out of 23 questions, the study examined the answers to six. The first angle of analysis was on perceptions of the EU's importance (in the present and in the future).[7] The second was on spontaneous images of the EU in general, and of key issues in EU-locality dialogue in particular.[8] The final angle was on the nature of personal/professional links with the EU and its member states.[9]

Perceived importance

Our first finding was that the general public in the six Southeast Asian locations did not perceive the EU as one of their nation's most important partners, either in the present or in the past (Table 5.1). Despite the EU's volume of trade, special trading and developmental arrangements with each nation in this analysis, the citizens of those nations assigned the top ranking in the perceived importance to either the existing 'super power' of the

Table 5.1 Perceived importance of the EU: in the present and in the future.

Year of the survey	Location	Currently, 1st place	EU rank	In future, 1st place	EU rank	Change
2006	Singapore	China	6	China	4	↑
	Thailand	China	5	China	4	↑
2008	Philippines	USA	5	USA	2	↑
	Vietnam	China	4	China	5	↓
	Indonesia	USA	8	USA	5	↑
2010	Malaysia	China	8	China	5	↑

USA (respondents in the Philippines and Indonesia) or to the rising 'mercurial power' of China (the rest of the sample). These two global actors occupied the top rank of importance both in the present and in the future. Taking into account the regional proximity of China and the colonial ties of the USA to the Philippines, these public choices are not that surprising. What is surprising is the gap between the actual and perceived importance of the EU (e.g. the EU was the second largest bilateral trading partner for Singapore after Malaysia according to 2006 statistics, yet the public ranked it only sixth). Somewhat encouragingly for the EU, its perceived importance was seen as growing by all respondents except the Vietnamese. The Philippines ranking was the most unusual with the EU's perceived importance in the future growing from the fifth to the second rank, trailing only the USA!

It is interesting to compare the perceived present-day importance of the EU with the perceived importance of former colonial rulers (a comparison non-applicable in the Thai case). The UK ranked eighth for Singapore and ninth for Malaysia. France ranked sixth for Vietnam, the UK ranked ninth for Indonesia, while the Netherlands was mentioned by only two Indonesians. Spain was not mentioned by any respondent from the Philippines (an unsurprising finding given that Spanish rule finished as early as 1898). In the Thai case, we looked into the perceived importance of the UK and France. The UK's ranking among Thai respondents was sixth, while France's was eighth. Significantly for EU PD efforts, the importance of the EU as a communal partner was ranked higher than EU member states/former colonial powers – an interesting finding possibly indicating that the absence of direct colonial experiences may facilitate a more positive perception of the EU's importance.

Spontaneous images of the EU

The summary of the top four spontaneous (stereotypical) images of the EU in six locations are presented in Table 5.2.

The analysis revealed a great degree of similarity in the stereotypical visions of the EU among the publics of the six Southeast Asian countries.

Table 5.2 Spontaneous images of the EU.

	1st	2nd	3rd	4th
Indonesia	Monetary/ economic union	Trade	Euro	Democracy, good governance, rule of law
Malaysia	Business/trade	Economic power	Education	Tourism
Philippines	No image	Union/ integration	Monetary Union	Development aid donor
Singapore	Union/ integration	Euro	Economic power	Individual countries
Thailand	Individual countries	Economic power	Trade	Euro
Vietnam	Union/ integration	Monetary/ economic union	Euro	Democracy, good governance, rule of law

One dominant perception was the EU as an integrationist entity. Many of those associations described the EU from either a neutral (a union of countries) or positive (a union of countries who stopped intra-European wars, improved the standard of living for the people of Europe, are using a single currency and providing each other with economic and financial support) perspective. Arguably, the existence of the intraregional ASEAN could have contributed to the prominence of the 'integrationist' image of the EU.

The second most visible theme was rather predictable – the EU as an 'economic giant', described in terms of its trade might and the success of the economy. Less frequent, yet still among the top four spontaneous images, there were the views of the EU as a political entity associated immediately with its individual states (most frequently the EU's 'Big 3' – the UK, Germany and France), as well as an agent of democracy, rule of law, good governance and aid donation. In the Philippines, the most typical response to the question about the three spontaneous images of the EU was 'none', arguably indicating a weak awareness of the EU.

Government policy relating to the EU

While the question about the three spontaneous images of the EU looked into general stereotypical views on the EU, one of the follow-up questions specifically sought perceptions of the EU's interactions with the locality in question. Respondents were asked to generate recommendations to their respective governments on policy making relating to the EU. The analysis of the answers marked several main themes in the perceptions of the EU as a local counterpart (Table 5.3).

Table 5.3 Issues recommended by the public to be stressed when their local governments formulate policy towards the EU.

		Indonesia	Malaysia	Philippines	Singapore	Thailand	Vietnam
Economy-related issues	Economy in general	230	72	60	144	277	246
	OFWs/job opportunity/labour rights	16	1	102	1	8	15
	Science and technology	22	0	1	3	1	8
	EU regulation	5	0	5	3	35	3
	Intellectual property	0	0	0	2	1	1
	Energy	0	0	0	0	3	0
	Environment	6	2	0	8	15	9
Political issues	Political affairs	38	12	2	41	30	43
	Human rights	7	3	16	28	10	5
	Rule of law, democracy, good governance	13	3	11	16	3	6
	Development aid/poverty alleviation	15	9	19	2	1	32
	Building good relations and cooperation with the EU	64	5	12	28	17	18
	Relations with individual EU member states	0	0	0	0	10	0
Cultural/civilizational issues	Social	25	4	1	4	3	19
	Education	21	3	1	2	1	31
	People-to-people exchanges	14	3	1	8	6	32
	Culture	21	3	0	25	1	11
	Religion	2	11	0	10	1	0
	Relation with former metropole	1	1	0	2	0	0
	Independence/non-interference	19	0	0	12	7	0
	Diversity within the EU	0	0	0	18	2	0
	Regionalism/globalization	0	0	0	15	3	0

Most frequently, the EU was conceptualized as an important yet demanding economic interlocutor, whose actions and decisions could disadvantage local economies. For example, Indonesian responses to the survey conducted in 2008 prolifically commented on the EU's ban on Indonesian airlines entering European airspace. In the same year a survey in the Philippines highlighted public demand for its government to improve dialogue with the EU on the issue of overseas Filipino workers (OFWs) in the EU. A 2006 survey in Thailand brought to the surface the issue of EU regulations on and quality requirements for imports impacting Thai industries. The 2008 Vietnamese survey answers stressed the reduction of tariffs on Vietnamese goods entering the EU's market. Most interactions between the EU and the various localities were seen in terms of trade, finance and business. Issues of science and technology, energy, environment and intellectual property in the official dialogue with the EU were considered peripheral in all locations.

The second most visible group of responses dealt with the EU as a political interlocutor. Building good political relations with the EU in general was a typical answer (and the most prominent in Indonesia in comparison with other locations). The issues of human rights were the most frequently mentioned in the Philippines and Singapore. The issues of democracy and good governance received greater recognition in Singapore, Indonesia and the Philippines. Relations with the EU in the areas of developmental aid were mentioned the most frequently in Vietnam, followed by the Philippines and Indonesia. In contrast, Thai and Malay respondents did not stress the need for their governments to engage in dialogue on the issues of human rights, democracy or developmental aid.

The third, less visible, group of responses was the description of the EU as an interlocutor belonging to a different culture and even civilization. For example, Malaysian respondents stressed the need to continue the dialogue on cultural and religious differences between the EU and Malaysia, especially in the context of globalization. A dialogue on religious differences was also urged by Singaporean respondents. Singaporeans also found such issues as diversity within the EU and regional cooperation in Southeast Asia as worthy for future policy dialogue with the EU. The Vietnamese respondents were the most vocal in requesting attention to education and people-to-people exchanges between the EU and Vietnam (possibly due to the fact that Vietnamese constitute a numerous ethnic minority from Southeast Asia living in Europe, or due to the fact that education remains one of the main state priorities for this communist country). Respondents in Indonesia, Singapore and Thailand specifically stressed their national independence and the importance of the EU's non-interference in their affairs. References to the 'colonial identity' of Europe/EU were prevalent in Indonesia, in contrast to the other locations. The Indonesian respondents were the most resentful, expressing sentiments against the EU while linking it to the past colonial legacies of Europe. Consider for example the following responses: 'Do not let Indonesia get colonized', 'Indonesia must defend the culture, do not let it be taken away', 'Indonesia should pay attention to its culture, do not get influenced by Europeans', 'Indonesia should not be dominated by Europe', and 'Limit European culture from entering in Indonesia'. This finding is hardly surprising considering the Dutch colonial experience/heritage and the strong influence of nationalism on today's Indonesian politics and society at large.

In summary, while the question about three spontaneous images evoked mostly positive and neutral visions of the EU, responses to the question about the EU-related government policy question brought to the surface a greater variety of attitudes towards the EU, and demonstrated public awareness of sensitive and contentious issues in the EU dialogue with the locations in question.

Personal and professional links with the EU member states

This analysis also looked at the interpersonal connections the citizens of the six Southeast countries have with the EU member states. Our assumption was that respondents from the former colonies will have stronger ties with their former metropoles, and through these links will get first-hand exposure to the realities of the modern integrating Europe.

Revealingly, the survey showed that the most typical answer in each location was 'no ties with any EU member states' (Table 5.4) – almost two-thirds of the total sample registered no personal or professional links with the EU member states. In Indonesia and Malaysia, less than a quarter of respondents had ties with the EU countries, and only a third of the Vietnamese respondents had links to the EU members. Respondents from Singapore and the Philippines had a slightly higher level of personal involvement with the EU's states. The public in the only non-colony in our sample, Thailand, appeared to be the most connected with the EU countries, with nearly half of the respondents reporting links to the EU member states (it may well be that Thailand, as the 'number 1' ASEAN tourist destination in the region (ASEAN,

Table 5.4 Personal/professional connections with EU member states

	Yes (%)	No
Indonesia	87 (21.5%)	318 (78.5%)
Malaysia	98 (24.5%)	302 (75.5%)
Vietnam	137 (34.2%)	263 (65.8%)
Singapore	175 (43.7%)	225 (56.3%)
Philippines	177 (41.7%)	233 (58.3%)
Thailand	193 (48.2%)	207 (51.8%)
Total	867 (36%)	1,538 (64%)

2010, online), is the one most exposed and connected with Europe that supplies it with tens of millions of tourists every year). In contrast, Indonesia, which experienced the rule of not one but several European colonial powers in the past, had the lowest share of personal connections with Europe in this survey.

Assessing the patterns of connectivity between the respondents from the six Southeast Asian states and individual EU member states,[10] in the total sample, the UK, which was a colonial ruler for three of the six countries in this analysis, was the state with the most professional and personal bonds to the six countries (Figure 5.1). The countries with the fewest connections with the locations were the smaller EU member states and those countries that joined the EU in 2004.

In terms of each individual country's Southeast Asian connections, the former colonial rulers have more contacts (Table 5.5). For example, the Netherlands was the EU country with whom the Indonesian public reported most personal/professional linkages, while for the Malaysian and Singaporean respondents, it was the UK, and for the Vietnamese it was France. It is worth noting that in Vietnam's case, other than France, the public's connections are predominantly with ex-Communist Central/Eastern European countries (including Germany with its former GDR). This is not unexpected – as a member of the ex-socialist camp, Vietnam enjoyed close links with the former USSR and its political allies in Europe.

The Philippines also presents an interesting (but not surprising) case. Its respondents reported more links to the UK, Italy and Germany than to Spain (unlike the other European colonial powers, Spain lost its supremacy over the Philippines much earlier). The uniqueness of the Filipino case can be

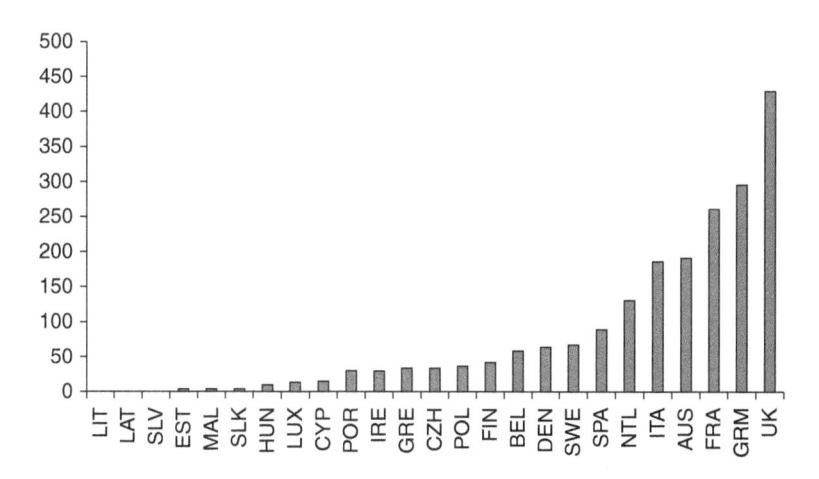

Figure 5.1 Personal and professional links with individual EU member states.

Table 5.5 The ten EU member states that feature most personal/professional links with the Southeast Asian public.

	Indonesia	Malaysia	Philippines	Singapore	Thailand	Vietnam
Austria	14	31	29	16	46	56
Belgium	7	4	16	14	19	0
Denmark	2	4	14	16	28	2
France	9	11	22	55	87	78
Germany	25	23	51	58	89	51
Italy	8	8	73	40	56	2
Netherlands	36	5	15	32	36	7
Spain	3	1	34	30	23	0
Sweden	1	4	14	20	23	7
UK	15	59	83	130	134	9

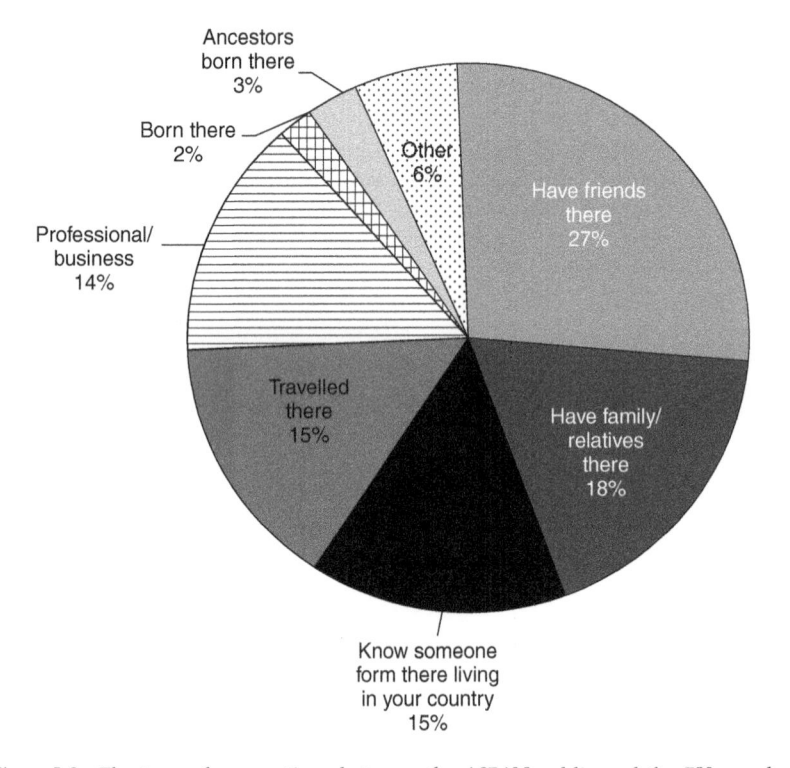

Figure 5.2 The type of connections between the ASEAN public and the EU member states.

explained by the large-scale emigration of OFWs.[11] In the EU, Italy has been the biggest employer of OFWs since 2004 (half of the OFWs in Europe), whereas the UK and Ireland are the second- and the third-biggest receivers respectively (the Philippines Overseas Employment Administration, 2009: online). In contrast, only 6 per cent of the OFWs are working in Spain.

Concerning the nature of connections to the EU member states, the two top categories were 'friends' or 'family members' living or working in the EU (27 and 18 per cent, respectively (Figure 5.2)).

Challenges and opportunities: EU public diplomacy in Southeast Asia

This comparative systematic analysis of EU external imagery among Southeast Asian publics proves the 'relevance of communications, cultural policy, ideology, psychology and propaganda for the study of international affairs' (Scott-Smith, 2008, p. 173). Arguably, the findings indicated problems in the EU PD monologue and collaboration activities in the regions, and outlined several promising messages on the dialogue level.

An essential advocacy tool, PD monologue is there to 'convey an idea a vision, or perspective and to present it eloquently and clearly' (Cowan and Arsenault, 2008, p. 13). Yet, not enough EU effort is currently 'devoted to developing a comprehensive and coherent communication strategy with third-countries' in order 'to project a much stronger and clearer identity to the rest of the world' (USC Centre for Public Diplomacy, 2010, online). Our findings seem to support the latter argument. The actual importance of the EU to each of the six countries and to the Southeast Asian region as a whole was not reflected in the public's perception. Moreover, for all locations, the most frequent spontaneous images of the EU did not include visions of it as an environmental 'champion', developmental actor, or contributor to poverty reduction in the region. The EU's most frequent spontaneous image in the Philippines was 'none'! These findings may indicate that the EU is still not seen as achieving and delivering internationally, while other major powers (e.g. the USA and China) have made relatively greater and more visible achievements in comparison with the EU (the ubiquitous 'capability-expectations gap' formulated for the EU by Hill in 1993). They may also indicate that the EU (even if it achieves) did not communicate its achievements to the external public effectively, while other players were more successful in it (a phenomenon we call 'EU external communication deficit').

Arguably, the findings of the EU's perceived peripheral status and invisible environmental, developmental and poverty-eradicating profiles indicate the need to revise the EU's PD monologue mode in the region within the framework of a newly established EEAS. Ultimately designed to make the EU's communal global performance efficient, transparent and attractive to third countries, EEAS is also expected to 'boost (...) the EU's cultural and public diplomacy activities' (Korski, 2008, online). If used skilfully, traditional one-way communication will result in a raised awareness of policies, identities or values. Moreover, EU PD's successful monologue can later be used as the basis for two other modes – dialogue and collaboration.

The European Commission (2007, online) claimed that the EU PD objective is in 'clearly explaining the EU's goals, policies and activities and fostering understanding of these goals through dialogue with individual citizens, groups, institutions and the media'. Several messages from the general public surveys indicated a strong potential for the dialogue mode in EU PD efforts in Southeast Asia. To begin with, our findings highlighted a positive popular predisposition towards the EU: the perceived importance of the EU in the future was seen as slightly increasing[12] and spontaneous images of the EU (question deliberately asked in the very beginning of the questionnaire to avoid the bias inflicted by later questions) profiled predominately positive typical visions of the EU (the EU was not treated 'with suspicion' due to the legacies of colonialism left by several EU member states in the region). Importantly, the images of 'union' and 'integration' were the predominant spontaneous associations of the EU in the minds of respondents. Thus, it is suggested that the public in the region can relate to the EU – the idea of regional integration in Europe is not an alien concept to the public in a region which has itself been involved in intraregional construction (ASEAN). The public also saw various facets of the EU's international persona. Unsurprisingly, the EU was recognized as an 'economic powerhouse' – a vision of economic might surfaced in the spontaneous images of 'trade' and 'euro'. The top four stereotypical images in four locations (with the exception of Singapore and Thailand) also included views on the EU as 'normative' and aiding agency, listing such attributes as 'democracy', 'good governance', 'rule of law' and 'developmental aid'.[13] In addition, the visions of the EU's interactions with the government reported in each respective location also highlighted the roles of the EU as a global political player, a culturally diverse entity and an important economic partner. These are images that can contribute to an understanding of the communal nature of the EU and its economic power in the world – a fundamental element of developing a successful dialogue facilitated by EU PD.

Importantly for EU PD dialogue mode, the general public was clearly aware of numerous contentious issues in the interactions between the EU and their locations (including economic tensions and a range of cultural/civilizational issues such as religion, culture, national sovereignty and the need for Europe's non-interference in local and regional affairs). This is significant as 'dialogue should first and foremost be approached as a method for improving relationships and increasing understanding, not necessarily for reaching consensus or winning an argument' (Cowan and Arsenault, 2008, p. 19).

This study argues that collaboration mode is the most problematic for EU PD efforts in the region. True cross-national collaboration is based on a meaningful dialogue as well as on joint projects when individuals from different cultures 'build or achieve something together' (Ibid., p. 21). Yet, this analysis revealed that two-thirds of the total were found to have no personal or professional links to any EU member states. Focusing on individual countries demonstrated that the two Muslim states, Indonesia and Malaysia, had the lowest level of personal links to the EU countries. If the lack of personal contacts in these two countries is somehow associated with the controversial yet popular idea of the 'clash of civilizations', this presents an additional challenge for EU PD. For those members of the public who did report personal and professional connections to the EU members, the 'geography of links' with the EU was somewhat limited (typically, the EU's 'small' and Central/Eastern European new member states were not well connected). The surveys showed that the EU's 'Big 3' were the major source of Southeast Asian linkages.

This situation is not that surprising – most of the links are to compatriots who are living and working in the more prosperous Western European countries in order to send remittances home. Among the 'Big 3', the UK was the most contacted EU state, suggesting that the British lifestyle, political, scientific and mass culture contributions have a higher visibility to the public in the region than any other EU member state. Indeed, the UK was a colonial ruler in three out of the six Southeast Asian countries in this study, yet two other locations that are not former UK colonies, Thailand and the Philippines, also had the most links with Britain. With the UK's infamous Euro-sceptic attitudes, the perceptions of the EU filtered through British personal and professional links is yet another point of concern for effective EU PD. More geographically diverse, intense and extensively supported people-to-people exchanges between various EU and Southeast Asian states are critical for EU PD efforts. While this study has shown how the colonial legacy in these Asian nations continues to significantly influence their contemporary engagement with EU states, the different connections reported in Vietnam, Thailand and the Philippines is indicative of how people's perceptions are also influenced by more recent historical developments, including migration and the spread of particular ideologies.

This analysis argues that a key factor in positively influencing popular Southeast Asian perceptions of the EU via dialogue and collaboration is to expand and diversify new people-to-people contacts (specifically, requested by regional public expansion and creation of educational exchange programmes as a more traditional means of PD), as well as cherish the existing ones (including diaspora links, a rather unorthodox means for PD). While establishing new educational exchanges and expanding existing ones could take a long time (mainly due to the need to secure additional funding), exploring the options of 'second-hand' exposure to the EU and its member states could be a short-term solution for EU PD in the region. This study revealed the lack of first-hand experiences of life in modern Europe (indeed, travel to Europe and contacts with Europeans were not among the most frequently reported links in our surveys). In contrast, a dominant type of personal contact with EU member states was friends and family members living there (the so-called diaspora). Scholars of PD conceptualize 'diaspora diplomacy' as one of the instruments of PD[14] (Leonard, 2002), yet '...Diaspora public diplomacy... has been relatively ignored' (Gilboa, 2008, p. 73). Cull (2008, p. 50) echoed this idea stating that only occasionally has PD purposefully used diasporas as 'a mechanism of intentional cultural transmissions'.

The survey in this analysis did not ask what those contacts were doing in Europe, but it is assumed that the majority of those contacts are working migrants (permanent or temporary, legal and possibly illegal) who live in the more prosperous Europe to survive and help families back home. In Cull's view (Ibid., p. 47), the creation of relevant PD policies should consider refugees, migrants (both documented and illegal), and workers who 'live in communities that exist simultaneously in both in the developed and developing world and spend time of the year in each'. Thus, post-Lisbon EU PD could consider taking the somewhat unusual step of promoting PD efforts with third countries within its EU member states (rather than only outside its borders) – in our case, to treat Southeast Asian links in the EU states 'as a public diplomacy resource... [not] merely a welfare problem to be managed' (Ibid., p. 50). These are individuals who possess first-hand experience of life in modern-day Europe, and thus they could become key players in EU PD collaboration efforts serving as nodes of information that disseminate opinions of the EU within their specific personal and professional networks in their country of origin.

Even though no political entity 'has made responding to international opinion central to its diplomacy or even its public diplomacy' (Ibid., p. 32), post-Lisbon EU has a realistic chance to upgrade its PD performance by paying systematic attention to its external popular perception. If the EU PD is still clear about promoting EU interests by '(understanding, informing and influencing' (European Commission, 2007) public attitudes abroad, then effective monologue, dialogue and collaboration PD efforts based on attentive and respective listening to its international partner are the key.

Notes

1. Several studies attempted to study the EU's external perceptions (e.g. GARNET, 2007; 2009; Murray, 2002). Yet, most of them focused on elite or media perceptions of the EU. In Asia specifically, several studies have touched on the EU's perception (Lisbonne-de Vergeron, 2006; 2007; Shambaugh, et al., 2007,

Tsuruoka, 2006, online). Specifically for EU-Southeast Asia interactions, several attempts have been made to explore the regional elites' views on the EU (e.g. EuropeAid 2003; 2007).
2. Public opinion in particular was occasionally mentioned in the perceptions analyses (GARNET (2007; 2009)), yet those remained unsystematic. Several notable exceptions of large-scale public opinion comparative surveys that explored the international public opinion on the EU are: US German Marshall Fund survey, September 2007 (*EUobserver*, 2007a); *World Powers in the 21st Century*, Bertelsmann Stiftung, June 2006 (it was conducted in nine countries – Brazil, China, Germany, France, the UK, India, Japan, Russia and the USA); 2007 'Voice of the People' annual survey has been carried out by Gallup International in collaboration with the European Council on Foreign Relations. It was conducted in 52 countries with 57,000 respondents (*EUobserver*, 2007b). A China-specific study of public opinion on the EU was undertaken by Zhou et al. (2010).
3. 405 in Indonesia.
4. In Thailand and Singapore the survey was delivered online. In Indonesia the survey was delivered in face-to-face format due to low level of ICT penetration. In all other locations, the survey was delivered by telephone.
5. For the EU, in 2009 Singapore was the 15th-largest trade partner (EUROPA, 2010), while in 2008 Malaysia was 23rd, Thailand was 26th, Indonesia was 32nd, and Vietnam was the 40th-largest trade partner (EUROSTAT, 2009). In contrast, the EU is among the top four largest trading partners for the six nations in this analysis. As an overall bilateral trade partner, the EU is the largest trade partner for Singapore in 2010 (de Gucht, 2010), second for Thailand (Thailand Business News:online) and Vietnam (*Deutsche Welle, 2010*: online) (both in 2009), and fourth for Indonesia in 2008 (European Commission, 2009b), Malaysia in 2009 (MITI, 2010: online) and the Philippines in 2009 (EUROPA, 2009).
6. Among the four, Vietnam is the largest recipient of the EU ODA – in 2007, 'the total EU pledge was €719.9 million' (ECD to Vietnam). In Indonesia, ODA from all EU donors in 2006 was US$335.5 million. In the same year, Thailand received US$149.86 million and the Philippines US$93.64 million. The largest of all EU donors in Indonesia is the EC, while France leads in Thailand and Vietnam, with Germany in the Philippines (*EU Donor Atlas*, 2008).
7. Questions: *Can you please tell me which overseas countries or regions, you think, are the most important partners for [your country]?* (open-ended question in telephone and face-to-face surveys (in the Philippines, Vietnam and Malaysia in the former case and in Indonesia in the latter case), and closed-ended rotating questions in online surveys in Singapore and Thailand); *How important to [your country's] future do you consider the following regions are, on a scale of 1 to 5, where 1 is not important at all and 5 is very important?* (closed-ended questions in all surveys).
8. When thinking about the term 'the European Union', what three thoughts come to your mind? (open-ended question in all surveys); In your opinion, what issues should be kept in mind when [your country] is developing government policy relating to the EU? (open-ended question in all surveys).
9. Which of the following countries [EU member states listed] do you have personal or professional connections/ties with? (closed-ended questions; option 'with none of the above' was also given); What type of connection/link is this? (closed-ended questions with a pre-determined set of options).
10. For comparative purposes, Bulgaria and Romania were not included in this analysis.

11. While according to the CIA Factbook (2010a: online), there are 'four-to five-million overseas Filipino workers', the census released by the Philippines government in 2009 stated that there were 1,912,000 OFWs around the world, and 8.3 per cent of them were in Europe (Philippines National Statistic, 2009), predominantly as domestic helpers or medical caregivers.
12. Vietnam was the only exception – its respondents saw the importance of the EU slightly declining in the future.
13. While the absence of such images in Singapore is understandable (the country is not the EU's ODA or GSP receiver), the Thai case remains intriguing.
14. On a par with NGO diplomacy, political party diplomacy, brand diplomacy and business diplomacy.

Bibliography

ASEAN (2009) 'ASEAN and EU Dialogue', http://www.aseansec.org/5612.htm, date accessed May 2010.
ASEAN official statistics, http://www.aseansec.org/stat/Table28.pdf, date accessed May 2010.
Balme R. and Bridges B. (2008) *Europe–Asia Relations: Building Multilateralisms* (London: Palgrave).
Bridges B. (1999) *Europe and the Challenge of the Asia Pacific Change, Continuity and Crisis* (Cheltenham and Northampton, MA: Edward Elgar).
Buber M. (1958) *I and Thou* (New York: Scribner).
Camroux D. (2008) 'The European Union and ASEAN: Two to tango?' in *Studies & Research 65* (Paris: Notre Europe). http://www.notre-europe.eu/uploads/tx_publication/Etude65EU-ASEAN-en.pdf, date accessed February 2012.
Chaban N. and Holland M. (eds.) (2008) *The European Union and the Asia–Pacific: Media, Public and Elite Perceptions of the EU* (London: Routledge).
Chaban N., Holland M. and Ryan P. (eds.) (2009) *The EU through the Eyes of Asia: New Cases, New Findings* (Singapore and London: World Scientific).
CIA Factbook (2010a) The Philippines, https://www.cia.gov/library/publications/the-world-factbook/geos/rp.html, date accessed May 2010.
CIA Factbook (2010b) Singapore, https://www.cia.gov/library/publications/the-world-factbook/geos/sn.html, date accessed May 2010.
Copland I. (1990) *The Burden of Empire: Perspective on Imperialism and Colonialism* (Melbourne: Oxford University Press).
Cowan G. and Arsenault A. (2008) 'Moving from monologue to dialogue to collaboration: The three layers of public diplomacy', *The Annals of the AAPSS*, 616, 10–30.
Cowan G. and Cull N. (2008) 'Public diplomacy in a changing world', *The Annals of the AAPSS*, 616, 6–8.
Cull N. (2008) 'Public Diplomacy, Taxonomies and Histories', *The ANNALS of the AAPSS*, 616, 31–54.
De Fleur N.A. (2010) *EU–ASEAN Relations: The Importance of Values, Norms and Culture* (EU Centre in Singapore Working Paper no. 1, June) http://www.eucentre.sg/articles/205/downloads/EUASEAN–AlecuFlers-8June2010.pdf, date accessed June 2010.
de Gucht K. (2010) *Europe and Singapore: partners in trade, partners for growth* (speech at the Lee Kuan Yew School of Public Policy, Singapore, 3 March) http://trade.ec.europa.eu/doclib/docs/2010/march/tradoc_145850.pdf, date accessed May 2010.

Depkat V. (2004) Cultural approaches to international relations: A challenge? in J. Gienow-Hecht and F. Schumacher (eds.) *Culture and International History* (New York: Bergham), 175–97.

Delegation of the European Union to Vietnam (2007) *Press release on 27 June 2007*, http://www.delvnm.ec.europa.eu/news/vn_news/vn_news10.htm, date accessed May 2010.

Deutsche Welle online (2010) *EU and Vietnam: free trade with conditions?* http://www.dw-world.de/dw/article/05312307,00.html, date accessed 2 March 2010.

Duong T.T. (2008) *Welcome Remarks at the Book Launch: The EU through the Eyes of Asia: Media, Public and Elite Perceptions in China, Japan, Korea, Singapore and Thailand* (Hanoi, Vietnam, 7 May 2008).

Elgström O. (2006) *Leader or Foot-Dragger? Perceptions of the European Union in Multilateral International Negotiations* (Report 1), www.sieps.se/publ/rapporter/bilagorf2006 I.pdf, date accessed May 2010.

Elgström O. (2010) *EU Leadership in an Emerging New World Order* (Paper presented at the 5th Pan-European Conference on EU Politics, Porto, 24–26 June), http://www.jhubc.it/ecpr-porto/virtualpaperroom/015.pdf, date accessed May 2010.

EUObserver (2007a) *Europeans want the EU to take more global responsibility* (7 September), http://euobserver.com/9/24717/?print=1, date accessed May 2010.

EUObserver (2007b) *World citizens favour stronger EU global role* (25 October), http://euobserver.com/9/25036/?rk=1, date accessed May 2010.

EUROPA Press release (2010) http://europa.eu/rapid/pressReleasesAction.do?reference=IP/10/228, data accessed 3 March 2010.

EUROPA Press release, 11 December 2009, http://europa.eu/rapid/pressReleasesAction.do?reference=IP/09/1904, date accessed May 2010.

EuropeAid (2003) Final Report 'Survey Analysis of EU Perceptions in South East Asia', January. Framework Contract AMS/451-Lot 7. A.R.S. Progetti S.r.l. Ambiente, Risorse e Sviluppo.

EuropeAid (2007) Final Report 'Perceptions of the EU's role in South East Asia', Framework Contract Commission, EuropeAid/123314/C/SER/multi, Lot n°4.

European Commission (2007) *The EU's 50th Anniversary Celebrations around the World: A Glance at EU Public Diplomacy at Work*, http://europa.eu/50/around_world/images/2007_50th_anniv_broch_en.pdf, date accessed May 2010.

European Commission (2008) 'EU Donor Atlas 2008', http://development.donoratlas.eu.

European Commission (2009a) 'Trade relation with the ASEAN', http://ec.europa.eu/trade/creating-opportunities/bilateral-relations/regions/asean/, date accessed May 2010.

European Commission (2009b) 'External Relations with Indonesia', http://ec.europa.eu/external_relations/indonesia/index_en.htm, date accessed May 2010.

European Commission, 'Development, Generalised System of Preferences (GSP)', http://ec.europa.eu/trade/wideragenda/development/generalised-system-of-preferences/, date accessed May 2010.

EUROSTAT *Trade statistic September 2009*, http://trade.ec.europa.eu/doclib/docs/2006/september/tradoc_113471.pdf, date accessed May 2010.

Fort B. (2008) *Can Asia and Europe Cooperate?* (Paper at the International Conference *EU–Asia Relations: A Critical Review*, CERC, the University of Melbourne, Melbourne, Australia, 27–28 March).

GARNET (2007) *The External Image of the European Union* (Working Paper No. 17/07 9 (edited by Sonia Lucarelli)). http://www.garnet-eu.org/index.php?id=27, date accessed May 2010.

GARNET (2009) *The External Image of the European Union – Phase Two* (Working Paper 62 (edited by Sonia. Lucarelli and Lorenzo Fioramonti)) http://www.garnet-eu.org/index.php?id=27, date accessed May 2010.
Gilboa E. (2008) 'Searching for a theory of public diplomacy', *The ANNALS of the AAPSS*, 616, 55–77.
de Gouveia P.F. and Plumridge H. (2005) *European Infopolitik: Developing EU Pubic Strategy* (London: The Foreign Policy Centre).
Haacke J. (2010) 'The Burma/Myanmar imbroglio and ASEAN: Heading towards the 2010 elections', *International Affairs*, 86, 153–174.
Hendrikson A. (2006) *What Can Public Policy Achieve, Discussion Papers in Diplomacy* (Netherlands Institute of International Relations 'Clingendael') http://www.clingendael.nl/publications/2006/20060900_cdsp_paper_dip_c.pdf, date accessed May 2010.
Hill C. (1993) 'The capability-expectations gap, or conceptualizing Europe's international role', *Journal of Common Market Studies*, 31, 3, 305–328.
Holland M. and Chaban N. (eds.) (2010) 'Special issue: Reflections from Asia and Europe: How do we perceive one another?', *Asia Europe Journal*, 8, 2.
Holland M., Ryan P., Nowak A. and Chaban N. (eds.) (2007) *The EU through the Eyes of Asia: Media, Public and Elite Perceptions in China, Japan, Korea, Singapore and Thailand* (Singapore and Warsaw: University of Warsaw).
USC Centre on Public Diplomacy at Annenberg School, 'European Commission Policies and Initiatives', http://publicdiplomacy.wikia.com/wiki/European_Commission_Policies_and_Initiatives, date accessed May 2010.
Islam S. (2010) *A new Asia–Europe partnership for development* (ASEM-8 visibility network correspondence).
Jones D.M. (2008) 'Security and democracy: The ASEAN charter and the dilemmas of regionalism in South–East Asia', *International Affairs*, 84, 4, 735–756.
Korski D. (2008) 'Making Europe's voice louder, European Council on Foreign Relations', 19 April, http://www.ecfr.eu/content/entry/commentary_making_europes_voice_louder, date accessed May 2010.
Leonard M. (2002) *Public Diplomacy* (London: Foreign Policy Centre).
Lisbonne-de Vergeron K. (2006) *Contemporary Indian Views of Europe* (London: Chatham House).
Lisbonne-de Vergeron K. (2007) *Contemporary Chinese Views of Europe* (London: Chatham House).
Lynch D. (2005) 'Communicating Europe to the World: What Public Diplomacy for the EU?', *European Policy Center, Working Paper 21*, http://epc.eu/TEWN/pdf/251965810_EPC%2021.pdf, date accessed May 2010.
Manea M.-G. (2008) 'Human rights and the interregional dialogue between Asia and Europe: ASEAN–EU relations and ASEM', *The Pacific Review*, 21, 3, 369–396.
MITI (Minister of International Trade and Industry of Malaysia), Press release on 13 May 2010, http://www.miti.gov.my/cms/content.jsp?id=com.tms.cms.article.Article_94a12d4e-c0a81573-7a0c7a0c-986d1203, date accessed May 2010.
Murray P. and Rees N. (eds.) (2010) 'Special issue: European and Asian regionalism: Form and function', *International Politics*, 47, 3–4, 308–323.
Murray P. (2002) 'Australian voices: Some elite reflections on the European Union', *CESAA Review*, 29, 5–18. http://www.cesaa.org.au/publications.htm date accessed May 2006.
Ociepka B. and Ryniejska M. (2005) 'Public Diplomacy and EU Enlargement: The Case of Poland' (Netherlands Institute of International Relations 'Clingendael')

http://www.clingendael.nl/publications/2005/20050800_cli_paper_dip_issue99. pdf/, date accessed May 2010.
Oerstroem Moeller J. (2007) 'ASEAN's relations with the European Union: Obstacles and opportunities', *Contemporary Southeast Asia*, 29, 3, 465–482.
Petersson M. (2006) 'Burma/Myanmar in EU–ASEAN relations', *Asia Europe Journal*, 4, 4, 563–581.
Philippines National Statistic (2009) http://www.census.gov.ph/data/sectordata/2009/of0902.htm, date accessed May 2010.
Philippines Overseas Employment Administration (2009) http://www.poea.gov.ph/stats/2009_OFW%20Statistics.pdf, date accessed May 2010.
Rüland J. (2001) *'ASEAN and the European Union: A Bumpy Inter-regional Relationship', ZEI Discussion Paper C 95* (Bonn: Center for European Integration Studies, Rheinische Friedrich Wilhelms–Universität Bonn).
Scott–Smith G. (2008) 'Mapping the indefinable: Some thoughts on the relevance of exchange programs within international relations theory', *The ANNALS of the AAPSS*, 616, 173–195.
Shambaugh D., Sandschneider E. and Hong Z. (eds.) (2007) *China-Europe Relations: Perceptions, Policies and Prospects* (London: Routledge).
Thailand Business News online (2010) 'Asean is now Thailand's top trade partner', 2 May, http://thailand–business–news.com/asean/14481–asean–is–now–thailands–top–trade–partner/, date accessed May 2010.
Tsuruoka M. (2006) 'How External Perspectives of the European Union are Shaped: Endogenous and Exogenous Sources', paper prepared for the *20th World Congress of the International Political Science Association (IPSA)*, Fukuoka, Japan, 9–13 July.
Tsuruoka M. (2005) *EU–Asia Relations and Security Matters (RCO3 on European Unification)*, web.uvic.cakeurope/ipsa-rc3/IPSMTsuruoka.pdf.
Twigg S. as cited in de Gouveia P.F. and Plumridge H. (2005) *European Infopolitik: Developing EU Pubic Strategy* (London: The Foreign Policy Centre).
Stiftung B. (2006) *World Powers in the 21st Century*, Berlin, June, www.cap.lmu.de/download/2006/2006_GPC_Survey_Results.pdf, date accessed June 2008.
Yeo L.H. (2007) 'The inter–regional dimension of EU–Asia relations: EU–ASEAN and the Asia–Europe meeting (ASEM) process', *European Studies*, 25, 1, 173–191.
Zhou H., Lisheng D., Long S., Jun Z. and Zuokui L. (2010) 'A survey and preliminary analysis of the Chinese perceptions of the EU and China-Europe relations' in P. Canelas de Castro (ed.), *The European Union at 50: Assessing the Past, Looking Ahead* (Macau: University of Macau), 109–178.

6
Law and Policy: A Useful Model for ASEAN?

Rachminawati and Anna Syngellakis

Introduction

It is widely accepted that the evolution of the European Union (EU) from an economic community to a supranational, multifaceted union with a global reach is a historically unique, unprecedented phenomenon. Given these characteristics, the question arises of whether the EU processes and resulting policies and laws offer themselves as a model of regional integration for others to emulate. Arguably, the EU model is worth careful examination precisely because of its pioneering development and its capacity to bring within its remit, through the unanimous political will of its member states, policies and law traditionally reserved primarily for nation-states. This is also the case with human rights, which evolved from being case-law based to being included in the EU Treaty and to being further enhanced by the Charter of Fundamental Rights. This development demonstrates that the pursuit of the original economic objectives led the EU, gradually but surely, to recognize explicitly, at treaty level, the rights and freedoms demanded by an advanced transnational market and society.

Given that the Association of Southeast Asian Nations (ASEAN) is aspiring to establish an ASEAN Community by 2015, it is an opportune time to ask in this paper how and why the EU human rights policy and law evolved, and what lessons the Southeast Asian grouping can learn from the EU model of a community based not only on common economic objectives, but on a recognition and implementation of the human rights of the people the community seeks to serve. Such a learning process means that ASEAN can move faster to a more advanced community, extending a human rights entitlement to its citizens and thus strengthening its legitimacy. This core inquiry furthermore leads us to address the issue of human rights universalism versus particularism in relation to the so-called 'Asian values', and also the question of soft versus hard human rights institutions. Our discussion is based on a comparative analysis of EU and ASEAN policy processes towards regional integration and the place of human rights policy and law in community building. ASEAN has already taken on board the issue of human rights in its charter. This accords well with our argument in favour of an ASEAN Community incorporating human rights from the start, and with the proposition put forward here that the EU offers a useful model for ASEAN to learn from and build on. Moreover, the EU experience shows that human rights issues will ultimately have to be addressed in the process of regional integration. As we also point out, even with its current, settled human rights policy, the EU still has some serious unfinished business to address, namely its accession to the European Convention of Human Rights. We are arguing, therefore, that there is an advantage for ASEAN in developing its human rights framework sooner rather than later. In doing so, ASEAN can avoid the perennial 're-inventing the wheel' pitfall and the fragmented, piece-meal process the EU experienced. Thus, ASEAN may pre-empt criticism, strengthen its legitimacy both internationally and in the eyes of the citizens in its member states, and generally bring all-round benefits from a comprehensively designed strategy for regional integration.

The evolution of EU Human Rights law

Human rights were not part of the design of policy and law underpinning the creation of a customs union and common market in the early stages of EU integration in the 1950s. The six founding member states did not at that time consider human rights as pertinent to the key objective of economic integration, and therefore they did not grant to the EU the competence regarding human rights protection (Neuwahl, 1995; Petersmann, 2002; Schlink, 1996). However, since the 1970s, the absence of human rights protection in the European legal order came into scrutiny from the national courts. In response, the European Court of Justice (ECJ) developed case-law protecting human rights in the context of market integration. Furthermore, through successive treaty amendments, the EU embraced the protection of human rights as a key tool in integrating not only the markets of its member states but also, importantly, in bringing together European citizens within a common human rights framework at EU level, which is now regarded as evidence of EU legitimacy.

The development of human rights protection at the EU level presented a paradox: rights without a constitution. The EU did not have a constitution in the classic sense guaranteeing human rights but, nevertheless, human rights were integrated progressively in EU law and policy, so that today they form an integral part of EU treaties.

The initial absence of human rights protection in EU policy and law has been explained by the fact that such protection was guaranteed by the constitutions of the EU member states and also because this level of protection was initially considered adequate (Levi, 2007). As a result, the founding fathers of the EU did not include human rights in the original EU Treaty. Furthermore, since member states had already committed themselves to all international and regional human rights conventions, such as the Universal Declaration on Human Rights (UDHR), the European Convention on Human Rights (ECHR), the International Labour Organization (ILO) Conventions and other related human rights conventions (El-Agraa, 2008; William, 2004, p. 137), it has been argued that the EU incorporated human rights indirectly (because human rights were already at the heart of the national legal orders of its member states). Nevertheless, the absence of human rights protection at EU level posed the possibility that the EU could infringe human rights. It also meant the absence of any institutional human rights framework at EU level: no directorate-general, no commissioner and no budgetary provision. The Court of Justice of the European Union became the first EU institution to address this absence of human rights protection in the EU by declaring in key judgements that human rights are recognized and protected by EU law.

The court's recognition of human rights in EU law led progressively to their political recognition and the introduction of explicit provisions on human rights in the treaty framework. The 1986 Single European Act (SEA) was the first to accord human rights a place in the treaties. However, the ground-breaking 1992 Maastricht Treaty signalled the transformation from an economic to a political community where human rights became a central issue, since they were acknowledged as a key notion for a democratic organization based on rule of law. As the member states were fully aware of the importance of integrating human rights in EU law and policy, the Maastricht Treaty declared in Article 6 (1) that the EU 'is founded on the principle of liberty, democracy, respect for human rights and fundamental freedoms and of the rule of law' and that the Union 'shall respect fundamental rights, as guaranteed by the European Convention for the Protection of Human Rights and Fundamental Freedoms signed in Rome on 4 November 1950 and as they result from the constitutional traditions common to the member states, as general principles of Community law.'

The EU Charter of Fundamental Rights adopted in 2000 also reinforced the strong commitment of the EU to human rights protection. In the preamble of the charter, it is stated that 'conscious of its spiritual and moral heritage, the Union is founded on the indivisible, universal values of human dignity, freedom, equality and solidarity'. The charter can be said to complete the shift from the original 1950s treaties towards placing human rights in the 'heart' of the EU. Arguably, it was a belated attempt to include in the text all those principles that had purportedly governed the EU throughout its existence (Williams, 2004). In other words, the aim of the charter was to codify and constitutionalize human rights at the EU level.

Four main reasons can be put forward to explain the adoption of human rights by the EU. First, given the evolution of the EU legal order and the growing activities of the institutions, peoples' daily lives are more and more affected by EU law. Second, human rights became more relevant because of the creation of a single market, the abolition of border controls within the community and the concomitant intensification of controls at its external borders and also within EU member states. This means that the 'social dimension' of market integration creates expectations of human rights protection at all levels, which a national legislator alone is insufficiently equipped to solve. Third, European identity is closely linked to the protection of human rights as a result of the history of violation of human rights in the European continent. Finally, an adequate protection of human rights strengthens the EU in relation to its member states and in its relations with third countries. EU law not in line with human rights risks being challenged by national courts, as has happened with the German and Italian Supreme Courts.

Another important factor increasing the relevance of human rights is the enlargement of the EU, which has posed several challenges. Candidate states are required to demonstrate their commitment to human rights protection, otherwise their accession to the EU is problematic, as has been the case with Turkey's application to accede to the EU. Naturally, the EU needs to demonstrate similar standards as the ones demanded by candidate states. The EU has to live up to the historic fact that after the end of World War II, the European continent had been the forerunner in the development of human rights through the Council of Europe (CoE) and its ECHR. The EU was, therefore, under pressure to follow in this historic tradition by adopting treaty provisions and the Charter of Fundamental Rights. Furthermore, the addition of new members makes the EU more diverse in many aspects and, unless the EU strengthens its institutions, there is a risk of the EU being diluted into simply a large free trade zone. Human rights provide a common basis for EU institutional and constitutional legitimacy, thus maintaining the momentum of the EU integration process. In this respect, the EU Charter of Fundamental Rights is said to be 'the expression of a process of constitutionalizing the EU, of the transition from a union of states based on single market and single currency to a union of citizens based on human rights' (Levi, 2007). In this context, we would argue that human rights in the EU became significant because of their role in overcoming the challenges facing the EU with further economic integration as well as continuous enlargements. Enhancing the protection and fulfilment of citizen's rights, respecting human rights, and proclaiming them to be an integral part of EU law and policy increases the value of the EU as an entity to be reckoned with.

Human Rights and market integration: assessing the role of the court of justice of the EU

Human rights are closely related to a wider conception of market integration and the transformation of 'market freedom' to a 'fundamental rights' approach to the market, in other words, to a more multidimensional market where economic rights lead to human rights. In the EU experience, the free movement of goods, persons, services and capital created rights of family life, property, social security and others (Howse, 2002).

In the EU context, the objective of European integration through market integration was the initial driver for the endorsement of human rights by the Court of Justice. The court started to integrate human rights in its case-law in the early 1970s, and, as often happens, this judicial innovation led to the gradual integration of human rights provisions in the EU treaties. This stance of the court was in line with its long tradition of case-law furthering European integration, a tradition regarded by some commentators as judicial activism (Schlink, 1996, p. 321). Although typically the subject-matter of ECJ case-law was mundane enough, the court built a human rights dimension derived from the constitutional traditions of the member states.

This is demonstrated by the Stauder case, which was about a decision of the commission authorizing member states to allow the sale of butter at reduced prices to persons in need. In order to prevent the abuse of this benefit by fraud, applicants had to produce certain documents, which in the German language version of the decision included their identity cards. Stauder, one such applicant, considered this requirement to be contrary to human dignity, and challenged the validity of the requirement before a German administrative court. When this case was referred to the court for a preliminary ruling, the court denied a violation of human rights, but stated in an *orbiter dictum* that fundamental rights are enshrined in the general principles of community law and protected by the court. By referring to general principles of law, the court was able to address the absence of explicit provisions on human rights in the treaty.

Furthermore, in the Internationale Handelsgesellschaft case (para 4), the court reaffirmed the Stauder case and stated that 'respect for fundamental rights forms an integral part of the general principles of law protected by the Court of Justice. The protection of such rights, whilst inspired by the constitutional traditions of the member states, must be ensured within the framework of the structure and objectives of the Community'. Significantly, the constitutional traditions of the member states were identified by the court as the primary source. In the Nold case, the court reaffirmed the importance of the constitutions of the member states in establishing protection of human rights as a general principle of law. The court would strike down any provisions of community legislation that were contrary to the fundamental rights protected by the constitutions of the member states. It clearly explained that the community did not form their own rights but the member states did within the framework of the ECHR. Neuwahl concludes as follows about the development of the court case-law regarding human rights:

> The review by the ECJ in compliance with human rights has developed from review of measures adopted by the Community institutions themselves (the second Nold case) to 'review' of measures adopted by member states in implementing community measures, (Wachauf) and more recently to 'review'of measures adopted by the member states which, in one way or another, fall within the scope of community law (the ERT case); 'the concern of human rights is recognised in the Community, and the case law of the ECJ is flourishing, even though there is neither bill of rights nor any general guarantee of fundamental rights in the Community treaties'.
>
> (1995, p. 11)

There are different arguments about why the EU finally integrated human rights into its law and policy. Two theories in particular can be discussed in this respect: constructivism and functionalism. Adler (2002) focused on constructivist theory and the concept of cognitive development in the study of 'common values' and their dissemination. This is also the starting point of institutionalization of values that develops into cooperative behaviours in the international society. As part of international relations theory, constructivism studies the social relations among states and non-state entities as well. This theory does not address the issue of how values can be studied through positivist approaches, and can be very subjective because norms and values depend much on the interaction of the people, and therefore it will be different from one community to another. Regarding human rights, the way they develop is influenced by social, historical, moral element and conditions. Donnely (2003) argued that human rights are constitutive no less than regulative rules. Therefore, constructivist theory can be applied in this 'ideational' condition.

In line with Donnely, Chryssochoou (2009) argued that a constructivist theory of integration can be applied in this area of human rights as it attempts to incorporate 'human consciousnesses' and 'ideational factors' into the process of understanding social reality. It aims to 'track norms from the social to the legal' (2009, p. 112). Accordingly, the way human rights are practised in the EU shows that the EU moves from social norms into legal norms. In this context, the constructivist theory explains the endorsement of human rights in the EU integration process progressively from case-law to the treaties and EU policies.

In a different line of argument, according to the functional theory, Petersmann (2002) argues that

> European integration confirms the insight of 'functional theories', for example, citizen-driven market integration can provide strong incentives for transforming: 'market freedoms' into 'fundamental rights' which – if directly enforced by producers, investors, workers, traders and consumers through courts (as in the EC) – can reinforce and extend the protection of basic human rights (e.g. to liberty, property, food and health).

Another analysis offered by functionalism is that EU member states support an integration strategy starting from economics – relying on the hypothesis that 'politics will follow' – because such a strategy allows them to proceed along the line of less resistance and to consign as far as possible into the future the issue of the transfer of sovereignty to supranational institutions (Levi, 2007). Member states have progressively moved in this direction, which, however, has brought persistent tensions between national and European institutions. Therefore, human rights are needed as a uniting factor to overcome the crisis.

It appears to us that functional theory is more capable of explaining how human rights came to be progressively integrated into this 'economic organization'. Human rights in the EU exist as a consequence of market integration. Human rights and market integration are closely intertwined. This argument is further strengthened by the key role human rights play in EU enlargement. As mentioned above, in the enlargement process, the economic criteria regarding the establishment of the free market economy in the candidate states are intertwined with the political criteria regarding the stability of institutions guaranteeing democracy and human rights. The combination of economic and political criteria highlights how economic integration, democracy and human rights go hand in hand.

The Charter of Fundamental Rights of the EU, as discussed earlier, was an advanced move to integrate economic and political rights into the supranational power of the EU and give them a binding legal effect. The legal status of the charter is now guaranteed under the Lisbon Treaty, which entered into force on 1 December 2009. Most importantly, the member states stipulated in the Lisbon Treaty that the EU will accede to the ECHR. To this effect, the EU institutions started the legal process of accession in March 2010 (Reding, 2010). This development is an impressive culmination of human rights integration in the EU legal order, although the accession process may take several years.

In conclusion, international bodies, including the EU, need to integrate human rights into their organizational law in order to enhance their legitimacy by according to citizens the concrete benefit of legally protected human rights provisions. EU integration in particular, demonstrates that nation-states with a background of centuries-old conflicts can come together in one institution to their mutual benefit. In this process, human rights have a decisive role to play in ensuring the future of EU integration.

The ASEAN path towards human rights: lessons from the EU

Incorporating Human Rights into ASEAN core integration objectives

ASEAN is the most prominent example of a regional organization in Asia-Pacific pursuing the most developed form of integration in the area (Cockerham, 2007). ASEAN was founded by Indonesia, Malaysia, the Philippines, Singapore and Thailand with the 1967 Bangkok Declaration as its constituent instrument. They were subsequently joined by Brunei, Cambodia, Laos, Myanmar (Burma) and Vietnam. Based on the 2007 ASEAN Charter, their new and legal binding constituent instrument, ASEAN members have emphasized regional cooperation in the 'three pillars' of security, socio-cultural and economic integration. ASEAN has made the most progress in the area of economic integration, aiming to create an ASEAN Economic Community (AEC) by 2015 (Sim, 2008). The foundation of the AEC is the ASEAN Free Trade Area (AFTA), a common external preferential tariff scheme to promote the free flow of goods within ASEAN.

In ASEAN integration, national sovereignty and non-interference are the main principles, as laid down in the ASEAN Charter. Lay Hong Tan (2004) stated that these principles have stymied closer and deeper integration in ASEAN for three decades. The behavioural norms occupy more importance than formal rules and regulation. ASEAN member states too often adopt a 'me-first' attitude instead of looking for collective benefits (Sim, 2008), thus presenting a major obstacle for ASEAN in moving towards a stable organization that is more rule-based and people-centred.

The 2007 ASEAN Charter is the first binding instrument of the institution since 1967. The adoption of the charter shows us that ASEAN aims to be a more integrated organization. Furthermore, this step will facilitate the achievement of the original aims of ASEAN stated in the Bangkok Declaration, namely to accelerate economic growth, promote regional peace and stability, foster collaboration in many areas of development and closer cooperation among member states. Therefore, the ASEAN Charter enhances the character of this Southeast Asian grouping as a regional organization in legal, social, economic and cultural terms. As we show next, the adoption of the ASEAN Charter marks a milestone towards the integration of human rights in ASEAN.

The integral place of human rights is declared by the ASEAN Charter in the Preamble, Articles 1 para 7 and Article 2 (i), which state explicitly the commitment of ASEAN and its member states to the principles of democracy, the rule of law and good governance, respect and protection of human rights and fundamental freedoms and pledges to act accordingly. Most importantly, an ASEAN Human Rights Body is to be established according to

Article 14. These provisions open up the path towards developing a rule-based human rights mechanism in the future AEC. Such a mechanism can be expected to establish rules determining the role and rights of the community's citizens, a development which we can argue to mirror EU developments. The inclusion of these provisions is therefore a significant step taking ASEAN closer to a people-centred organization.

Human rights were a major concern during the drafting process of the ASEAN Charter. The many violations of human rights in different Southeast Asian countries internally and externally, as well as the absence of any specific regional body which can settle or adjudge these violations, pose a challenge for ASEAN in achieving its aims declared in the charter. Therefore, there is an urgent need to incorporate human rights into ASEAN institutions, law and policy.

Building ASEAN human rights institutions: reconciling universal human rights with Asian values and particularism

As early as 1995, the ASEAN Human Rights Working Group was established by ASEAN with the task of setting up an intergovernmental human rights commission for the grouping. The group proposed in 2000 rules and principles, a commission and a court. This demonstrates that the idea to have a binding mechanism of human rights is not new, but the result of a long process of discussions and lobbying. There have been debates between stakeholders, especially between states and non-governmental organizations, as to whether ASEAN should have a binding human rights mechanism or not. In response to this, it is argued that the EU experience indicates that ASEAN should not postpone establishing a legal binding mechanism, which will enhance the protection of human rights in the region and also can accelerate the ASEAN integration (Aseanhrmech, 2007). The need to have a legally binding mechanism will be discussed in more detail in the next section.

The drafting of a human rights mechanism is at the level of ministerial meeting. The Terms of Reference (ToR) for the High Level Panel (HLP) on an ASEAN Human Rights Body (AHRB) was approved by the 41st ASEAN Ministerial Meeting on 21 July 2008. The HLP was to draft the ToR of the AHRB in line with the purposes and principles of the ASEAN Charter relating to the promotion and protection of human rights and fundamental freedoms (ToR AHRB, 2009). Therefore, a year later, in 2009, the ASEAN Summit launched the ASEAN Intergovernmental Commission on Human Rights (AICHR).

National Human Rights Institutions (NHRIs) are a prominent stakeholder in this process. Responding to the ToR of the AHRB, the NHRIs of Indonesia, Malaysia, the Philippines and Thailand welcomed the efforts of ASEAN to establish the AHRB and suggested that it should be an independent deliberative body providing an effective level of promotion, protection and monitoring of human rights throughout the ASEAN region. They further emphasized the importance of both the AHRB's functions of human rights promotion and protection (Aseanhrmech, 2007).

In the HLP debate over a 'soft' versus 'hard' body, only Indonesia sought to grant it more powers, while the other nine members preferred a less powerful human rights body. These stark differences in positions meant that in the end, the HLP decided in favour of the AICHR rather than a supranational commission or even a court (Tansubhapol, 2009).

This shows that the idea of having a legally binding human rights mechanism in ASEAN still faces significant opposition among its member states. However, the ASEAN regional integration would be advanced by the establishment of a supranational rather than an intergovernmental human rights institution (Tan, 2004). Such a development would reflect the universal nature of human rights within ASEAN. In the debate over the universalism or particularism of human rights in Asia, Southeast Asian governments tend to support 'Asian' values, thus favouring particularism. Non-governmental organizations strongly disagree with this position, arguing that state elites use 'culture' and 'Asian' values as one of the mechanisms preserving their political power (Arriola, 2004).

In the context of advancing human rights within ASEAN, the concept of 'Asian' values is pertinent and deserves further discussion. Even after the adoption of the ASEAN Charter mandating the establishment of a human rights body, ASEAN member states appear to resist the idea of such a body on the grounds of defending national sovereignty and maintaining 'Asian' values at the national level (Rüland, 2000). As mentioned earlier, with the exception of Indonesia, which supported a 'hard' human rights body, the other nine member states opposed it, possibly fearing exposing themselves to scrutiny and intervention (Tansubhapol, 2009).

The concept of 'Asian values' is at the heart of the conflict between universalism and particularism of human rights in ASEAN. Based on 'Asian values', the ASEAN leaders and member states convince themselves that they have their own human rights values, which are different from those in Europe or other regions around the world. Therefore, the approach to human rights in ASEAN reflects what Rüland (2000) calls ASEAN values, namely 'behavioural norms of ASEAN' characterized by an essentially personalistic, informal, non-contractual and little institutionalized style of politics in order to maintain social harmony and avoid confrontation. The state sovereignty and non-interference principles are applied with regard to human rights and create obstacles to accepting the universality of human rights and legally binding mechanisms and institutions. This tension is not, though, unique in the context of ASEAN. State sovereignty and non-interference present globally a potential obstacle to implementing human rights depending on circumstances and political expediencies.

The issue is how to avoid a dogmatic, rigid entrenchment behind a perceived divide, and how to make progress despite the existence of potentially conflicting principles. Given the commitment of both the EU and ASEAN to human rights principles, we would suggest that the EU offers a useful precedent towards integrated, legally binding human rights rules and institutions. The evolution of EU human rights conception, as discussed earlier, demonstrates a gradually maturing acceptance of the necessity to work with these potentially conflicting principles and reconcile them in a pragmatic manner, as and when any such conflict manifests itself in practice. In line with our central argument, we would suggest that ASEAN, taking into account the EU experience, may avoid the lengthy and piece-meal EU process towards human rights, littered with anomalies and necessitating continuous adjustments. Instead, ASEAN has the opportunity to endorse an advanced framework of human rights, gaining an advantage in human rights credibility.

To strengthen further this line of thought, we would suggest that, although particularism is arguably accepted in international human rights regimes (Steiner et al., 2008), there seems to be a mistaken understanding of the meaning of particularism by different actors within ASEAN. Particularism of human rights does not mean the existence of different human rights in different states or regions. It means that human rights values are universal in character, but that the implementation of those rights may be pragmatically different depending on socio-cultural background and conditions in any given circumstances. Legally binding mechanisms and institutions can accommodate this meaning of particularism. In their absence, the endorsement of human rights by ASEAN would only be seen as 'lip service'.

Achieving a mature ASEAN human rights regime: specific lessons from the EU experience

The adoption of human rights commitments in the ASEAN Charter presents an opportunity for ASEAN to develop similar mechanisms as the EU. The EU experience offers three important lessons of why human rights need to be integrated into the law of regional or international organization.

First, having all ASEAN member states party to an international human rights instrument assumes that ASEAN member states have a common understanding of human rights. However, individual ASEAN states adhere to their own respective human rights concepts based on their own values, and resist the introduction of a human rights mechanism. Nevertheless, there has been a gradual shift in this position since ASEAN leaders recognized the importance of human rights in a regional policy and law context, as we can now see in the context of the new ASEAN human rights body. From the perspective of citizens, the adoption of a binding human rights mechanism offers the prospect of self-development, peace and prosperity across frontiers, as evidenced by the EU case.

Second, by integrating human rights into its legal framework, the EU case illustrates that a regional organization subsequently improves its prospects across the board. The evolution of the original European Economic Community was in parallel with the introduction human rights in the relevant EU treaties. The rising status of the EU as an economic and political actor on the world stage was promoted by its increased moral standing accorded to the EU by the advancement of its human rights policy and law. The EU experience demonstrates the link between effective human rights protection, both at the national and regional level, and free, prosperous and stable societies in Europe. In contrast, conflict and poverty persist in the ASEAN region. The most poignant example is Myanmar, with a long history of human rights violations that no regional mechanism has been able to effectively address. The establishment of the ASEAN Intergovernmental Commission on Human Rights, as endorsed by the HLP, is not adequate to protect the human rights of the ASEAN countries' citizens. The function of the commission will be limited to the promotion of the rights. However, the example of the EU shows that a functioning community develops a dynamic that leads to the expansion of community functions into the human rights field. In this context, a binding human rights mechanism, and in particular the establishment of a regional human rights court through the ASEAN process, lends momentum to the vision of a ASEAN Community by 2015.

Third, integrating human rights promotes legitimacy, democracy and self-governance in regional organizations. It is very clear that the active protection of human rights in the EU by the judgements of the Court of Justice, which led to human rights being enshrined in the EU treaties and becoming a component of EU policies, strengthened the EU's democratic legitimacy as well as enhancing its capacities as a self-governing, supranational entity with global reach. The long-standing criticism of democratic deficit in the EU is significantly weakened by the fact that the EU provides mechanisms to empower its citizens who can then exercise their economic, social and cultural rights and enforce them in the Court of Justice. With respect to ASEAN establishing a judicial mechanism for human rights, we need to point to the risk of having two human rights frameworks: one under ASEAN and one under what we may call a potential Asian or Asian-Pacific Community, developing beyond the present ASEAN.

Such parallel establishment of two human rights frameworks is actually what happened in Europe in the post-World War II era: the adoption of the ECHR and the establishment of the prestigious European Court of Human Rights within the framework of the intergovernmental Council of Europe, followed by the establishment of the European Economic Community, now the EU, and its long, tortuous but inexorable process towards human rights law, policy and institutions. As a result, today we have parallel European human rights systems and, as mentioned earlier, in a further twist in the EU human rights saga, the EU is seeking to accede to the ECHR. Determining the respective jurisdictions of the ECJ and the European Court of Human Rights is a crucial issue in the accession process. Therefore, to avoid repeating a process of duplication, ASEAN should consider having a 'hard' human rights mechanism from the start, before another similar mechanism is also established. This will avoid potential future complexities with having two human rights systems at the regional level.

Turning now to the question of how ASEAN may proceed towards a mature framework for the human rights body and mechanism, we note that the AICHR presents itself as the initiating actor. The AICHR can undertake the task of developing the necessary texts of rules, procedures and institutions to promote and protect human rights.

From the analysis above, it is concluded that common perception and recognition of universal human rights in the ASEAN region is important in order to build a stable, rule-based regional organization. The objective of an ASEAN Community by 2015 offers ASEAN an opportunity to learn from the slow but inescapable EU process towards legally integrated and binding human rights mechanisms, take the bull by its horns and adopt an accelerated mode of human rights integration into the ASEAN Community framework.

Nevertheless, it has to be acknowledged that ASEAN, despite the necessity and opportunities to build legally binding human rights mechanism, faces constraints in realizing them. Such constraints flow from the more traditional view of Southeast Asia as structured around a strong concept of state sovereignty and narrow self-interests among states. Such a view then may lead to the argument that the ASEAN Charter may in reality have no influence at all in strengthening the organization, and that ASEAN regionalism will continue to be relatively weak in the face of external influences, such as globalization, the volatility of global finance and the growing power of China in Asia. In this context, the interest in ASEAN integration will decrease as member states perceive more benefit by integrating in the global arena than in ASEAN (Cockerham, 2007). For example, states perceive membership of the World Trade Organization (WTO) as according them more benefits at a global level, and therefore their integration in this organization and the commitments it involves are accepted more easily. In contrast, ambivalence about mutual benefits and interests among ASEAN member states slows down the ASEAN integration process. The EU experience shows the possibility and value of pragmatic dualism: the EU is a founding member of the WTO in its own right but has, nevertheless, to function within the WTO alongside its member states, who are also WTO members in their own right. Being integrated in a regional organization and being a member of a global organization are compatible.

Other potential constraints come from conflicts between different ASEAN member states, for example between Indonesia and Malaysia, namely over demarcation of borders, as well as over the issue of violation of the human rights of Indonesian migrant workers in Malaysia. As Indonesia and Malaysia are two influential member states of ASEAN, antagonism between them impacts on ASEAN progress. An analogy at the EU level could be the tensions between old and new member states regarding the free movement of workers and citizens. Territorial tensions exist between EU member states too, for example, between the UK and Spain regarding Gibraltar. These tensions, however, are not seen as a threat to EU regional integration.

Finally, it has been argued that the different legal systems of its member states constitute a further potential constraint in establishing an ASEAN human rights body (Jatna, 2005). Indonesia follows the European Continental Law system, while Malaysia, Singapore and the Philippines follow the Anglo-Saxon legal system. In this context, it needs to be emphasized that similar differences in national legal systems did not prevent the integration of human rights policy and law at EU level.

Conclusion: towards integrating human rights into the law and policy in ASEAN

The discussion offered here has charted the gradual progress of the EU over several decades towards today's mature state of human rights integration in EU law and policy. It was a slow process because of a gradual realization of the high degree to which human rights are intertwined with economic and social integration and a progressive acknowledgement that the EU stood to benefit from the synergies between human rights and integration.

ASEAN has the opportunity to adapt to its circumstances the EU learning process in human rights integration and quicken the pace of achieving the ensuing benefits. ASEAN today does not have to go through a slow learning curve. Of course, it is not all plain sailing. A number of obstacles in integrating human rights into ASEAN law and policy have been identified and discussed: first, cultural differences in the conception of human rights; second, ambivalent perceptions among member states regarding mutual benefits and interests leading to reluctance in integrating within ASEAN; third, antagonism between some of the ASEAN member states; and fourth, though a less acute problem, the differences between the legal system of member states.

The critical factor in addressing successfully these difficulties is political leaders who share a common understanding about the importance of human rights in establishing the ASEAN Community. Common perception and recognition of universal human rights in the ASEAN region is important in building a stable, rule-based regional organization embodying a new human rights culture and citizen-oriented policies. Legally binding human rights provisions enforceable in a court of law play a vital part in regional integration by providing citizens with tangible benefits and the regional organization with legitimate authority, as evidenced by the EU experience. Without binding legal force, human rights, both in member states and at regional level, remain rhetorical.

ASEAN member states have recognized the benefits of regional integration and have taken steps towards strengthening their relations and narrowing cultural gaps; they also understand that sovereignty has to be limited to some degree in favour of common institutions. Furthermore, they have taken the first steps towards including human rights in their integrationist framework. There seems to be a good chance, therefore, that ASEAN can avoid re-inventing the wheel by borrowing what is valuable and useful from the EU experience. By doing so, ASEAN can accelerate its own progress towards establishing a mature regional community that acts from the start on the synergies between the economic rights and the human rights of its people.

Bibliography

Adler E. (2002) 'Constructivism and international relation', in C. Walter, T. Risse, and B.A. Simmons (eds.), *Handbook of International Relations* (London: Sage Publication), 95–118.

Alston P. and Weiler J.H.H. (1999) 'An "Ever Closer Union" in need of Human Rights policy: The European Union and Human Rights' in P. Alston, M.R. Bustelo, and J. Heenan (eds.), *The EU and Human Rights* (Oxford: Oxford University Press), 3–66.

Asean Foreign Minister. (2009) *Press release on Human Rights Body and of the ASEAN Foreign Ministers*. http://www.scribd.com/doc/17477897/Press-release-on-Human-Rights-Body-and-of-the-ASEAN-Foreign-Ministers, accessed 12 August 2009

Arriola S. (2004). 'Proposing an ASEAN Human Rights Commission: A Critical Analysis', *Ateneo Law Journal*, 48(4), 906–945.

Aseanhrmech. (2007) *About Us*. Aseanhrmech website: http://www.aseanhrmech.org/aboutus.html, accessed 14 March 2009.

Association of South East Asian Nation (ASEAN). (2007) *The ASEAN Declaration*. ASEAN website: http://www.aseansec.org/1212.htm, accessed 24 February 2009.

Charter of Fundamental Rights of the European Union. (2010) Official Journal of the European Union C 83/389.

Chryssochoou D.N. (2009) *Theorizing European Integration* (London and New York: Routledge).

Cockerham G. (2007) *Regional Integration in Southeast Asia: Institutional Design and the Asian Way* [electronic version], Social Science Research Network website: http://www.allacademic.com/meta/p_mla_apa_research_citation/3/1/4/2/7/pages314277/p314277-1.php, accessed 3 September 2009.

Donnely J. (2003) *Universal Human Rights in Theory and Practice*, 2nd edn (Ithaca, NY: Cornell University Press).

El-Agraa A. (2008) EU 'Economic and Human Rights' examined within the context of regional integration worldwide, *Asia Europe Journal*, 6, 3–4, 391–399.

Howse R. (2002) 'Human Rights in the WTO: Whose Rights, what humanity? Comment on petersmann', *Jean Monet Working Paper* 12(2), Jeanmonnet website: www.jeanmonnetprogram.org/papers/02/021201-01.rtf, accessed 27 March 2009.

Internationale Handelsgesselscahft GmBH, Case 1/70 [1970] ECR 1125.

Jatna R.N. (2005) 'Analysing the European Law Integration and its global impact to the sovereignty of member states', *Journal of European Studies* 1(1), 50–61.

Levi L. (2007) 'The charter of Rights and the European Commission', *Journal of European Studies*, 3, 2.

Neuwahl N.A. (1995) 'The treaty on European Union: A step forward in the protection of Human Rights?', in N.A. Neuwahl and A. Rosas (eds.), *The European Union and Human Rights* (The Hague, The Netherlands: Kluwer Law International), 1–22.

Petersmann E. (2002) 'United Nation "Global Compact" for Integrating Human Rights into the law of world-wide organisations: Lesson from European integration', *European Journal of International Law*, 13, 3, 621–643.

Qazilbash A.M. (1977–78) NGOs Efforts towards the Creation of a Regional Human Rights Arrangement in the Asia-Pacific Region. *4 ILSA J. Int'l & Comp. L.603* http://heinonline.org/HOL/LandingPage?collection=journals&handle=hein.journals/ilsaic4&div=43&id=&page=.

Reding V. (2010) The EU's accession to the European Convention of Human Rights. http://ec.europa.eu/commission_20102014/reding/pdf/speeches/speech_20100318_1_en.pdf.

Rüland J. (2000) 'ASEAN and the Asian crisis: Theoretical implications and practical consequences for Southeast Asian Regionalism', *The Pacific Review* 13, 3, 421–451.

Schlink B. (1996) 'Are there equal standards for the protection of individual Rights and "State Rights"? The case of the European community', in A. Sajo (ed.), *Western Rights? Post Communist Application* (The Hague/London/Boston, MA: Kluwer Law International), 317–323.

Sim W.E. (2008) 'The ASEAN Charter: One of Many Steps towards an ASEAN Economic Community' *International Trade Law & Regulation: Legislative Comment*. Westlaw Databases, accessed 11 February 2009.

Steiner H., Alston P. and Goodman R. (2008) *International Human Rights in Context: Law, Politics, Morals*, 3rd edn (New York: Oxford University Press).

Tan L.H. (2004) 'Will ASEAN economic integration progress beyond a free trade area?', *International & Comparative Law Quarterly*, 53, 4, 935–967.

Tansubhapol. (2009). Indonesia nearly derails rights body talks, *Bangkok Post*. Published at July 21, 2009 from Bangkok Post website: http://www.bangkokpost.com/news/local/20636/indonesia-nearly-derails-rights-body-talks.

Williams A. (2004) *EU Human Rights Policies: A Study in Irony* (Oxford: Oxford University Press).

7
Energy Security in Southeast Asia: A Role for the EU?

William Kucera

Introduction

The industrialization of East Asia, including the Association of Southeast Asian Nations (ASEAN) region, is increasing the link between the region's prosperity and its dependence on the ability to secure undisputed access to energy and mineral deposits, which, in relation to human population, are unevenly distributed across the Earth's surface.

Across the ASEAN region, access to energy resources is hindered by political boundaries that cut across features of the natural terrain such as river basins, watersheds and seas. These boundaries serve to disrupt the geospatial thrust of human endeavour. ASEAN states face competition from external powers such as China and Japan, as well as from one another, when attempting to secure access to external energy supplies.

Under-investment in Southeast Asia's energy infrastructure, given the strong demand for energy in the region, is likely to contribute to high energy prices and threaten economic growth at the global level. Such a situation would threaten the well-being of European Union (EU) member states and contribute to undermining the European integration process itself.

The European experience has shown that a common market can facilitate the de-politicization of relations between supplier, transit and consumer countries. In encouraging ASEAN states to adopt a common legal framework to govern energy trade and investment based on this experience, perhaps via the introduction of energy-relevant provisions in its bilateral trade agreements with ASEAN states, the EU could make a long-term contribution to regional security in Southeast Asia.

The ECT as a multilateral legal framework

The historical legacy of conflict in Europe during the first half of the 20th century was the driving force behind the European Coal and Steel Community (ECSC), the precursor to today's EU, formally established in 1951 by six countries, who decided to pool their most important sources of industrial production for the common good. Diplomatic and commercial competition between France and Germany had manifested itself in the fragmented region of Eastern Europe prior to both world wars. It should be remembered that the respective triggers for both conflicts featured events that took place in Eastern Europe.

The genesis of the European Energy Charter (now the Energy Charter Treaty, or ECT) lay with the collapse of Communism in Eastern Europe. It began as a political initiative launched by Western European countries in need of imported energy supplies, which partnered with former Soviet republics in need of the hard currency provided by export revenues from oil and gas deposits. This in turn required significant foreign investment and technology. The European Energy Charter was signed in 1991. It consisted of a political declaration featuring a commitment to cooperation in the energy sector. This later evolved into the ECT, which was signed in 1994 and came into effect in 1998.

The ECT initiative of the 1990s echoes the earlier ECSC in creating a multilateral political and legal framework that seeks to create common interests through the pooling of the most important industrial inputs, and in doing so reduce or even eliminate the risk of conflict over sovereignty and resource access by removing the artificial political boundaries that are a defining feature of the modern age.

At the time of writing, the ECT is the world's only international energy investment treaty. Although certain other bilateral and regional trade and investment treaties (for example the North American Free Trade Agreement, NAFTA) do include provisions that cover energy, it is more often the case that energy is either only addressed by blanket rules applying generally all sectors, or specifically exempted. The complexity and inherently multinational nature of energy projects often leaves bilateral treaties inadequate. The ECT represents a multilateral approach to energy security that is fully compatible with the existing World Trade Organization (WTO) system, and goes so far as to extend the WTO framework to cover the energy sector of non-WTO states that have acceded to the Energy Charter Conference.

A key feature of the ECT is the stability that it provides in the investor-host government relationship. Although it recognizes the principle of national sovereignty over energy resources, there is a requirement for the rules governing the sector to be available, non-discriminatory and transparent. The ECT protects investors against the most important host country political risks, namely those of discrimination, expropriation, losses resulting from strife, transfer restrictions and breach of investment contracts.[1] Importantly, the ECT provides for a clear and comprehensive dispute resolution mechanism, with provisions for the settlement of trade disputes based on WTO rules, and application of the bilateral investment treaty (BIT) model for resolution of investment disputes. There are also dispute resolution mechanisms to cover transit by conciliation, competition by information and consultation, and the environment by review conducted by the Energy Charter Conference.[2] The ECT is an important component of the institutional framework that safeguards the prosperity and well-being of the EU and its member states.

The stalling of the General Agreement on Tariffs and Trade (GATT)-WTO process in the 2000s has seen a proliferation of preferential trade agreements (PTAs) between individual ASEAN states and external trading partners, such as the USA, China, Japan and India. PTAs are often driven by political considerations (such as competition for regional influence) and may even undermine free trade at the regional or global level through the creation of market distortions and the strengthening of rent-seeking lobbies at the domestic level.

Security of energy supply

Investment decision making in the energy sector differs from that of other industries for a number of reasons. First of all, energy (in particular hydrocarbons) is essential to the continued functioning of industrialized civilizations. Energy markets are therefore more likely to attract political intervention and investors must consider this risk alongside the long payback periods that are a common feature of energy projects. The technical and commercial complexity of capital-intensive energy projects, particularly those in the oil and gas sector, often requires the involvement of several national jurisdictions. The related investment protection concerns of the sector are more effectively addressed via a multilateral legal framework that is specific to the energy sector.

Increased demand for energy from countries in ASEAN and the broader Asia-Pacific region has not been matched by sufficient investment in the new infrastructure. Meanwhile, the region lacks a cohesive institutional structure to sufficiently address the specific demands of energy trade and investment. Although the WTO system (of which all ASEAN states save for Laos are full members) does cover trade in energy, it does not address the energy sector's challenges with regard to investment protection and export restrictions.[3] Nor does it address the concerns of producer country governments with respect to capturing maximum resource rent in support of national development needs, which may include certain domestic industrialization or social policy goals (Hunter, 2011, pp. 1–24).

The ECT was designed to balance the interests of energy producer, consumer and transit countries. In this regard it more closely matches the interests of ASEAN member states in a region that is characterized by differing levels of economic development and therefore a broader collection of national priorities. A critical factor in determining the future stability of the ASEAN region will be the question of whether market-based pricing emerges as the dominant model for transactions in energy resources and key industrial commodities. The outcome will to a large extent depend on the means that the largest Asian importers choose to secure their access to stable and affordable energy supplies.

The 'traditional' approach to energy security often involves securing exclusive access to supplies by locking producers into long-term supply contracts. This approach tends to be driven by concerns over price fluctuations but locks both parties into a long-term dependency that can be used to exert political influence. A market-oriented policy approach to energy security, on the other hand, will take the view that the diversity and flexibility of a regional or global market is systemically more resilient over the long term. It allows countries to pool their respective infrastructure and resources to create a shared common interest. It requires a common legal framework for trade and investment, such as that provided by the ECT in Europe, or NAFTA in North America.

India and China, the two largest emerging powers, have fundamentally different legal preferences and philosophical traditions, and these are reflected in their respective approaches to international law on which the current system of global trade depends, most notably in areas such as freedom of navigation and the delineation of maritime boundaries. While India has tended to uphold the norms of international law, China has to some extent followed in the tradition of other revolutionary states such as the Soviet Union in seeking to challenge these norms. The introduction of a multilateral legal regime that enhances access to energy resources and infrastructure in the ASEAN region would reduce the risk of conflict between states with different historical world views.

The ASEAN countries are key components of the global energy infrastructure in their respective roles as energy consumer, producer, and transit states. All will require substantial amounts of capital investment in their energy infrastructure over the coming decades to cope with rising domestic consumption, or to earn foreign exchange from exports of energy production.

Among ASEAN's key trading partners, the EU and its member states, Australia and Japan are all members of the ECT.[4] ASEAN, China and Korea have observer status, while Indonesia – ASEAN's largest member – recently began the Energy Charter process by signing the 1991 Energy Charter.[5]

Indonesia's move reflects its pressing need for infrastructure investment and follows over a decade of its energy infrastructure suffering from a lack of funding, resulting in overall economic growth being hampered by electricity shortages, foreign exchange earnings reduced by declining oil and gas export volumes.[6] Indonesia's status as the first ASEAN member state to begin the Energy Charter accession process is potentially indicative of two separate trends that could threaten to derail the ASEAN integration project.

The first is a divergence of outlook and interests between the maritime and mainland ASEAN member states. The archipelagic geography of Indonesia and the Philippines points towards the need for a more decentralized, diversified – and perhaps liberalized – energy infrastructure. Meanwhile, several of the other ASEAN member states are adopting energy policies that involve the construction of state-led mega-projects. These may have serious environmental and socio-economic negative impacts, while crowding out smaller-scale private investments and creating long-term dependencies that may be exploited by external powers to exert political leverage.[7]

The second trend would be a political and economic decoupling of Indonesia from the rest of ASEAN. Regardless of whether Indonesia chooses to open its energy sector to more foreign investment via the ECT accession or decides on a more protectionist approach to its energy policy, the country's renewed international stature based on a largely successful political transition to democracy and high rates of economic growth has led to increased self-confidence and a growing ambition to focus its influence on the global rather than regional stage. Unless ASEAN is able to deliver some tangible benefits to the Indonesian population, there is a danger that Indonesia's membership of the regional body will be perceived as an elitist distraction from more pressing domestic issues, and political leaders in Jakarta may come under pressure to reduce their involvement in the ASEAN regional integration project. Increased populism in Indonesian politics would feed resource nationalism, with consequences for the settlement of existing boundary disputes with neighbours, such as Malaysia, as well as for the maintenance of a stable investment climate.

Geography: Southeast Asia as a geopolitical 'pivot'

The UK Ministry of Defence (MoD) defines pivotal regions as 'those whose future paths are likely to have an effect on global stability disproportionate to their geopolitical status. They represent significant strategic choke points, where trends have the potential to converge to give them importance out of their economic, political or demographic standing. These regions include the Middle East, the Asian Meridian, sub-Saharan Africa, the Polar regions and the Korean peninsula' (MoD, 2010, p. 59).

The 'Asian Meridian' describes a crescent-shaped area from Hong Kong and coastal China in the north, through Southeast Asia to Darwin and northern Australia in the south. It is anticipated by defence planners to be an area of future geopolitical competition that sits astride major trade routes, such as the Malacca Straits, and contains major energy and minerals deposits, notably coal in Indonesia and Australia (whose combined exports account for over half of world exports). It also features the intersection of a number of strategic trends that could combine to create geopolitical instability. These could include internal security problems within regional states being exacerbated by environmental change processes, potentially leading to separatism and state fragmentation, as well as boundary disputes, which would in turn disrupt trading patterns, including the flow of energy supplies.

Factors such as increasing uncertainty over the ability to secure access to the resources necessary to maintain economic growth and well-being in the face of growing competition from other regional powers, the possibility of climate change and environmental degradation putting additional stress on existing resource availability, and the intentions of neighbouring states over disputed territories, and the changing distribution of power in the region (especially the prospects of rising Chinese and declining American influence) in combination pose a major challenge to the future security of the Southeast Asian region. If one takes into account the region's integration into global supply chains and manufacturing processes, any future regional instability could have serious implications for economic well-being in the rest of the world.

The ability of ASEAN's member states to maintain internal coherence and stability will directly impact on the security and well-being of immediate neighbours in the region and on the prosperity of major trading partners, such as the EU. The absence of such stability will increase the incidence of transnational security challenges including terrorism, undesired migratory flows, maritime piracy, overfishing and large-scale environmental degradation effects (such as haze). Unless elite consensus within can be crystallized around a political-economic order that delivers the aspirations of the population at large via efficient public expenditure, distributional conflicts may re-emerge as a major threat to social cohesion and political stability in future.[8]

Such a state of affairs would remove from world markets a significant amount of potential production capacity in food, primary energy sources, minerals and other natural resources, and in doing so, serve to intensify, rather than mitigate, the risk of growing international competition for resources. It would also limit the emergence of what is potentially one of the world's largest consumer markets, to the detriment of all other major economies.

Indonesia is the pivotal state in Southeast Asia, a region that, along with coastal China, constitutes the Asian Meridian. The economic and political development of the Asian Meridian will be a key determinant of the continued dominance of globalization based on maritime trade into the 21st century. The region is widely predicted as a future arena of geopolitical competition and is drawing increased interest from major powers such as the USA, India and China.[9] Likewise, the events of the 20th century were quite substantially shaped by political and military competition over Eastern Europe in order to influence the region described by Sir Halford Mackinder in his Heartland Theory as the 'Geographical Pivot of History' (Mackinder, 1904, pp. 421–437).[10]

The success or failure of Indonesia's economy will determine the future posture towards Southeast Asia likely to be adopted by external powers, such as the USA, China, Japan and India. At the global level, creating conditions that are conducive to trade and investment activity in Southeast Asia forms an important part of the effort to reduce international trade imbalances (such as that between China and the USA) and asset price bubbles in the industrialized economies, by providing a more diverse range of investment destinations for capital accumulated by the leading manufacturing exporters (such as Japan, Germany, China and Korea) and major commodity producers (the Gulf states, Russia, Australia, Canada).

The countries of maritime Southeast Asia also have the potential to set an example for the elites of other ASEAN states with substantial mineral wealth but lower levels of economic development, such as Myanmar, Cambodia, Laos and Vietnam. For Southeast Asia's main trading partners, a sustainable level of economic growth in ASEAN will have an immediate impact on key domestic sectors such as legal and financial services, property development, retail and tourism.

Were the EU in its bilateral trade negotiations with ASEAN states to introduce provisions covering energy trade and investment, based on the ECT framework, the potential for benefit-sharing would extend beyond opportunities for companies involved in bilateral trade.[11] A precedent would be set and, more importantly, a pro-ECT constituency created within the ASEAN state(s) concerned, to shape the domestic political and economic environment more favourably towards conditions favouring intra-ASEAN energy trade and investment liberalization.

A key challenge to extrapolating from Europe's 20th century experience is the absence of an overall strategic logic or geopolitical narrative to describe Southeast Asia's contemporary situation. Europe's wider institutional architecture, which in addition to the EU structures includes the North Atlantic Treaty Organization (NATO), the Organization for Security and Cooperation in Europe (OSCE) and the European Economic Area (EEA), is derived from the strategic logic of Mackinder's Heartland Theory. In the aftermath of World War II, this theory contributed to the formulation in Western capitals of the Cold War policy of containment. Following the collapse of Communism in Eastern Europe, the eastward expansion of NATO and the EU took place under the same strategic logic.

States, markets and the rule of law: the Southeast Asian experience

ASEAN took its first step towards creating a common framework for cooperation when in 1986 its member states signed the Agreement on ASEAN Energy Cooperation in Manila. This was further amended in 1992 to establish the consultative committee that is known as the annual ASEAN Ministers on

Energy Meeting (AMEM). The agreement contains provisions to cover cooperation in planning, energy development, conservation, training, security of supply, information exchange, and for the establishment of a consultative committee (later known as the AMEM). In 1999, this was followed by a Plan of Action for Energy Cooperation that focused on the establishment of an ASEAN power grid, a trans-ASEAN gas pipeline and the promotion of supply diversity. Material progress has, however, been slow in the absence of a mature institutional framework for regional energy cooperation.

The world economy currently faces the challenge of ensuring sufficient investment in energy production and infrastructure in the face of declining reserves of low-cost hydrocarbons, the rise of new consumer countries in Asia, and growing environmental awareness, which in practical terms has the effect of reducing Energy Return on Investment (EROI). A fundamental reordering of energy systems will have to take place, and the challenge in Southeast Asia will be to achieve this in the face of a grossly inadequate institutional framework. Although oil, gas and coal are freely traded at the international level, investment in production and distribution infrastructure is still governed by national legislation.

When it comes to energy, ASEAN member state governments often remain fixated with a statist 20th century paradigm of industrial development.[12] Many existing and planned transboundary energy projects in the region, including those that form the Trans-ASEAN Gas Pipeline and ASEAN Power Grid interconnection schemes, are state-driven and do not adequately reflect the changing structure of international energy markets. In particular, international energy companies and financial institutions play a key role in determining levels of investment, production and consumption. It is the market structure that regulates what price mechanism will be used to balance between the forces of supply and demand, and this in turn depends on the institutional framework.

Institutional frameworks exist primarily for three reasons, and these include the addressing of market failures, the lowering of transaction costs, and providing the rules and standards that govern market exchange (Goldthau and Witte, 2010, p. 7). Andreas Goldthau and Jan Martin Witte point out that the importance of assessing the political economy of rules and institutions has yet to enter the mainstream discourse on energy security, which has to date been dominated by a geopolitical competition, zero-sum game lens (Goldthau and Witte, 2010, p. 17).

The top-down approach adopted by several ASEAN member states to date tends to sidestep the geographic and political diversity that exists within ASEAN, both between as well as within the member states. Yet this has long-term implications for the social cohesion and territorial integrity of several member states in the region, as new grievances created by energy projects that do not take into account the need for equitable benefit-sharing among existing users of affected natural resources run the risk of creating tensions that may escalate into open conflict.

In terms of approaches to energy policy, however, the Philippines bucks the trend and it has been Southeast Asia's first-mover in many respects; as the first country in the region to build a nuclear power plant (completed in 1985, though never made operational); as the only country to have privatized both its electricity generation and transmission markets; and as a regional leader in the development of renewable energy sources (in particular geothermal and hydroelectric power).[13]

Indonesia may create more investor-friendly conditions by moves such as the ECT accession, or choose to become more inward-looking, in which case it would be unlikely to achieve sufficient energy production levels to warrant any substantial participation in the Trans-ASEAN Gas Pipeline or ASEAN Power Grid interconnection projects.

Singapore is moving away from reliance on piped natural gas from neighbouring Malaysia and Indonesia towards liquefied natural gas (LNG) purchased on the open market. In this regard, Singapore is best positioned among the ASEAN member states to benefit fully from energy security based on maritime globalization and the ability to access natural gas from an increasingly diverse portfolio of LNG exporters.

Thomas Barnett has pointed out the crucial linkages between continued global economic growth, access to resources for Asian countries, and infrastructure, all underpinned by a rules system (Barnett, 2002, pp. 189–200). Drawing on a US Naval War College research project (the NewRulesSets.Project) on globalization and international security, and how this is intertwined with Asia's future political and economic development trajectory, Barnett echoes many in the energy industry in pointing out that the challenge to meeting Asia's rising demand for energy lies not so much in the existence of sufficient fossil fuel reserves, but rather in the 'above-ground' political and economic factors that will determine whether these can be accessed on a commercial basis.

The economic rise of East Asia is creating interdependency between the economic stability of Asia and the political stability of the Middle East, in particular the Gulf states (Piggot, 2009, p. 1). The continuation of this relationship is reliant upon Asian economies gaining access to sufficient energy resources to fuel the demands of economic growth. Securing this supply of energy will require substantial investment in capital-intensive infrastructure. Attracting sufficient investment in turn will depend on whether investors can be confident in the existence of the rule of law to provide the necessary investment protection for capital to be disbursed. The existence of a sufficiently effective legal framework, in turn, is dependent on regional security arrangements capable of defending the trading system against potential threats. At the time of writing, these are underwritten by the USA and its military partners and allies.

Conclusion

A sense of urgency driven by the rise of China is currently working in favour of the political will to further ASEAN's economic integration, including the harmonization of the relevant national legislation. In this regard, ASEAN leaders have committed to a common market with the target date of 2015 for the realization of a single market and production base.

Andreas Goldthau, Wade Hoxtell and Jan Martin Witte argue that there needs to be a shift from the focus on energy security among countries, to global energy governance, in recognition of the emergence of the global interdependencies that characterize the energy cycle. These interdependencies create shared interests among producer, consumer and transit countries at both the global and regional levels (Goldthau and Witte, 2010, p. 342).

If ASEAN is to achieve substantive regional energy cooperation, it will require a common legal framework to govern cross-border energy trade and investments. Top-down attempts at cross-border energy cooperation have met with limited success. The ECT provides a framework whereby bottom-up projects can access international financing. A move towards joining the ECT by ASEAN states would create political momentum both at the national and regional levels that could be used to support further regional trade liberalization in future, thus strengthening the concept of an ASEAN economic community.

Despite the mutual interest among ASEAN states in developing their energy infrastructure to enhance regional energy trade flows, the large-scale investments that are needed will have to come from the private sector, and not governments. Attracting such investments will require a stable investment environment at the regional level due to the inherently multinational nature of large energy projects.

The ECT is a proven legal instrument that includes among its principles that of non-discrimination among participants; respect for state sovereignty over natural resources; and recognition of the importance of environmentally sound, energy-efficient policies. One particular comparative advantage of the ECT over the WTO system for those ASEAN states that do hold significant natural resource endowments is that it was designed to balance the interests of producer, consumer and transit countries. In this regard it contains a provision that confirms the principle of national sovereignty over energy resources. The ECT does not attempt to dictate what structure a country's domestic energy sector should take, or what form of ownership a country's energy companies should follow, and nor does it force a member state to allow foreign ownership of the energy sector or third-party access to the energy infrastructure.

Despite the clear recognition of the need for regional cooperation in energy security, ASEAN states have made little progress beyond symbolic declarations (Tan, 2008, p. 50). Part of the reason may be the absence of an underlying geopolitical concept to guide policy, equivalent to the existential threat of Communist subversion that provided the strategic rationale and logic for ASEAN's initial formation. If such a concept were to emerge, it would perhaps have to combine a sea power thesis based on the thought of Alfred Thayer Mahan and Julian Corbett, on which is built the system of maritime-based globalization that Southeast Asia has depended on for its economic growth since the colonial era, with a Mackinderian thesis of continental power, to form a synthesis explaining Southeast Asia's pivotal location at the intersection of maritime-based globalization and the industrialization process of mainland Asia, in particular China.

Notes

1. Part III of the treaty covers the provisions on Investment Promotion and Protection.
2. More details are available in *The Energy Charter Treaty: A Reader's Guide*, Brussels: Energy Charter Secretariat (2002). Available online at: http://www.encharter.org/.
3. Energy differs from other internationally traded commodities on account of its finite nature, its centrality to modern industrialized civilization, and the sovereign control exercised over its supply by a relatively small number of states. The WTO/GATT system, however, does not take into account these differences. For further elaboration, see Yuliya Selivanova, March 2011, 'Energy Challenges for International Trade Rules?', *Oil, Gas & Energy Law Intelligence (OGEL) Journal* Issue 2 (2011), Maris BV, Voorburg (Netherlands).
4. An overview of the implications of a non-European state becoming a party to the Energy Charter Treaty is provided by RJ Stevenson (2001), in 'Energy Charter Treaty: Implications for Australia', *Journal of Energy and Natural Resources Law* Volume 19.
5. On 18 June 2009, in Brussels. See *Indonesia Becomes the 74th Participant in the Energy Charter Process*, accessed November 2010 at http://www.encharter.org/index.php?id=471&L=0.
6. Indonesia in fact became a net oil importer in 2005 and left OPEC in 2008, following over a century as a leading hydrocarbons province.
7. These include the countries of the lower Mekong (Thailand, Laos, Cambodia and Vietnam) that have 134 hydroelectric power projects amounting to over 3,200 MW under construction and an additional 134 projects to join the 3,235 MW of existing capacity (see presentation by Lawrence Haas, Mekong River Commission, at the 3rd Regional Forum on Mekong Basin Development Plan, July 2010, accessible at: http://www.mrcmekong.org/free_download/BDP-3rd-reg-stakeholder-forum-ppt.htm), and Malaysia's Sarawak Corridor of Renewable Energy, which according to the Regional Corridor Development Authority, Sarawak (http://www.recoda.com.my) involves the construction of 20,000 MW of hydroelectric and 5,000 MW of coal-fired generation capacity in order to attract energy-intensive heavy industries to Sarawak.
8. During the late 1990s and early 2000s the possibility of a violent break-up of Indonesia was feared, and was driven at least in part by demands for a greater share of resource revenues by provincial elites. The Permesta/PRRI rebellion

during the 1950s, when parts of Sumatra and Eastern Indonesia turned against the central government, was also caused in part by government policies aimed at redistributing wealth from the outer islands to Java.
9. The writings of Robert D. Kaplan are proving to be particularly influential in Washington and New Delhi. These include recent articles in *Foreign Affairs*, 'Center Stage for the 21st Century: Power Plays in the Indian Ocean', March/April 2009, 'The Geography of Chinese Power: How Far Can Beijing Reach on Land and at Sea?', May/June 2010, and a book *Monsoon: The Indian Ocean and The Future of American Power*. Random House, October 2010.
10. Halford Mackinder (1904), *The Geographical Pivot of History*, presentation to the Royal Geographical Society, London. Mackinder was a key personality in the revival of the study of geography in modern times, and was involved in setting up the Department of Geography at Oxford University, and the founding of the University of Reading and the London School of Economics and Political Science. He also led the first expedition to climb Mount Kenya in 1899, served as a member of parliament from 1910 to 1922, and was appointed British High Commissioner to Southern Russia in 1919 as part of an attempt to consolidate White Russian forces. His Heartland Theory was highly influential during the 20th century, and was closely studied by strategists in Nazi Germany as well as the USA during the Cold War.
11. At the time of writing the European Commission was in the process of negotiating a bilateral free trade agreement (FTA) with Singapore. The EU-Singapore FTA is seen as a precursor to EU FTAs with other ASEAN states.
12. A notable exception is Singapore, which, despite having gas pipeline connections with both of its neighbours, Indonesia and Malaysia, is now constructing an LNG receiving terminal in order to be able to receive shipments purchased on spot markets. Singapore in this regard is joining the countries of North America and Western Europe in shifting towards a market-based pricing structure for natural gas.
13. After the USA, the Philippines and Indonesia are the world's second- and third-largest producers of geothermal power, respectively.

Bibliography

Barnett T. (2002) 'Asia's energy future: The military-market link', in S.J. Tangredi (ed.), *Globalization and Maritime Power* (Washington, DC: National Defense University Press).

Energy Charter Secretariat (2002) *The Energy Charter Treaty: A Reader's Guide* (Brussels: Energy Charter Secretariat).

Goldthau A. and Witte J. (2010) *Global Energy Governance: The New Rules of the Game* (Berlin: Global Public Policy Institute and Washington, DC: Brookings Institution Press).

Hunter T. (2011) 'The Energy Charter Treaty as a Means of Developing National Industry and Commerce in the Exploitation of Petroleum Resources: An Analysis of the Application of Articles 5, 10 and 22 of the Energy Charter Treaty', *Oil, Gas, & Energy Law Intelligence* (*OGEL*) *Journal Issue 2* (*2011*) (Voorburg, Netherlands: Maris BV).

Mackinder H.J. (1904) 'The Geographical Pivot of History', *The Geographical Journal* 23:4 (London: Royal Geographical Society).

MoD Development, Concepts and Doctrine Centre (DCDC) (2010) *Global Strategic Trends: Out to 2040*, Fourth Edition (London: Ministry of Defence).

Piggot L. (2009) 'Middle East outlook and energy security in the Asia-Pacific region', *ASPI Special Report 23* (Canberra: Australian Strategic Policy Institute).

Selivanova Y. (2011) 'Energy Challenges for International Trade Rules?', *Oil, Gas & Energy Law Intelligence (OGEL) Journal Issue 2 (2011)* (Voorburg, Netherlands: Maris BV).

Stevenson R.J. (2001) 'Energy Charter Treaty: Implications for Australia', *Journal of Energy and Natural Resources Law 19:2* (London: International Bar Association).

Tan A.T.H. (2008) 'The ASEAN countries' interest in Asian energy security', in A. Forbes (ed.), *Asian Energy Security: Regional Cooperation in the Malacca Strait* (Canberra: Seapower Centre, Department of Defence, Commonwealth of Australia).

Part IV
EU–ASEAN: Practitioners' View

8
ASEAN and the EU: Natural Partners

Jan Willem Blankert

ASEAN and the EU: similar but very different

The Southeast Asian region, which stands for more than the Association of Southeast Asian Nations (ASEAN) today in the same way as 'Europe' stands for more than today's European Union (EU), has for 45 years been seeking to achieve peace and prosperity for its peoples through regional cooperation and integration. Keywords guiding this process have been soft approach and multilateralism. After 50 years of quietly and cautiously – and slowly, some may add – progressing, Southeast Asian nations have accomplished three things in particular, which are easily taken for granted, but were certainly not the logically expected outcome 50 years back. Southeast Asia's three major successes are:

- Peace and stability in the region: there are still thousands of kilometres of disputed borders between different ASEAN member states, but (practically) nowhere has this unfinished business led to open conflict (I will discuss the skirmishes between Cambodia and Thailand later in this chapter);
- Slowly, but steadily, the ten ASEAN members today are integrating their economies and institutions. With the ASEAN Charter in place since the end of 2008, the pace of this integration has gone up;
- The steady rise of ASEAN as a well-respected bloc with the stated aim to push regional cooperation and integration beyond its own borders: the ASEAN Plus (ASEAN+) project or ASEAN's 'regional architecture'. The result of this third aspect is that ASEAN is increasingly recognized as a trusted stability-builder, as a go-between for the big players in the region.

Peace and stability did not come naturally to the region, and were not automatically the expected situation 50, 40 or even 30 years ago. The tensions between the nations that joined hands in 1967 were many, and the risk of serious conflict was always there. Once it is achieved, stability is easily taken for granted while the anguish and concern – or worse, war and destruction – that prevailed before stability was achieved are easily forgotten. People's memories are short. It is like in 'the West', where the widespread notion seems to be that democracy has always been there, although in reality it is a relatively recent phenomenon. It was only in 1949, for instance, that women in Belgium were able to vote for the first time. Singapore's success is taken for granted today. Singapore's Lee Kuan Yew's trepidation and deep concerns when Singapore separated from the Federation with Malaysia in 1965 are easily forgotten ('We faced tremendous odds with an improbable chance of survival').[1] In a climate of uncertainty and distrust, ASEAN started as a political project committed to by visionary leaders. Political cooperation was the principal goal. Only at a later stage did economic integration become part of the ASEAN agenda, and gradually a very important part. Economic integration, although not yet very far advanced, has been stepped up in the last few years, in particular since the ASEAN Charter came into force at the end of 2008. ASEAN's achievements at the political level, however, may be the most remarkable, in particular when it comes to 'reaching out' beyond its own region, which is referred to as 'ASEAN+' or regional architecture.

Again, ASEAN's economic integration process is advancing. However, when compared with the EU's economic integration, ASEAN's achievements in this area are still very modest. But we must remember that economic integration was the major explicit goal of what began as the European Economic Community and is the EU today. Behind the drive for economic integration was a strong political drive and ideal. Indeed, the early builders of European integration had 'no more war' as their common political motive, and quite a few dreamed of a federal state that would one day be represented by one flag. The idea and the ideal behind the European project was that the EU would become one integrated market where coal and steel would be produced according to one set of rules, cookies and cheese could travel unhindered from one country to another, and political integration of some sort would follow. The question of how far political integration should go was deliberately kept for later. Without doubt the flagship achievement of the EU to date is its Internal ('Single') Market. The single market project has always had the full support of a more sceptical UK, which chose to opt out of the more daring – and not risk-free, as we have since learned – euro project.

ASEAN's most impressive achievements are, not surprisingly given its birth certificate, more political in nature. Slowly, but steadily, ASEAN has developed into the platform for regional cooperation far beyond the strict ASEAN sphere. With its Treaty on Amity and Cooperation (TAC), ASEAN has created an ever-larger group of nations and 'regional integration organizations consisting of sovereign states' (as the TAC language was adjusted to enable the EU to join) that commit to the TAC's key elements of peaceful cooperation and non-interference. ASEAN is in the driver's seat during the meetings of the ASEAN Regional Forum (ARF), a varied group of countries who seek solutions through political dialogue and preventive diplomacy.

In 2010 Russia and the USA accepted the invitation to join the East Asia Summit (EAS) in 2011, a sign of recognition of ASEAN's regional role.

This said, ASEAN has also been making major steps forward in the economic area, but with an emphasis on 'widening' rather than 'deepening'. Most impressive, perhaps, is how smoothly ASEAN seems to be accommodating its giant neighbour China, including in the economic sphere. Since 1 January 2010, a Free Trade Agreement (FTA) between the ASEAN-6, the six most advanced ASEAN nations[2] (who account for 90 per cent of ASEAN GDP and trade), and China has been in full operation. It means there is now one free trade area from Beijing to Jakarta and from Singapore to Manila, accounting for 1.9 billion people and US$6 trillion in GDP. In late 2009, when the last step of this agreement was imminent, concern was expressed, for instance by Indonesian manufacturers, that the ASEAN home markets would be flooded with cheap Chinese products. Not much has been heard since then, and one would think that the fears were unfounded – as calls against free trade have always appeared to be unfounded throughout the centuries.[3] It seems that ASEAN is handling its relations with China with greater ease and agility than, for example, the EU has for a long time handled its relations with Russia.

ASEAN has concluded FTAs with other partners, among them Australia, India, Japan, Korea and New Zealand, which are now gradually phasing in, some of them over a very long period. Together with these partners and China, ASEAN has formed the EAS, which Russia and the USA joined in 2011. Is it a 'talk shop' only, as is the often-heard criticism of the ARF, or a serious force for the better? Only time will tell, but perhaps not even time. Indeed, nobody will ever be able to establish with certainty which conflicts have been prevented by these initiatives for confidence building and preventive diplomacy.

Let me try to explain what I see as the most important differences and similarities between ASEAN and the EU, and hence the challenges and opportunities for the relationship between the two:

- ASEAN started in the first place as a political project. Economic integration came as an afterthought, inspired by enhanced economic integration in Europe. The EU started as an economic organization, which had political integration as an important, but secondary (or perhaps one should say 'hidden') goal;
- ASEAN focuses more on 'widening' than 'deepening'. Examples of ASEAN's widening efforts are: (i) the ASEAN+ initiatives and its activism in the area of regional architecture, which remains a loose cooperation structure; (ii) fairly shallow FTAs with a large number of non-ASEAN countries in the region, not least China, which are in the first place about tariff reductions; it appears as if these FTAs develop at a faster pace than ASEAN's own economic integration;

- The EU focuses more on 'deepening' than 'widening'. Let me stress that I consider the often-heard notion of the 'inward looking' EU as nonsense: the EU has its neighbourhood policy, is the world's largest donor of development aid, has peacekeeping operations all over the world, and is among the world's most active advocates for human rights and action against climate change. This said, it is true that because of the very strong internal EU systems, EU core business concerns food safety, product standards, competition policy standards and many other aspects of the EU internal market – all being very laudable causes that serve EU taxpayers much better than they usually perceive it.

In the period 2008–2011, both ASEAN and the EU faced very serious challenges in their 'core business'. ASEAN saw a worrying eruption of violence at the border between two of its member states, Cambodia and Thailand. It was perhaps the most serious challenge to date to the effectiveness and credibility of ASEAN. In the ASEAN context, the conflict is an anomaly. It should not have happened or, in the words of one of the ASEAN foreign ministers, it was 'unacceptable' – if not ridiculous. One can only hope that the conflict will remain limited to isolated skirmishes. Any serious violent conflict between two ASEAN members would put the credibility of the whole ASEAN project at stake.

With the euro crisis still unfolding, the EU was and still is facing a very serious problem in what actually is its 'core business'. The crisis puts an important aspect of the EU economic integration project into question. During 2011 it became clear that getting out of the crisis would take much more time, effort and money than initially thought. In early 2012 there was renewed confidence that the euro zone would be able to cope provided that EU members would accept a greater degree of economic integration. The policy measure under discussion in early 2012 implied a further deepening of the EU integration process. The measures being considered – more budgetary coordination among euro member states and stricter controls that the rules are respected – are indispensable aspects of any monetary union. However, at the time of the introduction of the euro it was still too difficult for all EU member states to accept such measures.

ASEAN and the EU – like each and any timely and successful preventive diplomacy operation – share the fate that much of what they accomplish inevitably remains unnoticed and undervalued. Failure, havoc and disaster, as much as houses on fire or that collapse, grab the headlines. Happy houses do not get media attention. Hard power is daily news; soft power rarely is. Europe's divide over Iraq in 2003 made, quite understandably, headlines. The dozens of instances of agreement among EU member states usually do not. ASEAN and the EU must accept this as a fact of life, although they may try to better explain their cause.

The most remarkable fact remains that the EU and ASEAN, 'the two quiet actors', have been able to achieve peace in their regions (with the caveat mentioned above), and to varying degrees have also been able to extend their peace message to their wider 'neighbourhood', to use a term from the EU dictionary. The similarities beg the question as to what extent the two regions can strengthen the relationship between them and better achieve common goals. The relationship is warm enough, but on both sides there is a feeling that something is missing, that the relationship should be made more effective, and that there is a potential that should be better explored. Or could it be that the differences between the two blocs stand in the way and form an insurmountable obstacle to bringing the relationship to a higher level?

ASEAN, smooth global player

Taking the optimistic view, one can stress that ASEAN, one of the most comprehensive and committed regional integration initiatives in the world, is a natural partner for the EU. In this view, the EU and ASEAN share their multilateral approach to political and economic issues. It is their multilateral 'DNA'. The EU is ASEAN's oldest dialogue partner (from 1977). It has from the very beginning been a supporter and an ally of ASEAN. ASEAN is a champion of regional integration, multilateralism and preventive diplomacy, which are among the main planks of EU foreign policy. This is all fine, but if we stress these similarities, we may easily gloss over the differences, mostly given that ASEAN's construct is more shallow and political in nature when compared with the EU, which is – first and foremost – an economic giant.

First, ASEAN has been steadily developing, primarily, its ambitious ASEAN regional integration project among its ten member states. In 2008, with the adoption of the ASEAN Charter, the integration effort was stepped up with the construction of the 'three communities': (i) Political/security; (ii) Economic; and (iii) Social/cultural and the goal of 'a single market and production base' by 2015. Second, ASEAN has been developing an 'ASEAN-centred regional architecture'. This is the growing network for multilateral dialogue and consultation, including at the highest level, that is at the level of heads of government/state, where ASEAN and its partners address a wide range of strategic issues, from economic cooperation and climate change to North Korea and maritime security in the Strait of Malacca and the South China Sea.

- The first ring of ASEAN partners comprises China, Japan and Korea (ASEAN+3).
- The second ring adds Australia, India and New Zealand (ASEAN+6, at leaders' level referred to as the East Asia Summit – EAS). In October 2010, the USA and Russia were officially invited to join the EAS in 2011.

- The third ring is formed by the additional members of the ARF, in which security issues are discussed with other relevant actors in addition to those already mentioned and including the EU.

In doing so, ASEAN has worked on fostering peace, stability and security in its region and beyond. Important players in the region – China, India, Japan and South Korea – have so far accepted ASEAN's lead in the construction of these regional arrangements. Even the USA has followed suit more recently following the Obama administration's growing emphasis on Asia and Southeast Asia. In both 2009 and 2010, US Secretary of State Hillary Clinton travelled twice to the region, followed by a much larger number in 2011. Also, after the first ASEAN–USA summit in Singapore, in 2009, ASEAN and the USA had their second summit meeting in August 2010 in New York.

ASEAN's regional architecture from ASEAN+3 to the EAS is about more than political and security cooperation. As mentioned earlier, in the last few years ASEAN has established FTAs with all its ASEAN+6 partners. These are now gradually coming on stream, even though for some of them the complete implementation of the FTA will take more than ten years. The FTA between ASEAN and China is the most advanced. After gradually phasing in from 2005, this latter agreement came into full implementation with ASEAN's six most advanced member states on 1 January 2010. On that date, the FTA among ASEAN's six most advanced nations themselves also came fully into force, whereby practically all trade tariffs between these six were abolished. It is paradoxical that international media hardly paid attention to this landmark development.

It is striking how relatively easily China was integrated into all these FTAs with ASEAN, especially considering the sometimes very explicit fear of competition from China in other parts of the world, not least the USA still supposedly being the strongest economy of the world. It is impressive to see how ASEAN is quietly and unassumingly accommodating and actually integrating with its big and rising neighbour. Is this not a big risk for Indonesian and Thai manufacturers? The jury is still out – provisional data indicate that Chinese exports to the region have indeed been rising, but so have ASEAN exports to China. Perhaps ASEAN leaders have found that Chinese exports to ASEAN are about much more than the presumed 'cheap consumer' goods. For example, ASEAN countries hope to benefit from Chinese investments, such as when it was announced that certain segments of China's coastal manufacturing industry would be relocating to Indonesia.

I may be too much of an optimist, but I see the above as signs that ASEAN is confirming its role as a confident driver and a centre of the ongoing process of regional political and economic cooperation. ASEAN leaders like to refer to this as 'ASEAN centrality': 'a process of ASEAN centred, inclusive regional cooperation' as the official ASEAN reference is. In 2009, the then Japanese prime minister Hatojama and the Australian prime minister Kevin Rudd drew headlines with far-going proposals for 'a new approach' to cooperation in East Asia. The Japanese prime minister suggested an EU-like economic area with its own currency. ASEAN seemed somewhat taken aback by the proposals of the two prime ministers. Less than two years later, both prime ministers had been replaced and their proposals forgotten. ASEAN is still there and, with its confidence regained, is quietly continuing its regional cooperation project, 'ASEAN driven' indeed.

In 2010, with Vietnam as ASEAN Chair, ASEAN presented its Master Plan for Inter-Connectivity (MPIC). Of the three major pillars of the plan, the first is infrastructure, 'physical inter-connectivity'. The maps of the plan, which one can look up on the website of the ASEAN Secretariat, show ASEAN's plans for further improving and connecting roads, railways and pipelines in the region. ASEAN leaders stress that the MPIC is no more than an inventory, or a map, of what is going on or decided already – as Ong Keng Yong, former ASEAN secretary general, argued, 'there is nothing new in the plan, it only serves to remind us what we have been talking about for more than 40 years.'[4] The MPIC is more than a plan or a dream – it rather appears to be the satellite photo of a building site. The second pillar of the MPIC concerns 'institutional inter-connectivity', which I interpret as 'making the single market work': improving border crossings, facilitating transport across borders and customs procedures, and improving cooperation between institutions in different countries. It entails much tedious technical work on standards and norms and involves, for example, the mutual recognition of diplomas or driving licences. Again, not very exciting 'stuff' for the media, but if it works it will lead to very direct, tangible benefits for the ordinary people.

ASEAN: the China factor

On the occasion of the official application of East Timor for ASEAN membership in March 2011, Indonesian authorities were unusually outspoken about the role of ASEAN in its role to counterbalance Chinese influence. The Indonesian foreign minister expressed his warm support for the application, saying that a negative reaction could only lead to greater Chinese influence in East Timor. It showed that at least Indonesia sees ASEAN as a force to counter (or to express it in more diplomatic language, to 'balance') Chinese influence in the region. It is ASEAN's hidden and usually grossly underestimated force. It again begs the question: think of what the region could look like without ASEAN.

The Indonesian president backed the statement of his foreign minister by promising assistance to East Timor in areas such as infrastructure, oil exploitation, military equipment and diplomatic training, typically areas controlled by Chinese interests. When asked about China's role during a meeting with members of the European Parliament, the Indonesian foreign minister stressed that there was 'no need to create a new Cold War climate'. Later, in other meetings with Indonesian interlocutors, the European parliamentarians were told that Indonesia welcomed a prosperous China – 'Indonesia is better off with a prospering China than an impoverished one'. The intention is, it seems, to be firm vis-à-vis China, but to keep a cool head.

As mentioned earlier, under the Vietnamese chair, ASEAN presented its MPIC. The plan is a useful inventory of ongoing and planned infrastructure investment both within ASEAN and in the wider region. Especially in the poorer Northern ASEAN member states (Cambodia, Laos, Myanmar and Vietnam – CLMV), China is a major investor in infrastructure and also in other sectors. The possible political implications of this development are clear enough. On more than one occasion, some analysts have pointed out that China's influence is a threat, which might even lead to a 'split' within ASEAN.

It makes me think of similar analysis with regard to Europe in the 1960s when French author Jean Jaques Schreiber made headlines with his warning against American 'colonialism' which would lead American businesses to overtake (and 'colonize') European economies. The excessive concern about Japanese economic and financial 'colonialism' so prevalent in the USA in the 1980s comes also to mind. How simplistic and outdated these warnings sound today! Taking a more long-term view (and with this I mean that we should analyse these developments in terms of decades), I am of the opinion that Chinese investments in the Northern part of Southeast Asia should be seen as a welcome factor helping these countries to catch up and 'bridge the development gap'. Chinese investments should help them better connect not only with China, but also with the more prosperous Southern part of Southeast Asia.

I fail to see how roads, railways and ports financed by Chinese investment in countries that account for no more than 10 per cent of the ASEAN economy could lead to a 'split' in ASEAN, as long as the countries concerned are sovereign states who have firmly decided to anchor their fate and future in ASEAN. Let me quote the Rwandan president Paul Kagame, who, when asked about the role of China in Africa, said: 'In the end, it is up to African countries and their leaders, not the West or China, to define the terms under which they want to cooperate with China and/or the West.'[5] The same applies to Asian countries, one would think. Moreover, and more importantly, it can only be an advantage that these developments take place within the ASEAN context – within ASEAN's protective fence as it were. In exactly the same way as small EU member states see sometimes greater advantage of EU membership than the larger ones, also in ASEAN the relatively small members, such as Cambodia and Laos, will find that ASEAN membership, instead of weakening them, will make their voice better heard on the international stage. China's dominant position in the northern ASEAN area is mentioned as a possible factor behind ASEAN's decision to present its MPIC. With the MPIC, these Chinese investments were put in an ASEAN context as it were, fenced by ASEAN by giving them an ASEAN label.

ASEAN and the EU: natural partners?

So are ASEAN and the EU 'natural partners'? Do the two share a multilateral 'DNA' and multilateral reflexes? True, the EU is ASEAN's oldest dialogue partner and supporter. However, being courted by important players on the world stage, it seems that ASEAN has started wondering how deep the EU interest in the region is, and especially how serious the EU is in its voiced intention to politically engage with the region. The point comes up in many private conversations and can be paraphrased as: 'We respect and like the EU as an economic partner, the EU remains a source of inspiration, we appreciate EU support programmes to support ASEAN's integration effort, but what is the EU's political engagement with the region?'

ASEAN has made it clear it doesn't want to turn into an EU-like structure. As ASEAN states stress, giving up or pooling sovereignty – a sovereignty only recently obtained – is not considered as an option. Still, the EU will continue to serve as an inspiration for ASEAN's integration effort. ASEAN officials stress that the EU experience will remain of great use and serve as an example, albeit not one that will be directly copied. This said, basic technical features of the integration of markets are inevitably similar whatever the envisaged final outcome (technical product standards, the simplification of border facilities, the recognition of diplomas and certificates, and the integration of customs systems that is 'institutional inter-connectivity'). Also political and psychological resistance to any integration effort will have common, universal characteristics. ASEAN is increasingly becoming aware that concluding a regional agreement is fine, but factual implementation of agreements at national level, that is making them actually work, is the more difficult part. Implementing a regional agreement, that is, transposing it from the plan on paper to day-to-day practice (faster border procedures, region-wide food standards) is not only technically challenging in its own right, but factors such as administrative inertia and active resistance from vested interests can lead to additional headwinds. 'You have gone through this and we want to learn from you,' ASEAN officials tell the EU.[6]

EU assistance in customs and standards remains useful and has led to tangible results. After the completion of the EU support programme ASEAN Programme for Regional Integration Support (APRIS II) of €7.2 million in March 2011, a new larger programme, of €15 million over the period of four years, again to support economic integration, will come on stream in the second half of 2012. Also 'exchanging experiences' and 'lessons learnt' are likely to be a constant in the EU–ASEAN relationship. In July 2010, the ASEAN Committee of Permanent Representatives (CPR), an important novelty of ASEAN's institutional structure, visited Brussels and Berlin to gain first-hand experience of how integration works in the EU. Furthermore, in 2011, the ten members of the ASEAN Human Rights Commission (AICHR) visited Europe. Although the Human Rights Commission had visited the USA already in 2010, the EU, as another bloc of sovereign states that seek to integrate, provides a unique example for ASEAN.

Many, if not all, areas where the EU and ASEAN cooperate or may cooperate serve mutual interests. Stability in the ASEAN region and ASEAN achieving its integration goals is also very much in the EU's interest. Cooperation in disaster relief/management is, first and foremost, designed to benefit the ASEAN region. However, in today's interconnected and interdependent world, achieving and maintaining stability and security in ASEAN will also be to the benefit of other parts of the world, including the EU. 'A strong ASEAN is probably the best guarantee for peace and stability in the region,'[7] the Commission Communication on Southeast Asia of 2003 (it may be time for an update) stated. The instruments proposed for the EU–ASEAN cooperation in the communication were 'for conducting policy dialogue and providing expertise in regional integration',[8] meaning that officials and experts of the two regions working in similar areas (be it automotive spare parts or food safety) will sit together and compare notes. It continues by arguing that the EU stands ready to continue 'support to actions in the area of mediation, conflict prevention and conflict settlement'.[9] Individual ASEAN member states have demonstrated the capacity of their own in these areas, but not as ASEAN as a whole. In July 2010, the EU delegation in Jakarta and the ASEAN Secretariat organized, together with the Crisis Mediation Initiative, the first joint workshop on crisis mediation.

The thriving trade and investment relationship would certainly warrant greater political engagement of the EU. The EU is the biggest investor in the region, and ASEAN is the EU's fifth largest trade partner (the EU is ASEAN's second after China). The negotiation of a region-to-region ASEAN–EU FTA may have faltered, but negotiations on different bilateral economic and trade agreements are ongoing (Singapore, Malaysia, the Philippines and Vietnam) or were scheduled to begin by the end of 2011 (Indonesia, Thailand). Both sides have committed to intensify the trade dialogue. As a sign of this new dynamism, in May 2011, the first-ever ASEAN–EU Business Summit was organized in Jakarta, on the eve of the second meeting of the EU trade commissioner with his ASEAN counterparts, the ASEAN economic ministers (the ASEAN–EU Economic Ministers Meeting – AEEM).

The EU and ASEAN: strategic engagement – or not?

As already mentioned, the EU serves as an inspiration for ASEAN integration, and the EU supports the ASEAN integration efforts with funds and expertise. And yet ASEAN feels that the EU should or could show greater political engagement with the region. Why? ASEAN feels that the EU has difficulty in being present at EU–ASEAN events at what ASEAN partners consider a sufficiently high political level. This has given rise to doubts over whether the EU is genuinely and strategically interested in the Southeast Asian region.[10] Also, when the ASEAN Charter entered into force at the end of 2008, the EU upgraded the relationship with ASEAN, but other important partners upgraded their relationship with ASEAN more comprehensively.[11]

Obviously, the inclusion of Myanmar as a member of the ASEAN bloc (in 1997) complicated the relationship for a long time. The EU, because of its background as an human rights advocate, its accountability to national parliaments and the European Parliament and the constraints posed by the fact that its foreign policy formulation is based on the principle of unanimity, had great difficulty in coping with the inclusion of Myanmar in ASEAN as a member. ASEAN, on the other hand, felt that the EU, a friend, should not interfere in the other friend's choice of partners. ASEAN doesn't have the strict membership criteria the EU has and hence does not have the in-built political litmus test. This notwithstanding, the world and the people of Myanmar are probably better off with Myanmar within ASEAN than outside it. At the time of Myanmar's accession to ASEAN, the China factor played as much a role as now in the case of East Timor. The obvious difference is that East Timor, although as poor as ASEAN's poorest member states, is a young, thriving democracy.

The USA had a similar problem with Myanmar. However, once the USA decided to 're-engage' with the region, starting in 2009, Washington made it clear that it would take a pragmatic approach and was open to dialogue on the matter. In addition, the USA took the 'presence' issue at heart. Secretary of state Hillary Clinton travelled twice to the region in both 2009 and 2010 and visited three times in 2011. The USA opened a mission fully dedicated to ASEAN in 2011 – as did Japan. This said, the EU has also taken an increasingly pragmatic approach on the Myanmar issue. Myanmar participates fully in the EU–ASEAN technical cooperation programmes. And when the newly established ASEAN Committee of Permanent Representatives was invited by the EU and Germany to visit Brussels and Berlin in July 2010, the participation of the Myanmar permanent representative was not even a question.

Reviewing the two paragraphs above about Myanmar, which I wrote in early 2011, one year later, in early 2012, I am struck again when I think of how little credit, let alone praise, ASEAN has received for the changes that have taken place in Myanmar during the course of 2012. ASEAN's quiet diplomacy has without doubt helped – and probably has helped a lot – to make these changes happen. ASEAN's diplomacy on the matter has been so quiet that it has hardly been heard, in fact it has remained practically unnoticed (certainly by the international media).

The reason that the EU is not a 'state' has delayed EU membership of the ASEAN Treaty of Amity and Cooperation (TAC) already for more than five years. This ASEAN peace treaty enjoys a growing popularity, with 18 non-ASEAN signatories in early 2011 and a growing number of other countries showing interest in joining.[12] As early as 2006, ASEAN and EU officials agreed that the EU should join the TAC. There was a snag, however. The treaty text speaks of 'states', so an amendment was needed to accommodate EU membership, because the EU is not a state. This was essentially a technical detail, but, as it appeared, a treaty text is always more than technicalities alone as every word counts. Initially proposed wording would, in theory, open the possibility for Taiwan to join the TAC, which bothered China (already a TAC signatory), so an alternative had to be found. In 2009, a text was agreed by ASEAN members,[13] and which was approved by other TAC signatories in 2010. This approved text has now to be ratified by all 28 TAC signatories – 10 ASEAN states and 18 non-ASEAN ones. It is expected that this process will be completed in 2012, after which the EU can join the TAC.

Membership of the TAC may be rather symbolic and not have any serious political or strategic implications. But again: in diplomacy symbols matter and membership of the TAC is the minimum requirement for joining the EAS. To date, 8 out of 18 non-ASEAN TAC signatories have joined the EAS. Membership of the latest two, the USA and Russia, were officially confirmed at the EAS meeting in 2011. Given the US military presence in the region, the invitation to join the EAS so soon after its re-engagement with the region and its joining of the TAC should not come as a surprise. On the other hand, the invitation extended to Russia, which had been kept waiting for almost five years, seemed less obvious. Russia has, however, its champions in ASEAN and one would think that it was above all invited to counterbalance the US membership and make it more easily acceptable for other EAS members, not least China.

The EU has expressed its interest in joining the EAS. This meeting of ASEAN leaders with important players in the region and beyond is increasingly considered as a gathering with great potential. However, ASEAN's reaction so far can be summarized as 'not now, perhaps later'. The explanation given privately relates to how the EU interests and its role in the region are perceived – this is also reflected, as I pointed out earlier, in the usual reply in private by ASEAN policy makers and diplomats: 'We respect and like the EU as an economic partner, we appreciate EU support to ASEAN, but what is your political engagement with the region?' And when it comes to the EAS, ASEAN interlocutors add to that: 'What could the EU add to the EAS or how could the EU contribute to the success of the EAS?' One high ASEAN official expressed it even more clearly: 'Why do you ask for an entry ticket? Better make sure you earn it and we beg you to join.'

So it would seem that the EU, because of the lack of high-level political engagement, its principled stance on the question of Myanmar and some practical matters, is considered as a second-tier partner by ASEAN. This said, at working level the relationship is excellent. The various EU-supported programmes are well appreciated. ASEAN officials are very explicit in expressing their appreciation, including with regard to the special role of the EU as a similar organization. With the EU Lisbon Treaty and the ASEAN Charter in place, it may be the right time to energize and reinforce the EU–ASEAN relationship. In particular, both partners should strive to enhance their political cooperation in areas where the EU and ASEAN can act together as natural soft-power allies in addressing global challenges, namely issues of migration, trafficking in human beings, money laundering, piracy, organized crime and drugs. All these issues 'need to be incorporated systematically into our regional and bilateral dialogues with Southeast Asia', says the European Commission Communication of 2003.[14] This commitment could be updated with a focus on assistance to develop physical and legal infrastructure that will facilitate ASEAN integration.

Conclusion: ASEAN and the EU – from pragmatic approach to higher strategy

The EU and ASEAN may be well advised to take for the time being a pragmatic approach and not set their goals too high. EU membership of the TAC may take a long time, but will soon be reality. Who knows, the EU will be invited to join the EAS one day. But in the meantime, there is enough day-to-day practical work to do.

First, after negotiations for a region-to-region FTA between the EU and ASEAN were halted, the EU has been actively engaging with individual ASEAN member states. For example, in August 2010, the EU trade commissioner met with ASEAN economic ministers when the latter gathered in Vietnam. It should be stressed that the EU considers the country-to-country talks and possibly future agreements as stepping stones to an over-arching region-to-region agreement, which remains the ultimate goal. This pragmatic approach has led to progress in bilateral talks and, at the same time, a deepening of the region-to-region dialogue.

Second, support programmes for the integration effort of ASEAN, including technical matters such as customs, trade facilitation and border management will continue. As already mentioned, the EU has been, throughout its existence, considered as a unique partner to support the more technical aspects of ASEAN economic integration. In March 2011, a new large (€15 million) programme designed to support the ASEAN economic integration was launched. Other support programmes are about to begin. An FTA support programme, aiming to strengthen ASEAN capacity to negotiate FTAs (€2.5 million) came on stream in 2011. The Regional ASEAN Dialogue Facility (READI, €4 million) became operational in early 2012. Programmes for border management (making the single market work), higher education (scholarships), human rights (support to the Human Rights Commission) and regional statistics, totalling up to €30 million, are being designed. Given the considerable length of EU and ASEAN procedures, these programmes may not become operational before 2013.

Third, the EU helps strengthen the capacity of the ASEAN Secretariat (ASEC). With some 80 professional staff dealing with the political and technical files, the ASEC is too small and weak to fully support, let alone drive, the integration process. It may be unfair to compare the ASEC with the EU Commission bureaucracy, which comprises about 15,000 professionals supporting the EU integration effort. The EU Commission is a unique institution and nothing comparable is foreseen in the ASEAN context. However, the work of the ASEC could be compared with the Council Secretariat of the EU, which directly supports the work and the meetings of ministers and officials of member states. The Council Secretariat amounts to about 4,000 officials, interpreters and other support staff included and some 2,000 professionals. Assuming that the tasks at the heart of the integration machinery of the EU and ASEAN are in principle similar or comparable, it would suggest that even a doubling of staff in the ASEC might even not be enough to solve all their problems. The new EU support programme of €15 million includes a sum for direct funding of the ASEC. Also, other donors – or 'dialogue partners', as ASEAN prefers – have support programmes for the Secretariat.

The READI programme in particular should facilitate and intensify dialogue between experts and practitioners in sectors such as food safety, consumer protection, transport, science and technology, ICT, health and energy. The EU has its very specific expertise in these areas, which can be put to good use by ASEAN (and in part already is). The programme may also help to familiarize officials in line ministries and the public at large with the implications of ASEAN integration. ASEAN and ASEAN integration can, very much like the EU and its integration machinery and policy outcomes, be difficult to understand. The first ASEAN–EU Business Summit that took place in May 2011 brought together some 500 business people from the two regions. There are many other practical areas where the EU and ASEAN can enhance their cooperation.

Somehow ASEAN and the EU have to seek to overcome the constraints that apparently exist at the highest political level. In the meantime the two regions can continue and extend their cooperation at a more practical and down-to-earth level as described in the last four paragraphs above. Actually, they do. People in ASEAN may be better helped with the very concrete assistance ASEAN receives from the EU in its economic integration effort. Possibly the best sign of all of how vibrant the relation is, are the trade data. Total trade between the EU and ASEAN, exports and imports taken together, was US$220 billion in 2011, with a surplus for ASEAN of US$25 billion. The flow of tourists, scholars and business people who travel each year between the two regions is about 10 million. This may be of greater importance for the day-to-day life of people in ASEAN and the EU and a better sign of how they interact than grand strategy statements.

When the relationship will be lifted to a higher political level one day one can only conclude that the grand strategic statements are not hollow words, but simply the recognition at high political level that ASEAN and the EU are two thoroughly intertwined regions with similar goals, and that they are natural partners indeed.

Notes

1. Lee Kuan Yew, The Singapore Story, Singapore (1998, pp. 15–16).
2. The ASEAN-6 are Brunei, Indonesia, Malaysia, the Philippines, Singapore and Thailand.
3. Britain's repeal of the Corn Laws in 1846 is still as a symbolic landmark decision. It was a significant triumph indicative of the new political power gained by the English middle class, a triumph of consumers over producers.
4. Ong Keng Yong, at a Seminar on the MPIC, in Ho Chi Minh City on 17 December 2010.
5. During a public presentation in Singapore on 22 May 2008 (his remark led to enthusiastic applause from the audience); from 'China rising: will the West be able to cope?', p. 96, Singapore, 2008.
6. The headline scoreboard success percentages on ASEAN economic integration – of close to 75 per cent – are about ratification of agreements, and do not tell us anything about factual implementation or operation on the ground of these agreements.
7. European Commission, Communication on South-East Asia (2004, p. 5).
8. Ibid.
9. European Commission, Communication on South-East Asia (2004, p. 18).
10. Examples are (i) EU presence at EU/ASEAN ministerial meetings and the one-off ASEAN–EU Commemorative Summit in 2007 in Singapore; (ii) few visits by high EU officials to the ASEAN Secretariat; (iii) most recently difficulties with sufficiently high EU representation at the ARF.
11. In early 2009, the EU appointed its bilateral head of delegation in Jakarta as representative to ASEAN and upgraded its ASEAN activities. EU member states present in Jakarta all appointed their bilateral ambassadors as representatives to ASEAN. Japan was the first to appoint a dedicated ambassador to ASEAN in 2010, followed by the USA. Japan and the USA opened dedicated missions to ASEAN in 2011. China announced it is working on doing the same.

12. The most recent newcomers are the USA, Turkey and Canada, whereas Brazil has shown its interest in joining (situation in early 2012).
13. This agreement by ASEAN member states was marked with a festive ASEAN–EU signing ceremony in Phnom Penh in May 2009. It led some to think that the EU actually joined the TAC at that moment.
14. European Commission, Communication on South-East Asia (2004, p. 5).

Bibliography

Blankert J.W. (2007) *China Rising: Will the West Be Able to Cope?* (Singapore: World Scientific Publishing Company).

European Commission (2004) 'A New Partnership with South-East Asia', Commission Communication, COM (2003) 399 (Brussels).

Yew L.K. (1998) *The Singapore Story: Memoirs of Lee Kuan Yew* (Singapore: Prentice Hall).

9
Bringing Europe and Southeast Asia Closer Through ASEAN and the EU

Ong Keng Yong

Introduction

The Association of Southeast Asian Nations (ASEAN) has a long-standing partnership with the European Union (EU). This relationship is not a frivolous one. Many mechanisms for cooperation have been established and numerous projects have been implemented. It began informally in 1972, five years after ASEAN's birth. At the ASEAN Foreign Ministers Meeting in July 1977, the dialogue and cooperation was formalized. Dr Surin Pitsuwan, the current secretary general of ASEAN, put it this way in a recent commentary: 'Since 1977, ASEAN and the EU have formalized and nurtured their dialogue relations. This was further institutionalized with the signing of the ASEAN–EC Cooperation Agreement on 7 March 1980, and this year, we celebrate its 30th anniversary. Since then, the EU has become an important ASEAN Dialogue Partner. It is also the only regional organization which has a full dialogue partner status with ASEAN' (ASEAN, 2010c).

Collectively, the ten member countries of ASEAN have more than 590 million people. The EU has 27 member states and almost 500 million people. In 2008, the gross domestic product (GDP) per capita of ASEAN was US$4726, while that for the EU reached US$32,708 (ASEAN, 2010a, pp. 1, 3).[1] ASEAN's total trade with the EU amounts to more than US$200 billion per annum (ASEAN, 2010a, p. 10).[2] The recent global financial crisis had decreased this trade, but the EU was still ASEAN's second-largest trade partner, while ASEAN was the EU's fifth-largest trading partner in 2009. The EU's share of ASEAN's total trade with the world in 2009 accounted for 11.2 per cent. The total EU foreign direct investment (FDI) flows to ASEAN totalled US$7.2 billion in 2009, accounting for 18.4 per cent of FDI received by ASEAN for the year. There were 7.14 million tourists from the EU who visited ASEAN in 2009, up from 6.97 million in 2008 (ASEAN, 2010b).[3]

ASEAN and the EU are often described by analysts as the two most advanced regions in the world in terms of regional economic integration.

Officials from ASEAN and the EU countries have always stated that their unique partnership is based on the spirit of equality and mutual respect, and both sides have learned to appreciate each other and have worked on their common interests rather than let differences divide them. In reality, the ASEAN–EU ties have been hampered by disagreement between some governments from both regions over political and economic issues, and the future direction of the relationship. Some European quarters, including members of the European Parliament and non-governmental organizations, have repeatedly criticized a number of ASEAN governments for their lack of human rights protection and political freedom. The European media has also complicated the relationship by its reporting on sensitive issues such as cultural and religious subjects.[4]

Indeed, without the pro-active stance of the professional staff and officials at the European Commission in Brussels and the support of a few EU member states with strong economic and trade interests in Southeast Asia (notably Germany), ASEAN–EU relations would not have made the kind of progress witnessed so far. Let us examine the interactions between ASEAN and the EU on a few specific topics to get a better picture of what has troubled the relationship between the two regional organizations.

Expectations

On an intellectual and philosophical level, officials at the European Commission in Brussels have consistently supported ASEAN's integration efforts. They believe that the success of ASEAN in community building in Southeast Asia will help their own push of strengthening European economic and political integration. The European experiment or Project Europe would become a more validated example for others to follow. ASEAN's goal of a single market and regional production base by 2015, envisaged under the ASEAN Economic Community (AEC), is seen as similar to the common market and associated initiatives of the EU's antecedents.

The European Commission in Brussels has consistently supported programmes to intensify capacity building and regulatory cooperation between ASEAN and the EU. For example, under the Trans-Regional EU–ASEAN Trade Initiative (TREATI), cooperation focused on areas closely linked to ASEAN's own economic integration: sanitary standards for agriculture and fisheries, standards for specific industrial products, and technical barriers to trade. Training and technical assistance to improve the capacity of government agencies and the capability of officials to handle the negotiation of Free Trade Agreements (FTAs) have also been undertaken by the EU in the less developed ASEAN countries. For the period 2007–2013, almost €70 million has been allocated for various forms of technical assistance to ASEAN, according to the secretary general of ASEAN Surin Pitsuwan (ASEAN, 2010c).

Specific models of harmonization and standardization of rules and standards were shared with ASEAN officials in the hope that the latter's learning curve would be shortened and that European examples would be adopted. Indeed, the ASEAN Harmonized Cosmetic Regulatory Scheme, covering the mutual recognition arrangement of product registration approvals, and the ASEAN Cosmetic Directive (which is a comprehensive document to regulate the trade in personal beauty products across the ten ASEAN economies) drew heavily from the EU model. For statistical collection and analysis, protection of intellectual property rights, administration of customs procedures to clear imports and exports, the ASEAN countries took in many of the EU's ideas and practices. In specialized fields such as the cogeneration of energy from biomass, the efficient use of energy, and the protection of biodiversity and marine ecology in the ASEAN region, the EU provided significant technical assistance as well as funding support for the ASEAN Energy Centre in Jakarta and the ASEAN Centre for Biodiversity in Manila. Very often, the arrangement would be for an initial period of support for ASEAN work in these sectoral areas, followed by a gradual scaling down of the EU's financial and technical involvement as ASEAN assumed greater responsibilities for these respective projects.

Unfortunately, in many cases, the ASEAN counterparts would not be ready to take over the projects and operate them on ASEAN's own resources. The problem seems to be that many ASEAN bodies prefer to continue the donor–recipient relationship and do not wish to take more ownership over relevant activities. This resulted in many projects being managed on short-term funding provisions with limited sustainable arrangements. In the worst-case scenario, the project concerned could be wrapped up prematurely when financial support from the EU is curtailed or withdrawn. One example is the ASEAN–EC Management Centre in Bandar Seri Begawan, which was closed.

The overall effect of ASEAN indifference to the continuation of such joint projects has led to a stiffening of bureaucratic attitudes in the European Commission in Brussels. A lot of diplomacy and time was expended by the ASEAN Secretariat in Jakarta to keep the viable programmes 'alive' with a minimum level of maintenance financing from EU and ASEAN sources. In the long run, such an approach is not tenable. To compound the situation, there seems to be insufficient political cognisance in ASEAN of the corrosive nature of these developments for the overall ASEAN–EU dialogue partnership.

This came about because the ASEAN–EU relations are largely driven by the foreign ministries in the ASEAN member countries, while many of the functional and technical cooperation projects between ASEAN and the EU are initiated and implemented by the other agencies and bodies across a wide spectrum of the ten ASEAN governments. Coordination among national-level authorities in ASEAN is patchy, and bureaucratic turf wrangling is a common occurrence. For example, few officials in the domestic ministries in ASEAN follow what is happening in the ASEAN–EU Ministerial Meeting, which is under the purview of the diplomats from the foreign ministries. At the same time, some foreign ministries have not attached enough weight to certain ongoing programmes initiated by the sectoral bodies. The different structures under the EU and their particular institutions to handle the variety of issues and projects also make things complicated for the ASEAN side. At one point, a lot of effort and time was spent on arranging different representations from the European Commission, the European Presidency and the European Council for participation in ASEAN-related meetings. Questions are still being asked from time to time by the ASEAN side about who from the EU side would chair specific fora in engaging the ASEAN ministers and leaders.

Another divergence occurred in the approach of ASEAN and the EU towards the institutionalization of regional integration. The European historical experience and political development reinforce the belief in institution building, legislative promulgation, the formalization of regulations, and enforcement of the rule of law and the principles of accountability and transparency. On the other hand, the organic Southeast Asian way is based on informal interaction and consultation, flexibility in rule making and reliance on the rule of man rather than the rule of law.

While some countries in ASEAN have modernized their governance and governments with Western-style formalities and institutions, ASEAN as a group still sees institutionalization as expensive and the last course of action. The Southeast Asians prefer to work on substance and a track record. Only when the specific benefits and habits of cooperation have been rooted would permanent architecture and the required edifice be erected. This is a fundamental difference in governance and it has irritated the relationship between the two sides persistently. It has manifested especially in the way EU officials see the role of the ASEAN Secretariat in Jakarta, which is regarded by them as the only body in the region to ensure the implementation of the ASEAN agenda. As the name suggests, the ASEAN Secretariat is not a commission like the EU has in Brussels. The working levels in Brussels probably appreciate this, but many in the respective European capital cities might not fully realize this.

ASEAN officials see the ASEAN Secretariat only as an administrative and clerical resource to keep track of what has been decided and to remind them what needs to be followed up on for the region-wide plans already agreed to by the ASEAN leaders. They do not accept the ASEAN Secretariat as having the authority to tell them what to do. For example, the ASEAN Secretariat could not initiate work on an ASEAN position on energy or food security or climate change issues without the prior approval of all ASEAN member countries. In fact, the ASEAN Secretariat is like the council secretariat in the EU, which is involved only in preparing ministerial meetings and their agenda. For most policy makers in ASEAN, this body is still an intergovernmental regional organization, and the ASEAN Secretariat does not have any mandate or power to get the sovereign member countries of ASEAN to perform. Even though the secretary general of ASEAN has been given specific roles in using his good offices to promote and preserve the interests of ASEAN, member governments must be consulted beforehand on any move to be made.

ASEAN Charter

There was a quiet admiration among European officials towards the establishment of the ASEAN Charter. The process started in December 2005 when the ASEAN leaders agreed to proceed with the drafting of the charter, and by December 2008, the final document was ratified by all ten ASEAN member countries and entered into force. The eminent persons group from ASEAN who conceptualized the key elements of the charter and the ASEAN High-Level Task Force drafting the charter visited Europe on separate occasions to engage their European counterparts on the best ideas to adopt. Several reference points from the EU experience in constitutional and legal development were considered by the ASEAN eminent persons and drafters of the ASEAN Charter.

When the ASEAN Charter came into being within a relatively short period of three years, many EU officials felt that the institutionalization of ASEAN was gathering momentum. However, this is only the first of many steps towards an ASEAN community based on the three pillars of political-security cooperation, economic integration and socio-cultural cooperation. ASEAN continues to be an intergovernmental regional organization, and officials from the ten member countries still jealously guard their national sovereignty and independence. The ASEAN identity and region-wide plans would have to be realized in a step-by-step manner, at a pace comfortable for the national ego of the member countries even though the top political leadership in ASEAN has envisioned a model of collective action and development to advance the group's interests.

The implementation of the ASEAN Charter is unlikely to satisfy the expectations of those in EU circles who want a more rapid pace for integration of the Southeast Asian countries. Some quarters within the ASEAN membership have been slow in moving forward the advantage gained in having the charter. Nevertheless, the European side is likely to continue pushing for specific areas of cooperation between ASEAN and the EU by using the ASEAN Charter. One particular area of interest is the development of the Committee of ASEAN Permanent Representatives in Jakarta and the human rights body as envisaged in Article 12 and Article 14 of the ASEAN Charter respectively. The ASEAN Intergovernmental Commission on Human Rights (AICHR) has been established pursuant to Article 14. European parliamentarians and decision makers in the European Commission in Brussels are keen to engage the AICHR to promote and protect human rights in Southeast Asia.

On the other hand, most ASEAN governments are not ready to move quickly into this field of engagement, whether among the ten member countries of ASEAN or between ASEAN and any other country or organization.

Obstacles

The misgivings in ASEAN over the EU's interest in human rights originated from specific bilateral contexts as well as the stand of certain EU member states on ASEAN's position regarding the situation in Myanmar. The Myanmar issue has been a constant obstacle in the search for a deeper and wider relationship between ASEAN and the EU. Many EU sanctions against Myanmar have been in place for many years.[5]

Basically, there is insufficient recognition in Europe that ASEAN has limited influence to change things in Myanmar. The leadership of that country perceives its position as a life and death struggle, and any concession could mean the disintegration of its regime in the Union of Myanmar. However, the expectation in various European circles is that ASEAN could bring about a political solution and help to transform the political order in Myanmar. Even when there is some realization that ASEAN cannot change things in Myanmar, some governments in the EU do not have enough political strength to ignore lobbyists and non-governmental groups that agitate intensively against the military government of Myanmar. Such quarters insist that ASEAN should find a way to meet their demand on regime change in Myanmar. Consequently, Myanmar has not been able to accede to the ASEAN–EC Cooperation Agreement of 1980, even though Myanmar was admitted into ASEAN in 1997. Myanmar is denied other benefits which Cambodia and Lao PDR receive from the EU, after joining ASEAN in 1999 and 1997, respectively.

The initiative to develop an ASEAN–EU FTA has been abandoned in favour of separate bilateral FTAs between individual ASEAN member countries and the EU because of the lack of political support to overcome the opposition of the anti-Myanmar lobby in the EU. The negotiations for an ASEAN–EU FTA were first launched in 2007. However, progress in these talks was slow and both sides agreed in March 2009 to pause negotiations. The proposed ASEAN–EU FTA would have reduced or abolished the existing tariff and non-tariff barriers to trade and investment in a number of ASEAN markets so as to further strengthen the EU's commercial ties with Southeast Asia. At the same time, ASEAN exports to the EU would have increased as a result of the removal of the EU barriers. In earlier estimates, ASEAN could see its exports to the EU go up by at least 18.5 per cent and expect economic gains equivalent to 2 per cent of ASEAN's GDP by 2020. The EU's exports to ASEAN would have also increased significantly. It was calculated that the EU's total global exports would go up by 2 per cent with an ASEAN–EU FTA. One of the biggest areas of gains for both sides would be in the trade in services, as business services had been showing impressive growth in recent years.[6]

According to the media release from the European Commission in Brussels (European Commission, 2009), then EU Trade Commissioner Benita Ferrero-Waldner made this statement: 'Creating new business opportunities for European companies in the dynamic ASEAN countries will strengthen the competitiveness of manufacturers, farmers and service providers in the EU. While we don't lose sight of our ultimate goal of achieving an agreement within a regional framework, I welcome today's decision [to start negotiations with Singapore for an EU–Singapore FTA] which will allow us to move forward and re-engage with this important region through negotiations with individual ASEAN member states.' Singapore is the most important trading partner of the EU in ASEAN, with bilateral trade mounting to more than €55 billion annually and where the bilateral stock of investment reached €100 billion in 2007. The negotiation for an EU–Singapore FTA was eventually launched in March 2010, and officials from both sides are talking purposefully with each other to reach an agreement as soon as possible.

There appears to be no prospect of ASEAN and the EU moving forward to accomplish more substantive cooperation without the settlement of the Myanmar question, notwithstanding the substantial benefits from having more trade and other connections between ASEAN and the EU. In fact, there is much that the two sides can do together to strengthen their respective strategic interests. For example, they can work jointly to help in the reform of the international financial system through the Group of Twenty (G20) and other multilateral mechanisms, and to get more international consensus on climate change issues. There are benefits to be gained from joint initiatives to build up the capacity of ASEAN governments in international trade negotiations and the management of natural disasters.

Most recently, ASEAN has embarked on the ASEAN Connectivity Initiative to connect member countries more effectively in various fields such as air, road and sea transportation, information and communication technology (ICT), energy (especially in electricity production and transmission, and oil/gas pipelines), trade facilitation and related institutional linkages, the management of cross-border issues, culture, education and tourism. There are many infrastructural projects and commercial opportunities that the EU ought to capitalize on to further its interests in Southeast Asia. The more significant thing about the ASEAN Connectivity Initiative is its link-up with other dialogue partners of ASEAN, particularly Australia, China, India, Japan, the Republic of Korea, New Zealand and the USA, in various connectivity activities and strengthening substantive collaboration with them in enhancing ASEAN's status as a business and transportation hub in Asia. The EU should be part of this new buzz.

Bigger canvass

ASEAN is in the driver's seat of regional architectural development in East Asia and Southeast Asia. ASEAN is actively engaged in multilateral diplomacy with major powers in the region and those outside but interested in the region. ASEAN has developed several overlapping but strategically important fora to build mutual trust, manage common challenges and entrench the conditions for peace, economic growth and prosperity. These powers have confidence and trust in ASEAN and they participate annually in ASEAN-centric meetings.

The most significant forum that ASEAN has developed in the last few years is the East Asia Summit (EAS). This platform is attended by the top leaders of the ten ASEAN member countries, China, Japan, the Republic of Korea, India, Australia and New Zealand as founding members while Russia and the USA joined the EAS in 2011 with their presidents participating for the first time in the EAS summit that was held in Bali, Indonesia, in November 2011. The EAS will become the top table for discussing the region's strategic concerns and global affairs and challenges. At present, the priority areas of cooperation that the leaders talk about at the EAS revolve around energy, trade and finance (especially on developing a Comprehensive Economic Partnership for East Asia, which is in fact a wide-ranging FTA), education (notably the building of the Nalanda University in India), health care and communicable diseases, natural disaster management, and environment and climate change. A number of mechanisms involving the senior officials and Track II experts of the EAS participating countries have been activated to implement the initiatives approved by the leaders.[7]

As a dialogue partner of ASEAN, the EU is in the ASEAN Regional Forum (ARF) and the ASEAN Post-Ministerial Conference Plus One. The EU should build on its decision to accede to the ASEAN Treaty of Amity and Cooperation in Southeast Asia (TAC) and demonstrate more commitment in participating as an entity in the political, security and strategic developments of the region. ASEAN has undertaken the time-consuming task of amending the TAC to allow a 27-member regional organization like the EU to accede to the treaty. It is anticipated that the EU will sign the accession document for the TAC at the ASEAN Post-Ministerial Conference Plus One in 2011. There is a positive feeling in Southeast Asia towards expanding economic, political and strategic ties with the EU. The European preoccupation with sorting out the internal problems of the EU – such as budget deficits, financial instability, low economic growth and other pressing socio-economic issues – should not hold back the EU from getting more involved in ASEAN and its neighbourhood.

In fact, ASEAN has tried to forge closer understanding between the two sides by establishing the Asia–Europe Meeting (ASEM) in 1996 and including other key Asian countries such as China, Japan, the Republic of

Korea and India in this forum. In recent years, Australia, Mongolia, New Zealand, Pakistan and Russia have joined the ASEM. The ASEM provides an important venue for discussion on cooperation across a broad range of political, security and strategic issues. However, after almost 15 years, the ASEM has not delivered any 'big bang' outcome and the only concrete result on the ground is the Asia–Europe Foundation (ASEF) based in Singapore, and a few cultural and educational projects. Set up in 1997, ASEF has brought more Asian and European artistes, thinkers and young people together through its numerous activities for cultural, educational and other people-to-people exchanges. This is good and more must be done through ASEF.

ASEM's political dialogue and strategic discussions have suffered from inadequate commitment from the top-level leadership in several EU member states. It is natural for EU governments to focus on domestic concerns and relations with big powers or historical partners like the USA, Russia and Latin American countries. Yet, it is in the interest of ASEAN and the EU to strengthen the ASEM platform. The engagement of the Asian giants like China and India through the ASEM process would add value to the existing bilateral ties between individual EU member states and these Asian nations. Going forward, it might be more useful to identify a few priorities for ASEAN and the EU to focus on jointly within a specific time frame to get concrete results, instead of dealing with the whole package of long-standing issues usually surfaced at each ASEM gathering.

Conclusion

Looking ahead, there are many global issues that ASEAN and the EU can cooperate on and derive mutual benefits from. For example, in the 18th ASEAN–EU Ministerial Meeting in Madrid in May 2010, both sides looked at the global financial and economic crisis following the collapse of US fund management companies in Wall Street, and examined how they could work towards achieving a more balanced international financial architecture, including a more equitable representation of developing countries, and more effective global governance. The ASEAN and EU ministers agreed that by promoting trade, investment and financial links between ASEAN and the EU, growth and prosperity would be enhanced in both regions. In this respect, they reaffirmed their commitment to the initiative for bilateral FTA negotiations between the EU and individual ASEAN member countries, and the early conclusion of the Doha Round of multilateral trade negotiations under the World Trade Organization (WTO).

On climate change, the ASEAN and EU ministers stated that the two sides should work together to help achieve a comprehensive post-2012 climate agreement under the auspices of the United Nations Framework Convention on Climate Change. To achieve closer cooperation in environmental conservation, sustainable development and natural resource management, both sides considered the available policy frameworks and measures. They expressed their support for ongoing initiatives to get consensus in the international arena for concrete cooperation to deal with the effects of climate change. This is a good start. For ASEAN, the ministers from the two sides agreed that the ASEAN Centre for Biodiversity in Manila could be utilized to do more for environmental sustainability and the protection of ASEAN's rich biodiversity. This augurs well for the future of the centre, where many experts from ASEAN and the EU have devoted much energy and time to the cause of preserving the region's biodiversity.

There are other global challenges such as food security, energy security, combating terrorism and the non-proliferation of weapons of mass destruction, which the ministers from ASEAN and the EU highlighted as areas for taking cooperative action. Furthermore, the spread of communicable diseases and the occurrence of natural disasters are now becoming more frequent. From the various completed and existing joint initiatives, there is substantial expertise and knowledge in ASEAN and the EU for tackling such health threats and reducing the potential damage caused by earthquakes, floods and other natural calamities. The problem is one of coordination across the government agencies and removing bureaucratic red tape. The EU has enhanced ASEAN's disaster management and humanitarian assistance capabilities, and more programmes are being planned to strengthen ASEAN's preparedness and public education.

In conclusion, there is no doubt that ASEAN has benefitted from the EU's generosity and sharing of the European experience and resources in integrating its economies and strengthening its social fabric. However, the vast potential of ASEAN–EU cooperation has not been fully realized. More can be obtained out of the partnership.

There is also no doubt that the differing perceptions in Europe and Southeast Asia about political and social development of human society, and divisive issues like the situation in Myanmar and the human rights agenda, will always hinder progress. This is more so now with the growth of civil society and the increase in non-governmental organizations in ASEAN and the EU. At the same time, the urgency in dealing with domestic priorities in each of the member countries means that there is a limited bandwidth to settle the whole array of issues needing attention in the ASEAN–EU partnership. A balance and recalibration of expectations are obviously needed. In doing so, it is important for both ASEAN and the EU to learn from the relationship of the past three decades and capitalize on the equity acquired from such collaboration and cooperation to do more to move forward.[8] The sooner the big picture and long-term strategic interests are converged, the better it will be for the future of Europe and Southeast Asia, and their unique regional systems – ASEAN and the EU.

Notes

1. Based on PPP International Dollar for the year 2008.
2. Total trade figures between ASEAN and the EU refer to the EU25, due to non-availability of data for new EU member countries.
3. Statistics obtained from the ASEAN Secretariat.
4. European media reports on Islamophobia and on the public debates on the freedom of speech with regard to the writing about Islamic beliefs fuel emotional reactions from both sides and widen the perception gaps. For a recent example, see Hermawan (2010), which reflects the divergence of views and what ASEAN and EU are trying to do to address the issues.
5. For example, see Vogel (2009).
6. More details on ASEAN–EU trade relations and the FTA are available on the Asia–Europe Meeting (ASEM) website.
7. Track II is the generic term used to describe the academics and scholars from non-governmental affiliations. Track I refers to officials and representatives of government agencies and bodies.
8. The conclusions of the 3009th Foreign Affairs Council Meeting of the Council of the European Union in Luxembourg on 26 April 2010 have given some room for optimism on moving forward and not letting Myanmar be the stumbling block in ASEAN–EU relations. The outcome of this meeting was more positive in tone, and could perhaps pave the way for ASEAN and the EU to reconcile their differences.

Bibliography

ASEAN (Association of Southeast Asian Nations) Secretariat (2010a) *ASEAN Community in Figures 2009*, http://www.aseansec.org/publications/ACIF2009.pdf

ASEAN (Association of Southeast Asian Nations) Secretariat (2010b) *ASEANstats: Building knowledge in the ASEAN Community*, http://www.aseansec.org/22122.htm

ASEAN (Association of Southeast Asian Nations) Secretariat (2010c) *Press Statement by Dr Surin Pitsuwan at the 18th ASEAN-EU Ministerial Meeting Press Conference*, 26 May 2010, http://www.aseansec.org/24740.htm

European Commission Directorate-General for Trade (2009) *Press Release: EU to launch FTA negotiations with individual ASEAN countries, beginning with Singapore*, 22 December 2009, http://trade.ec.europa.eu/doclib/docs/2009/december/tradoc_145651.pdf

European Commission Directorate-General for Trade (2010) *Regions: ASEM (Asia-Europe Meeting)*, 21 June 2010, http://ec.europa.eu/trade/creating-opportunities/bilateral-relations/regions/asem/

Hermawan A. (2010) 'Can Asia, Europe agree on freedom of faith?', *The Jakarta Post*, 19 April, http://www.thejakartapost.com/news/2010/04/19/can-asia-europe-agree-freedom-faith.html

Vogel T. (2009) 'EU tightens Myanmar sanctions', *EuropeanVoice.com*, 17 August 2009, http://www.europeanvoice.com/article/2009/08/eu-tightens-myanmar-sanctions/65698.aspx

10
EU–ASEAN Relations in the 21st Century: In Search for Common Values to Forge a Partnership

Xavier Nuttin

A shift in the global balance of power

A rising Asia

In the last 25 years, Asia has been going through dramatic changes and has emerged as the world's fastest-growing region. The rise of Asia as a new global player is no longer in doubt, and will continue in the next decade to transform the world's geopolitical landscape. The region has indeed demonstrated a remarkable resilience during the 2008–2009 world economic and financial crisis – despite smaller growth rates, most Asian economies have continued to expand and through the crisis have reinforced their position on the world stage. Asia could be a major contributor to global economic growth in the coming years (co-chair's statement of the 18th ASEAN–EU ministerial meeting, 26 May 2010).[1] For now, growth is generating wealth, respect and freedom of action. Confident in its economic power and relying on the sheer size of its population, Asia is naturally claiming a new position on the world scene. But will Asia's growing economic power translate into political and military power? While the global power shift will certainly lead to a multipolar world in the economic sphere, Pax Americana in the region is likely to remain unchallenged for the foreseeable future, despite noises about the decline of American power.[2] During the transition period conflict between states could arise, and regionalization may offer a better way of governance.

ASEAN centrality in the regional architecture

For the last 30 years, the Association of Southeast Asian Nations (ASEAN) has been at the centre of Asia's regional architecture made up of concentric circles: ASEAN+3, ASEAN+6, the East Asia Summit. ASEAN continues, however, to be seen more as a collection of diverse states rather than as a single bloc. The world is changing – China and India are altering the balance of power; Indonesia is a full member of the G20 and develops its bilateral relations with the USA. New regional initiatives, such as the Asia-Pacific Community and the East-Asia Community, are being proposed to enhance regional integration. They may challenge the current set-up and marginalize ASEAN in favour of a kind of concert of regional big powers.[3]

If ASEAN, which remains more process-oriented than results-oriented, wants to retain its central position in the regional architecture, as declared by the ASEAN foreign ministers at the 43rd ASEAN Ministerial Meeting held in Hanoi on 22 July 2010, it will need to consolidate its strengths and deepen its integration both politically and economically. ASEAN must reposition itself to address the growing challenges and opportunities of regional integration, the major shifts in the Asian landscape brought about by the rise of China and India and Asia's widening links with the rest of the world.

The EU supports ASEAN's central role and has developed an interregional relationship since the early 1970s that fosters mutual cooperation und understanding. The EU is one of the most active promoters of ASEAN's cooperative efforts, through financial and technical assistance, and is eager to share experiences of regional integration.

The EU has no real 'look east' policy

Yet, despite those interregional links, the European Union (EU) doesn't pay sufficient attention to the fundamental evolutionary processes at work in Asia and in ASEAN, and sends contradictory messages.

For example, as a signal of its deep interest and commitment to East Asian stability, security and development, the EU is eager to accede to the ASEAN Treaty of Amity and Cooperation (TAC) – and the ASEAN states are working on the necessary amendments to the TAC to permit the EU's accession. The EU is also keen to be associated as closely as possible with the evolving structure of the East Asia Summit. But on the other hand while, among others, the Chinese, American, Japanese and Russian ministers of foreign affairs were personally attending the ASEAN Regional Forum and Post-Ministerial Conference in Hanoi in July 2010, the European high representative for foreign affairs and security policy, appointed in December 2009, was notably absent, and the EU was represented by the foreign minister of Hungary. This kind of political mistake is not specific to the relations with ASEAN – at the SAARC summit in Bhutan in March 2010, where the EU has obtained observer status since 2006, the EU was represented by a highly knowledgeable but middle-ranking official of the European Commission. This is clearly perceived in Asian official and diplomatic circles as a lack of interest in the region.[4]

Added to these worrying signals is the EU's perceived lack of credibility in Asia as a united and coherent actor, as it has not yet been able to define a clear common foreign policy. For all these reasons, the level of expectation at the political level from the EU is rather low, and the USA remains the power to be reckoned with. The EU must come to terms with the changing balance of power and look East if it is to live up to its global responsibilities and consolidate its way of life. Promoting a secure and stable region is a key long-term EU interest, which requires moving beyond its current role as economic player to become a global player.

The first point is therefore to see if there is any political will to work together beyond the current level of exchanges. Failure to understand and accept the key role of Asia in the new global balance of power may indeed confine the EU – particularly if it remains divided – to a second-class role on the margins of the new international system. In an increasingly interdependent and multipolar world, both sides must build stronger ties and engage actively with each other. But in the absence of a clear, well defined and coherent EU Common Foreign and Security Policy – CFSP – which makes it difficult for third countries to understand what the EU stands for – the EU lacks political clout commensurate with its economic power. How, therefore, should the EU engage the region while at the same time the links between ASEAN and the two other regional powers, India and China, are fast developing? And what are the tools that the EU needs to develop in order to strengthen the political relationship?

ASEAN and the EU – two different models of regional architecture

The intraregional institutional architectures of the EU and ASEAN are obviously very different – while the EU pursues a supranational model and relies on formal institutions, ASEAN is an inter-governmental organization based on informal networks. Nevertheless both try to consolidate their architecture to become more unified and assertive powers in a globalized world. It is a fact that globalization has challenged the Westphalian order of states and led to the emergence of regional organizations as an alternative. The EU is the best example of an increasingly integrated player particularly following the ratification of the Lisbon Treaty, while Asia is increasingly proactive in global affairs. ASEAN is already invited to the G20 conferences, but a more integrated ASEAN would give it a stronger voice in the international arena.

The EU is on the move

The EU is the most successful and advanced example of regional integration in the world. It is a model of regional integration aiming at reducing development gaps and increasing territorial cohesion. Its member states are convicted of the need to join forces to promote their interests and achieve their objectives. They have agreed to transfer part of their sovereignty to a supranational level as the fundamental principle of the EU's construction and development.

Despite ups and downs, what has been achieved since the Treaty of Rome was signed in 1957 is impressive – besides the well-known achievements of the single market, the abolition of internal borders and the common currency, few people know that today more than 60 per cent of all legislation that is enforced in the EU finds its origin at the European level rather than at the national level.

Since December 2009 the EU has operated under the Lisbon Treaty, which extends its democratic legitimacy by increasing the powers of the European Parliament and enhances its profile on the world stage through the appointment of a European high representative for foreign affairs and security policy. The Lisbon Treaty also increases the number of areas where qualified majority voting is the rule, although the inter-governmental principle still governs the CFSP. The treaty will nevertheless allow for better coordination between the political dimension and trade, environmental and development matters. While there is some resistance in a few member states, the drive towards further European integration continues. And the current financial and economic crisis may well help to push it further – history shows that most of the progress in European construction was made at a time of crisis.

At the global level, the EU is a champion of multilateralism and believes in a multipolar world where the international community increasingly acts in concert to tackle the causes as well as the symptoms of the threats the world faces in common – from security threats to global diseases, environmental challenges, organized crime or human trafficking. Those threats ignore the borders and can only be addressed through a concerted and collective effort. They will shape the conduct of relations among states and regions. The present economic and financial crisis further proves the interdependence between states and re-values the economic and financial tools of diplomacy. Regional cooperation is the only way for most countries to rise to the challenge of globalization. There is a growing interest in different parts of the world in the process of European integration, not just from an institutional point of view, but also in terms of the policies that promote cohesiveness – for example China, Russia and Brazil have entered into agreements with the EU on regional policy cooperation.

The development of regional entities is supported by the EU in all parts of the world. But this is not sufficient with regard to Asia. Asian powers can be strong allies in the pursuit of the EU strategic interests such as effective multilateralism provided that the EU clearly supports and accommodates their increasing role. The new emerging powers are challenging the current international order – their demand for a greater say in international fora deserves respect, as existing multilateral institutions were designed for a different geopolitical order and do not reflect the current global balances. The steps taken by the EU in June 2010 to increase the voting power of developing and transition countries at the World Bank and to come up with an agreement on the IMF reform during the G20 meeting in Seoul in November 2010 are heading in the right direction, as they allow for a better representation of the emerging economies in global economic governance.

ASEAN regional construction

On the other hand, ASEAN's current level of regional integration remains limited. ASEAN still needs to build strong regional institutional frameworks to tackle the main challenges of the 21st century such as security, energy, financial issues or the growing inequalities.

But some important steps, such as the entry into force of the ASEAN Charter in December 2008, have been taken. Despite its shortcomings,[5] the charter is no doubt a positive development that binds ASEAN members together into a rule-based group and is a cornerstone of the institutional framework that is required for an ASEAN that is able to achieve its objectives. It attempts to create greater internal cohesion, to promote an ASEAN identity and seeks to compensate for a lack of institutionalization – the secretariat has been strengthened, although sadly there will be no additional finance to support its extended role. The ASEAN Charter also makes commitments to preserve a nuclear weapon-free Southeast Asia – something that the EU is still struggling to achieve. While the EU certainly acted as a model – the Eminent Persons Group had several meetings with the EU institutions during its visit to Brussels in July 2006 – the charter is neither an adaptation nor a copy of the European approach, which is based on the transfer of sovereignty.

From the EU point of view there remains, however, much room for improvement – first the charter confirms the ASEAN principle of working by consensus, rather than by binding agreements, even though this has been relatively ineffective in the past. As we have learned in the EU, unanimity often ends up with no agreement or an agreement based on the lowest common denominator. The charter also confirms the guiding principles of non-interference and non-intervention, allowing each member country to lead its own affairs independently: the lack of condemnation of the dictatorial regime in Burma/Myanmar is an obvious example. ASEAN's poor record in the resolution of the Thai-Cambodian conflict over the temple Preah Vihear is another one.

Second, the failure of leaders to agree on an ASEAN Development Fund to narrow the development gap between the economies of the region is also most regrettable. Such a fund could have played the role that the EU regional funds are playing, but there was obviously no consensus on that proposal. Regional gaps are a threat to social and economic stability and should be fully addressed.

ASEAN has the ambition to create an ASEAN community by 2015 and to build a single market modelled on that of the EU.[6] This is an essential element for ASEAN to keep its influence. Enhancing economic integration may pave the way for better political integration, but progress in this field is hampered by the non-interference principle, which is the cornerstone of ASEAN. One of the major differences between the EU and ASEAN indeed relates to sovereignty: while the former bases its development on the concept of sharing sovereignty in most areas (the CFSP being a notable exception), the latter is more concerned about reinforcing national sovereignty and is based on inter-governmental cooperation.

With all its diversity, ASEAN will now have to find its own way to move from an economic integration approach based on trade and investments to an approach covering global issues in order to compete with the rest of the world.

Common values within different structures

2007 marked the 30th anniversary of formal relations between the EU and ASEAN, and today there is no global issue that can be meaningfully addressed without the participation of the two blocs. Both sides are seeking to deepen regional cooperation and integration between highly diverse member states. Both sides cherish the respect for their many cultural, religious and linguistic identities, but struggle to define a regional identity. Both regions are committed to a multipolar world based on strong international institutions. Both sides rely on economic growth to achieve sustainable development. With so many key values in common, both sides are made to be natural partners.

But how to enhance ASEAN's and Europe's ability to work together and to forge a strategic partnership? Regional cooperation offers both sides greater opportunities to boost prosperity and secure peace and stability. The EU will continue to support and encourage ASEAN's continued integration and welcomes the steps recently taken.

Building a stronger EU–ASEAN partnership

Due to the nature of the problems[7] faced by a globalized world which require a common effort, developing relations among structured regions is a strategy that needs to be actively pursued to achieve better global governance. Of course EU-style regional integration is unlikely to happen in Asia for several decades, if ever: ASEAN is not looking for an EU-type of supranational architecture, and its level of integration remains limited. Despite the wide differences between ASEAN and the EU in their approach to build a regional architecture, both sides have indeed much to learn from each other – from joint responses to common challenges to the use of soft power; from the single market to the pooling of financial resources there is growing interest in many Asian countries in the EU's approach, and by building a closer partnership both sides could offer the world new alternatives. What is needed is to create space for dialogue that is respectful of different views and using diversity as an asset in international collaboration.

But how can the EU, a non-regional actor, contribute to and participate in the stability and development of ASEAN? The EU is not a traditional security actor in the region and its capacity to bring security deliverables is limited,[8] but it has important economic interests, is a major aid donor and is willing to play an important role in non-traditional security issues. Indeed, besides poverty, which remains a significant challenge (Asia is home to two-thirds of the world's poor), major threats like terrorism, human trafficking, a revived drug production and the risk of nuclear proliferation are also prevalent. Many parts of the region are prone to natural disasters and suffer from infectious diseases. Ongoing conflicts or tensions in several countries, coupled with generally weak civil societies, add to vulnerability and contribute to human rights abuses, including discrimination of minorities. Most Asians regard the EU as a soft power with a non-threatening influence in their regional security, and that should facilitate cooperation in all those sectors.

Realizing the extent to which the security and well-being of Europeans depend on external relations, the EU has the ambition to become an effective global player. To achieve this goal the EU must define a political vision to respond to the new world order in the making, and particularly to deal with a rising Asia – and ASEAN – the continent that will be the engine for change over the next decades.

To guide the future development of its relations with Asia into the coming decade, the EU must focus on strengthening its political and economic presence across the region, and raising this to a level commensurate with the growing global weight of an enlarged EU. Today the EU is seen as a market and an aid donor, but to be a global political player it must begin to integrate its economic engagement with a more visible political presence, which remains under-developed. This requires a good understanding of the region's priorities – one has to take into account that foreign policy is all about the domestic policies of others[9] – and a clear definition of the EU's security and economic interests in Asia that must be well articulated with the values the EU wants to promote. The EU needs to assert itself politically and ASEAN can be an ally with whom it can work to achieve common goals. 'Today the main challenge for the EU is no longer about avoiding war or establishing democracy in Europe but how to deal with the rest of the world, how to defend our interests and to promote our values.'[10]

Where EU and ASEAN meet – or not – and what should they do together?

In addition to the many sectors where the EU and ASEAN are already engaged in cooperation at the regional level, such as trade, public health, migration, human trafficking, climate change, energy security, development aid or disaster relief, the EU should be active on such issues as economic governance, security, non-proliferation, good governance and democracy. This can partly be done through existing cooperation mechanisms such as ASEM and the ASEAN Regional Forum, but they must be strengthened. There is no global issue that can be meaningfully addressed without the participation of the 1.1 billion populations of ASEAN and the EU. New partnerships can therefore be built in several spheres of concern, but I will here concentrate on two of them that are at the core of EU's values and architecture – first, the EU model of economic integration and second, democracy and the rule of law.

The EU model of economic integration – economic integration is a corner stone of European integration. EU policies have always played a key role in promoting economic and social cohesion and to narrow the development gap between regions and between member states. They are thus an important expression of the solidarity within the EU through increased territorial cohesion. The EU helps regions that are less prosperous to achieve a faster rate of economic development in a sustainable way. Creating the internal market and speaking with a single voice in international trade negotiations are major economic achievements of the European construction process. Of course more remains to be done, such as establishing common socio-economic policies to create a coordinated European Economic Governance – the economic and financial crisis indeed obliges the EU to go further on the economic integration path, as national policies will remain inefficient to address global imbalances. And this is also required to maintain the EU's economic weight, which will determine its place in the world – 'An economically weak Europe is prone to lose its political importance.'[11]

Regional integration is a stabilizing factor, and ASEAN's deeper integration will accelerate growth and economic dynamism to the benefit of itself and its trading partners alike. Building institutional capacity to support ASEAN's regional economic integration is an avenue that the EU has and will continue to use to develop closer links and better mutual understanding. The EU is more than ready to continue to share with ASEAN its experience, lessons learned and best practices, while recognizing the differences between the two blocs.

In 2009, EU–ASEAN trade represented almost 1 per cent of total world trade. EU is ASEAN's second-largest trading partner after China, and ASEAN as an entity represents the EU's fifth-largest trading partner.[12] But despite the current level of trade, there is enormous potential for enhancing the economic partnership between the two sides. Measures to step up economic and trade relations between the EU and ASEAN can also help to consolidate overall relations between the two regions. This led the EU and ASEAN to launch in May 2007 negotiations on a region-to-region Free Trade Agreement – FTA – as, among the major powers, only the EU – and the USA – has no FTA with ASEAN.

An EU–ASEAN FTA could produce substantial economic advantages for both parties, and the EU believes that interregional agreements can usefully supplement the multilateral system – provided that they are complementary to it and fully respect World Trade Organization rules. The EU's objective was to conclude a wide-ranging and ambitious FTA with ASEAN that would go well beyond tariff reductions and cover the qualitative conditions associated with trade, including effective provisions on human rights, and social and environmental standards.

But things did not go as smoothly as expected by some – despite several rounds of discussions there has been no real progress in those negotiations. This was partly because of a lack of ambition on the ASEAN side or, as seen from the ASEAN perspective, because the EU has set too ambitious a goal. Differences over the participation of Myanmar in the negotiations also made it difficult to reach an agreement. In 2009, both sides decided to 'take a pause' in the regional negotiations, in effect putting them on the shelf for an indefinite period. The EU has now retreated to a fall-back position and has launched negotiations in a bilateral format, starting with Singapore, Vietnam and Malaysia.

Democracy, good governance, rule of law and human rights

The EU's democratic model is another cornerstone for foreign relations, but the EU should not take for granted that this model will be accepted by, and much less can be imposed on, the Asian countries that have different views based on different history and culture. Indeed very different political regimes continue to coexist within ASEAN (authoritarian, communist, democratic, monarchic, dictatorial) and, despite an obvious dynamic in the transition to democracy during the past two decades, democratization in the region remains a fragile process. Democracy is often reduced to elections, its main visible feature. Asian countries sometimes refer to EU idealistic attitudes, but also to EU double standards when addressing governance issues. They have a different view of the same concept and there has been little room for the Western liberal model in Asia. Rather a 'state capitalism' model, where the state has a prominent role in economic management, has developed. Although most governments in Asia follow a strategy of free market economic reforms, the levels of their accomplishments vary widely – 'The overall trend in the region is not one towards democracy and market economy but one of a pronounced decoupling of both transformations.'[13]

Nevertheless, with economic success and greater wealth also come greater political consciousness and demand for more participation from among the new emerging middle classes, and also from discriminated minorities.[14] How the regimes in place will be able to answer the increasing demands for political rights while avoiding social instability and centrifugal forces will be central to their political future and shape the long-term face of the region.

The need to address the democratic deficit in most Asian countries is vital, but there is also an urgent need to build political common ground and to avoid promoting those concepts from a high moral ground. EU member states that have experienced a transition from dictatorships to democracies accompanied by a modernization of their economic and social structures have much to share in that field. ASEAN and the EU can and must work together to contribute constructively to the promotion and strengthening of democracy, the enhancement of good governance and the rule of law, as well as the promotion and protection of human rights and fundamental freedoms. The differences between the two sides remain important but bridges can be built. They can best be understood through two different test-cases for the EU's ability to cooperate on basic human values: the ASEAN Charter and Myanmar.

Myanmar became a member of ASEAN in 1997 partly with the aim to balance growing Chinese influence. Its membership has never been made conditional to political reform. The regional group's philosophy was, and remains, based on a strict non-interference principle as the adoption of the ASEAN Charter has confirmed. ASEAN fully supports the UN efforts to launch a dialogue between the junta and the opposition, but this may also appear as recognition of its own failure to obtain results.

What does the EU expect from ASEAN on the Myanmar issue? Both sides broadly agree on the objectives – national reconciliation and free and fair elections – but not on the means to achieve these objectives. The EU is pressing ASEAN to intervene and encourage Myanmar as a fellow member state to listen to international appeals for reform for its own economic interest and regional stability. Without political reform it is clear that Myanmar will not be able to achieve fast economic growth like other ASEAN economies. Through the ASEAN Charter, the group has opened the door for a more assertive policy and given itself the basis, with the ASEAN Intergovernmental Human Rights Body, to promote human rights. ASEAN can take the diplomatic lead and play a strategic role in finding a common ground and a solution to a problem that has become an embarrassment and has a major impact on the association's image, reputation and relations with the rest of the world. For example the negotiations for an EU–ASEAN FTA, after having faced much difficulty, were put on the shelf in 2009 mainly because of Myanmar. In the end ASEAN needs to work out a coherent policy on Myanmar and to come out of its non-interference policy if it wants to keep some credibility.

The ASEAN Charter, which came into force in December 2008, stipulates adherence to the rule of law, good governance, democracy and respect for fundamental freedoms: a most welcome statement that entirely fits into the EU views. But the lack of mechanisms for dispute settlements and sanctions in case those principles were to be ignored, puts into question the implementation and enforcement of those principles, a key issue that remains one of the main problems of ASEAN.

Another major shortcoming concerns ASEAN's democratic machinery. With ASEAN's official choice to move from a state-centric to a people-oriented organization, the role of parliaments and civil society groups must be enhanced. However, ASEAN remains state-driven: while the organization acknowledges the usefulness of the ASEAN Inter-Parliamentary Assembly

(AIPA), it fails to give it any democratic power. The charter itself fails to make any reference to parliamentary activity,[15] let alone to the establishment of an ASEAN parliament, despite repeated calls from AIPA. ASEAN leaders have also agreed to meet briefly civil society representatives during their annual summit. But there is not yet a permanent consultative process to institutionalize people's participation and facilitate a transparent and inclusive decision-making process. Those are major gaps that contribute to the democratic deficit of ASEAN.

Finally, the Intergovernmental Human Rights Body established under Article 14 of the ASEAN Charter has the declared objective 'the promotion and protection of basic human rights and fundamental freedoms'. It does not give power to investigate human rights violations, and its mandate is therefore limited. ASEAN remains reluctant to hold any of its members accountable, and the human rights body will follow the principles of 'non-interference in the internal affairs of member states'. There are fears that the body will only be allowed to address external threats and to promote the concept of human rights. With no means to intervene in domestic policies and to investigate human rights violations within ASEAN, it could well remain a toothless consultative body.

Conclusions

In a globalized world no country can set the world agenda on its own. The world is changing and the nature of the challenges faced by mankind today – climate change, economic and financial reforms, energy security, epidemics or the fight against extremism – require a concerted effort towards common objectives. This is why the development of regional entities, and cooperation among those entities, is supported by the EU in all parts of the world.

The EU has learned from its own history that regional integration, at economic and political levels, is a stabilizing factor that largely contributes to enhance socio-economic development. It is also an efficient way to achieve better global governance at the time when state-centred solutions are fast reaching their limit.

ASEAN is far away from the EU level of integration but is building, at its own speed and with its own patterns of cooperation, a regional entity that is evolving and has an important role to play in the new geopolitical world order. ASEAN and the EU can complement and learn form each other in many areas – the sum of all their member states can achieve more together than one country or, indeed, the EU on its own or ASEAN on its own. However, much remains to be done to consolidate democracy, foster sustainable development, encourage the smooth integration of ASEAN into the world economy and improve the environment and the management of natural resources.

A strengthening of the relationship between the EU and ASEAN can contribute to those goals, but that would require the EU to make some hard political choices. Indeed, while the balance of power, starting with economic power, is shifting towards the East, this has not yet been reflected in EU policies. The EU is keen to engage with Asia, but lacks a strategic vision and struggles to find ways to move beyond its role as economic player and become a global player.

ASEAN was established 40 years ago as a security organization; it is now fast moving towards economic integration. The EU was launched almost 60 years ago – not yet under that name – as a steel and coal economic community. Despite the fact that the goal was also related to security (no more wars), its construction took place on economic criteria and it started as a market. It is only now slowly moving towards a political union with a common security and defence policy, and still needs to secure a stronger presence on the world stage. Different paths have led to the same broad conclusion – the importance of pursuing regional integration to confront the global challenges, to promote socio-economic development and to reinforce peace and security.

Notes

While I am an official of the European Parliament, I write in my personal capacity and do not represent officially any EU institution.

1. Co-chair's statement of the 18th ASEAN–EU ministerial meeting, 26 May 2010.
2. ASEM Conference on Europe–Asia interregional relations, Discussion paper, Brussels, 12–13 July 2010.
3. Douglas, Webber (2010), *'The evolving regional institutional architecture in Asia'*, ASEM conference on Europe–Asia interregional relations, Brussels, 12 July.
4. Low level of EU attendance is common at ASEM summits or ASEAN foreign affairs ministerial meetings when they take place in Asia.
5. The mandate of the Eminent Persons Group that prepared the first draft of the charter was to be 'bold and visionary'. The final version which has been adopted suffered from considerable modifications and is much more conservative.
6. ASEAN countries still trade more with third countries than among themselves.
7. Already described in Chapter 2, under 'Europe is on the move'.
8. With the exception of the key role played by the EU in the monitoring of the Aceh Peace Agreement.
9. Javier Solana (2009) *'Five lessons in global diplomacy'*, Financial Times, 20 January.
10. H.Van Rompuy, president of the European Council, (2010) speech at the College d'Europe, Bruges, 25 February 2010.
11. Gordon, Bajnai (former) prime minister of Hungary, (2010), in a letter to H. Van Rompuy, January 2010.
12. European Commission (2010), DG Trade website, August, www.ec.europa.eu/trade/.
13. Aurel, Croissant (2005), *'Can you have one without the other? Transformation towards market economy and democracy in Asia'*, Strategic Insights, December.

14. Michael, Wesley (2009), Far Eastern Economic Review, April.
15. AIPA is only listed in an annex as an entity associated with ASEAN; the ASEM dialogue also has a parliamentary window, the Asia–Europe Parliamentary Partnership (ASEPP), but which also lacks a clear role.

Bibliography

ASEM Conference (2010) Discussion paper, on Europe–Asia interregional relations, Brussels, 12–13 July 2010.

Aurel, C. (2005) 'Can you have one without the other? Transformation towards market economy and democracy in Asia', Strategic Insights, December.

Co-chair's statement (2010) 18th ASEAN–EU ministerial meeting, 26 May 2010.

Douglas, W. (2010) 'The evolving regional institutional architecture in Asia'. ASEM conference on Europe–Asia interregional relations, Brussels, 12 July.

European Commission (2010) DG Trade website, August, www.ec.europa.eu/trade/.

Gordon, B. (2010) (former) prime minister of Hungary, in a letter to H. Van Rompuy, January 2010.

Javier, S. (2009) 'Five lessons in global diplomacy', Financial Times, 20 January.

Michael, W. (2009) Far Eastern Economic Review, April.

Van Rompuy, H. (2010) Speech at the College d'Europe, Bruges, 25 February 2010.

11
The EU, ASEAN and the Challenges of the 21st Century: Conclusions and Recommendations

Pascaline Winand

Introduction

The European Union (EU) and the Association of Southeast Asian Nations (ASEAN) were both created during the Cold War. They had similar purposes. In a way, it was all about peace. It was about preventing recurring conflicts between member states in their respective regions while facing up to external threats together: security from each other and security from the external world. Although much has changed in the international arena since the creation of the European Communities and ASEAN, much also remains the same. Both organizations still fulfil important security functions in their regions, and both still have an important stake in improving their collaboration to enable them to tackle better the challenges of the 21st century. Yet the picture is not one of unalloyed success, and the future of their relationship is fraught with perils as much as it offers potentialities for cooperation.

Dealing with powerful neighbours: US–EU–ASEAN–China relations

The new world appears riddled with new crises and challenges, some of which can be traced back to the end of the Cold War and would seem to warrant a collective response from Europe and ASEAN. Yet both regions find it difficult to define their own contribution to security challenges, traditional or not, *vis-à-vis* the superpower of the day, the USA, and key actors such as China, India and Japan. For example, the EU faces divisions within its own ranks on what kind of security actor it should be and on the division of tasks between the EU, NATO and the USA. At the same time the global financial crisis has dented the superpower status of the USA while tainting the aura of the euro and prompting doubts about the viability of certain European economies, whereas Asian countries have weathered the crisis relatively well. With the growing power of China and India, and the declining power of Japan and the USA, the EU now seeks to learn from Asia to promote growth and to deal better with the world economic and financial crisis. Meanwhile the Obama administration has stepped up its involvement in Southeast Asia, and particularly with ASEAN and the East Asia Summit (EAS). The USA now appears intent on recognizing the important stabilizing role of ASEAN in the region. As the USA seeks extra avenues of cooperation with the Chinese economic giant, ASEAN and its network of cooperative frameworks with China and other political and economic giants in the Asia-Pacific region appear an attractive way to also help control Chinese military power in the Asia-Pacific and its claims to energy-rich areas. By joining in cooperation frameworks such as the EAS, the USA intends to help define the agenda in the region by having a seat at the table in an organization with Southeast Asia, nominally in the driver's seat that has the potential of exerting some degree of control over China. This new interest of the USA in Southeast Asia and ASEAN could compete with the EU's own engagement in the region, especially as the economic rise of China would seem to render ASEAN less important to the EU in economic terms, thereby undermining mutual collaboration. The EU and the USA also entertain competing visions of the use of regionalism and on how to defend their interests in Asia, while ASEAN is involved in a delicate balancing act in which it seeks to control powerful neighbours while keeping the USA and the EU engaged in the Asia-Pacific region.

EU and US competing visions of regionalism

On the one hand, the USA promotes regional and transregional arrangements such as the North American Free Trade Agreement (NAFTA) and the Asia-Pacific Cooperation (APEC), in which it seeks to retain a defining influence. The creation of a regional framework such as NAFTA can be seen partly as a reaction to the success of the EU and to American frustrations of relying on multilateral frameworks to liberalize trade. In the Asia-Pacific region, the Obama administration has made overtures to step up its involvement in Southeast Asia, with a recognition of ASEAN as a key partner in helping to stabilize not only Southeast Asia, but also Northeast Asia, by addressing security concerns such as nuclear proliferation and maritime security. This is in marked contrast with the Bush administration, which showed little interest in ASEAN. On the other hand, the USA also uses transregional fora. APEC[1], a transregional framework launched at the initiative of Australia with strong Japanese support, and which does not include the EU, offers a good platform for the USA to maintain its presence in the Asia-Pacific region and to bolster its bargaining power *vis-à-vis* the EU in World Trade Organization (WTO) trade negotiations. Likewise, the USA also participates in security fora such as the ASEAN Regional Forum (ARF), and, most recently, the EAS.

By contrast, the EU has adopted strategies of dialogue with regional organizations such as ASEAN – through EU/ASEAN summits – or the creation of interregional fora such as the Asia-Europe Meeting (ASEM), to counterbalance the power of the USA in Asia and to better defend its economic interests in this region. The EU is more inclined to think in interregional terms[2] than the USA. While the USA uses transregional frameworks such as APEC to put pressure on the EU in trade liberalization, the EU uses interregional arrangements such as ASEM[3], of which the USA is not a member, to harmonize positions with Asian countries, thereby bolstering the EU bargaining position towards the USA in multilateral negotiations. Initiated in 1996, ASEM is an interregional dialogue that includes EU and ASEAN member states and a wide range of other Asian countries such as China, South Korea, Japan, India, Pakistan and Mongolia. However, the definition of ASEM as an interregional organization could be disputed as it includes Australia, New Zealand and the Russian Federation, which joined the dialogue in 2010. It could be argued that ASEM is now more akin to 'a transregional forum' or a 'dialogue process with a more diffuse membership which not necessarily coincide with regional organizations, and which may include member states from more than two regions' (Loewen, 2010, p. 25; Rüland, 2006, p. 296). Yet ASEM is different from APEC as it has a broader mandate than economics and trade. ASEM indeed covers cultural, political and people-to-people as well as economic issues in its discussions. However, although the EU seeks to gain further access for its exports in Asia's dynamic economies via ASEAN and ASEM, it lacks a coherent strategy towards Asia and its growing importance in the world economy, and towards ASEAN in particular.

ASEAN: peace through enmeshment

ASEAN countries have devised strategies to deal with powerful neighbours such as China, Japan and India, as well as the USA, while keeping their own identity. The rise in power of China has had consequences for both the EU and ASEAN. To deal with China, Japan, India and South Korea, while also keeping the USA engaged in the region, ASEAN has devised an intricate web of organizations, of which it is the centre and from which it propagates its own values of regional cooperation. This is soft power at its best. The so-called 'ASEAN way' is based on consultation, the search for consensus via informal negotiations, the respect for the sovereignty, territorial and national identity of its member states and the peaceful settlement of disputes (Simon, 2008, pp. 264–292). The propagation of ASEAN-style regionalism allows ASEAN to keep its own identity while significantly contributing to security and peace in the region and keeping control of the agenda. Critics are perhaps too quick to dismiss ASEAN+3, the ARP and the EAS as inconsequential additions to the already crowded 'alphabet soup' of regional organizations, mistaking them for mere talking shops. Appearances are deceptive. Behind these organizations lies perhaps the greatest achievement of ASEAN: peace through enmeshment or embracing of the big powers in an architecture of dialogue and security, which it has largely initiated.

While ASEAN+3 was created in 1997 in the context of the East Asian financial crisis, the EAS met for the first time in 2005. ASEAN+3 includes ASEAN plus Japan, China and South Korea. The EAS currently gathers the same members as ASEAN+3 plus Australia, New Zealand, India, and, since 2011, Russia and the USA. Intent on maintaining a dominant influence in East Asian frameworks, China prefers ASEAN+3 to the EAS, in which its role is effectively balanced by key players such as the USA. With the recent entry of the USA and Russia and Presidents Obama and Medvedev having participated in the last summit, China will now in all likelihood have to upgrade its representation to the EAS to the presidential level, with President Hu Jintoa already participating in G20 and APEC meetings, of which the USA and Russia are also members (Cook, 2011). ASEAN+3, China's preferred forum, has been mainly active in the financial sector with the 2000 Chiang Mai Initiative, which promotes regional monetary cooperation and has the potential of reducing reliance on the US dollar (Beeson, 2009, pp. 75–87). The EAS is broader both in its membership and its scope. It is Japan's preferred forum as it has the potential of diluting Chinese political and economic influence in a wider framework by working together with democracies such as Australia, New Zealand, India and the USA. The EAS is also a way for ASEAN to keep the USA involved in the Asia-Pacific region and to guarantee Japanese security. The EAS is now turning out to be a major forum to discuss strategic, finance, trade, education, health, energy and environmental concerns in Asia-Pacific, with China having to share the lead with other important players.[4] This shows the consummate craftsmanship inherent in the ASEAN approach, balancing, as it does, Chinese power in the region, while keeping the USA involved, thereby helping to make the EAS a more effective forum to address disputes in East Asia. The mediating role of the USA in fostering dialogue between ASEAN members Japan and China on claims over the resource-rich South China Sea is a case in point. Unfortunately, the EU is not a member of the EAS. A key precondition to accede to the EAS is to sign the ASEAN Treaty of Amity and Cooperation (TAC), to be a dialogue partner of ASEAN and to maintain in-depth relations with ASEAN. The EU was initially divided on whether to sign the TAC and join the EAS. When it did finally decide to sign, ASEAN raised the price of the admission ticket by insisting upon the need to amend the TAC to allow the EU to join, as it is not a state. The lengthy amendment process has now been completed and should see the EU sign the TAC in 2011, and, perhaps, accede to the EAS (Murray, 2010; Parello-Plesner, 2011).[5]

While the USA is a member of the ARF and the EAS, the EU is also member of the ARF and is, additionally, a member of ASEM, of which the USA is not a member. The USA can accordingly use APEC, the EAS and the ARF to promote its security and economic interests in Asia, while the EU does not participate in either APEC or the EAS, but can use EU/ASEAN summits and ASEM to defend its own agenda in the region. The ARF was inaugurated in 1994 and again stemmed from an attempt by ASEAN member states to control Japan and China's strategic appetites in the region by inviting them to participate in a large regional framework with ASEAN as a core and which worked according to the principles of the ASEAN TAC. But the broad membership of the ARF has proved to be something of a double-edged sword. As it meets at foreign minister level and its reach encompasses states such as North Korea, it has found it difficult to address key security issues such as nuclear proliferation, terrorism and disputes over energy-rich regions such as the South China Sea (Beeson, 2009, pp. 56–73; Foong Khong and Nesadurai, 2007, pp. 58 and ff.). It does seem likely, then, that the EAS will increasingly overtake the ARF in the future in addressing regional security issues. If that is the case, EU membership in the EAS is a must, if it does not want to be marginalized from one of the key discussion tables in the Asia-Pacific region.

ASEAN: a strategic partner for the EU?

Even though, or perhaps, because ASEAN and the EU both face their own challenges in their own regions and have to cope with an uncertain international environment, their engagement with each other remains important. As stated in the introduction to this volume, 'from the geo-strategic point of view', these two regions may not be 'of central importance to each other and there is a 'stark economic imbalance' between the two. While the EU is 'among the top four largest trading partners' for most ASEAN member states, ASEAN countries rank lower on the list of the EU as trade partners.[6] Yet this may be about to change. The European Commission states that 'ASEAN as a whole represents the EU's third-largest trading partner outside Europe (after the USA and China)' (European Commission, 2011). The Commission sees the long-term potential of Southeast Asia for its exports and investment, and while a Free Trade Agreement (FTA) between ASEAN and the EU did not materialize, the EU is negotiating FTA agreements with individual ASEAN member states. EU member states such as Germany also have important economic interests in the region.[7] In addition, certain EU member states with a colonial past in Asia view ASEAN as a part of a pivotal region for worldwide security. Along with 'the Middle East, [...] sub-Saharan Africa, the Polar regions and the Korean peninsula', the UK Ministry of Defence considers 'the Asian Meridian', 'a crescent-shaped area from Hong Kong and coastal China in the north, through Southeast Asia to Darwin and northern Australia in the South' (MoD Development, 2010) as one of the key geopolitical 'pivots' of the 21st century. The region 'sits astride major trade routes such as the Malacca Straits, and contains major energy and minerals deposits, such as coal in Indonesia and Australia'. Environmental degradation in Southeast Asia, coupled with internal conflicts and insecurity from the rise of China, could lead to territorial disputes with neighbours, thereby fuelling terrorism, further environmental damage, piracy and migration. All of these developments could significantly affect global trade flows and access to energy supplies. This helps explain the growing interest of the USA, India and China for ASEAN, as its stability is pivotal for prosperity and security in East and Southeast Asia, and globally.[8] As stated by Sheldon Simon: 'the most dangerous disputes lie in Northeast and South Asia while the region's multilateral institutions designed to manage and reduce conflict have originated in Southeast Asia' (Simon, 2008, p. 265).

The EU established formal relations with ASEAN as early as 1977, with informal relations dating back to 1972. Having renewed its strategic partnership with ASEAN in 2003, it sees ASEAN is an engine of integration and cooperation in Asia as a whole and not just in Southeast Asia. The EU also perceives ASEAN as one of the building blocks of a world of regions, patterned in part on the EU model of integration. According to the EU vision, group-to-group cooperation will help to enhance global prosperity and stability by preventing conflicts. From this perspective, the EU is a model for peace that works, and is to be emulated. The more other regions choose to emulate the EU, the more recognition it also brings to the EU as a significant actor on the world stage. This in turn has the potential for strengthening EU political and economic integration.[9] Thus, in its brochure for the Commemorative EU/ASEAN Summit in Singapore in 2007, the Commission stated:

> The EU and ASEAN have a shared commitment to regional integration as a means of fostering regional stability, building prosperity and addressing global challenges. Thus the EU fully supports ASEAN's renewed efforts to build a closer relationship among its member countries [...] European history bears testimony to the fact that greater integration is the best guarantee of stability and prosperity, and Southeast Asia can find inspiration in this. A strong and united ASEAN will contribute to a secure and balanced future in Asia and the wider world.
>
> (European Commission, 2007)

The EU vision also encompasses the crucial nexus between regionalism and multilateralism. The EU views its relations with ASEAN and dialogue with ASEM as a way of advancing its agenda in support of multilateralism in the United Nations, the WTO or in G20 summits, by coordinating its positions with Asian partners prior to meetings in these frameworks. This is a way of balancing American influence in Asia, as the USA is not a member of ASEM. In trade, the EU sees interregional cooperation as a way of fostering and supplementing a new multilateral agenda with more emphasis on trade liberalization. This means that even though the EU is a significant donor of Official Development Aid (ODA) in the region,[10] the emphasis is now relatively less on development cooperation and more on non-aid or smart-aid policies in the framework of ASEM and in keeping with the WTO. At the same time, frustrations with multilateral trade negotiations in the WTO, which are marking time, have prompted the EU, the USA and other key actors to look for regional or bilateral options to obtain further trade liberalization.[11] Neither the EU nor ASEAN have chosen to put all their eggs in the interregional basket. Launched in 2007, negotiations for a FTA between the two regions have now been put on the back burner, with a preference for bilateral agreements, even though these agreements are mostly seen by the EU 'as stepping stones to a regional agreement'.[12]

The EU – a strategic partner for ASEAN?

If ASEAN is important to the EU for political, economic and security reasons, how important is the EU to ASEAN? As we have seen, the EU is currently relatively more important to ASEAN from a trade and investment viewpoint than the reverse, although this could change. According to the European Commission, the 'EU is ASEAN's second-largest trading partner after China, accounting for 11 per cent of ASEAN trade' and the 'EU is by far the largest investor in ASEAN countries' with EU FDI outflows to ASEAN totalling € 9.1 billion as an average for the 2000–2009 period (European Commission, 2011). By contrast, ASEAN was the EU's fifth-largest trading partner in 2009.[13] The EU is also negotiating a series of bilateral FTAs with individual ASEAN member states, and will soon provide financial support 'to strengthen ASEAN capacity to negotiate' such agreements (€ 2.5 million). A further € 15 million are to be given to bolster ASEAN economic integration, including by helping the small ASEAN Secretariat to develop.[14] Over the 2007–2013 period, the EU will have disbursed about € 70 million in technical assistance to ASEAN.[15] The EU is also a major aid donor and was involved together with ASEAN in a successful mission in Aceh to monitor the peace agreement on disarmament.

But the EU is also important to ASEAN, inasmuch as it contributes to strengthen ASEAN stability by helping to balance powerful neighbours such as China and the USA or by helping to further economic growth with a rising standard of living for ASEAN populations (Moeller, 2007, pp. 471–472). Does ASEAN seek to emulate the EU as a model of integration? Here ASEAN elites would seem to mostly agree in their assessment that the EU can be tapped for good ideas – for example on monetary and economic integration, customs and standards, disaster relief and management, or on how to tackle environmental challenges.[16] Yet the EU is generally not seen as a model to be emulated by ASEAN. The EU is deemed too different from ASEAN, as the latter encompasses countries with huge disparities in economic development. The EU's preference for a legal approach and a high level of institutionalization is further contrasted with the ASEAN preference for a more informal grouping.[17] As far as the EU as an example of reconciliation of past enemies is concerned, while some ASEAN elites showcase the EU as a successful experiment in the peaceful resolution of disputes, ASEAN is also 'happily equated to the EU' in having already accomplished reconciliation in its own right. In fact, the EU example is sometimes used by a specific ASEAN country or a group of ASEAN countries to promote a particular agenda in support or against further ASEAN integration. ASEAN accordingly seeks to develop its own model. One area in which this is particularly so is the field of human rights, as some of its elites fear that human rights could be used 'as an excuse for outsiders to intervene into ASEAN own affairs' (Nguyen, 2009). Finally, the Australian initiative for an Asia-Pacific Community modelled on the EU or the Japanese proposal for an East Asian Community, also modelled on the EU, would seem to have triggered little enthusiasm in ASEAN. The region's leaders tend to show a certain degree of 'regionalism-fatigue' as they are 'already overwhelmed with numerous regional forums, committees, meetings and acronyms'.[18]

Challenges and misunderstandings

There are indeed many challenges and misunderstandings in ASEAN–EU relations. The EU's emphasis on supranationality, legal agreements and institutions is not always understood or accepted by ASEAN countries. There is also a 'gap between the actual and perceived importance of the EU' as a trade, environmental or development actor in the region.[19] Likewise, ASEAN's emphasis on informality, state sovereignty and non-interference, its lack of a legally binding human rights mechanism[20] and its poor record of implementation of regional agreements at national level[21] have been a source of frustration for the EU. The inability of ASEAN to find a political solution to human rights issues in Myanmar has led to recriminations on the part of EU elites and non-governmental organizations (NGOs), only to be matched by ASEAN misgivings that the EU is seeking to interfere in its affairs.[22] Another source of concern on the European side is the close connection between political classes and business elites in Southeast Asia, which is perceived as leading to corruption (Beeson, 2009, p. 28). All of these tensions may be due in part to different approaches in Asia and in Europe on sovereignty, democracy and human rights and thus rooted in different cultures and histories. Cultural misunderstandings are rife between ASEAN and its European partners in their dialogue at the regional level. While Europeans have a 'very short-term conception of time', their Asian partners tend to 'operate only in the long term'. While Asian partners prioritize 'stability, harmony and security', Europeans emphasize democracy and a legal approach to human rights, often with a certain 'complacency' and 'sense of moral superiority' which is resented by their partners (Letta, 2002, pp. 26 and 435). The different origins and evolution of the EU and ASEAN also help explain why ASEAN is not interested in replicating the EU model of 'deeply integrated political structures' and the 'pooling of sovereignty'. Having only recently gained their independence, ASEAN states have been keen to 'protect and reinforce rather than pool their often fragile sovereignty' (Beeson, 2009, p. 21). At the same time, there are many historical, economic, political, administrative and cultural differences within ASEAN itself which make cooperation within the regional grouping, and with the EU, more difficult. Some countries, such as Vietnam and Indonesia, have experienced rapid economic growth, while others have lagged behind; the role of the state, of the army and of religious parties is different, with six major religions and many languages in the region. This is compounded by rivalries within ASEAN, for example between Indonesia and other member states over a leadership role in the region or by unresolved conflicts between certain member states such as Thailand and Cambodia.

ASEAN is also situated in a 'more conflictual security environment' than the EU. This includes tense Sino-Japanese relations and the development of nuclear weapons in North Korea. This sense of insecurity in turn leads ASEAN member states to maintain or develop security ties with the USA, while some states such as Singapore are 'pursuing a self-avowedly "promiscuous" foreign policy aiming at developing close ties with as many powers as possible and ensuring that they all have a stake in regional security and stability'.[23] Again, this contributes to a lack of coherence in the relations of ASEAN with an external actor such as the EU. While ASEAN faces internal and external challenges and tries to deal with powerful neighbours such as China, Japan and India, while also keeping the USA involved, it may also be paying less attention to its relationship with the EU. Meanwhile, the EU itself, intent on developing better ties with China, also tends to see its relationship with ASEAN as relatively less important than in the past.

Challenges and potential for cooperation

Yet ASEAN and the EU face common challenges. One of these is the increasing gap between elites and citizens in their regions. While the French and the Dutch voted 'no' to the EU Constitutional Treaty and the Irish first voted 'no' to the Lisbon Treaty, ASEAN citizens and NGOs seem to be increasingly frustrated at being shunted away from 'elite talk-fests', which conclude agreements without consulting them. This may ultimately result in even more difficulties on the ASEAN side in implementing agreements concluded with the EU if ASEAN populations should come to oppose ASEAN.[24] Another challenge which both the EU and ASEAN faced after the Cold War was how to address the potential for domination by certain nation states within their region, such as Germany in the EU and Indonesia in ASEAN, and, more generally, how to maintain a delicate balance between larger and smaller member states. The need to enlarge while maintaining an adequate decision-making capacity has also been a challenge. Last but not least, both regions have had to respond to financial crises and to an international environment characterized by traditional and non-traditional security threats.

Cooperation between ASEAN and the EU could help to address some of these challenges. In July 2010, the Belgian vice-prime minister and minister of foreign affairs Steven Vanackere gave the closing speech of the ASEM Public Conference on Europe–Asia Inter-Regional Relations. He implied that the EU and ASEAN could learn from each other in obtaining sustainable economic development:

> [...] Europe is fascinated by Asia and vice-versa. Europe envies the growth rates achieved by the Asian economies. It understands that the future of its economic and social model depends on major structural reforms unleashing entrepreneurship and competitiveness. Conversely, Asia understands that economic growth alone does not produce stable and harmonious societies. It is interested in the European practice of shared prosperity through the combination of income redistribution and public services. Also, the management of conflicting economic, social and environmental demands in Europe's pluralistic societies through dense webs of consultation and participatory mechanisms catches attention in Asia.
>
> (ASEM, 2010)

Recommendations

While the EU seeks to learn from Asia to promote growth and to better deal with the world economic and financial crisis, Asia could learn from the EU in developing more participatory modes of governance. ASEAN could also usefully look into the EU experience of progressively integrating human rights into regional law and its potential for increasing democratic legitimacy.[25] A frequent complaint on the ASEAN side is the lack of high-level political participation in EU interaction with ASEAN, although 'at working level of officials the relationship is excellent'.[26] To maintain and develop a fruitful dialogue with ASEAN, the EU would do well to increase the level of its political representation to keep pace with American and Chinese increasingly high-level interaction with ASEAN and participation in the EAS. The EU could also develop a more coherent political strategy towards ASEAN now that the Lisbon Treaty has entered into force and that the new External Action Service is in place. Both the EU and ASEAN could also further develop professional, educational or business people-to-people links as well as the involvement of NGOs to improve dialogue and collaboration between the two regions. To this effect, direct contacts could be supplemented by 'diaspora public diplomacy', by making use of workers, migrants and refugees from Asia in the EU to increase knowledge about the EU in their countries of origin.[27] The same could be done for EU expatriates living in ASEAN countries in promoting understanding of ASEAN and more dialogue between the EU and ASEAN. This would supplement ongoing ventures such as the Asia–Europe Foundation (ASEF), which encourages links between governments and civil society in Asia as well as policy and academic cooperation and debates on themes of common concern, or the Trans-Eurasia Information Network (TEIN), which connects about 60 million researchers in Asia and Europe via 'the first large-scale research and education internet-based network' (MTR Document, 2010, pp. 3 and 15). Another encouraging development is the inaugural Business Summit between the EU and ASEAN, which took place in May 2011 and led to discussions among business leaders and between business and governmental leaders from both regions. Such discussions could go a long way towards improving trade and investment cooperation between ASEAN and the EU (ASEAN, 2011).[28]

While some EU-funded projects in ASEAN have been largely successful, others were less so because of the lack of commitment on the part of ASEAN in contributing its own resources to the projects once EU funding was scaled down. This has led to unhappy episodes where the projects were discontinued or kept barely 'alive' by minimum financial contributions from the EU and ASEAN. An additional problem is the lack of administrative capacity on the part of some ASEAN countries in implementing region-to-region agreements. This is compounded by the fact that relations between the two regions 'are largely driven by the foreign ministries in the ASEAN countries', while initiation and implementation falls to a wide range of agencies in the ASEAN governments with lack of coordination between them.[29] Clearly this situation needs to be improved as it is damaging to good relations between the two regions.

In many ways, ASEAN and the EU could 'act together as natural soft power allies in addressing global challenges' such as 'migration, trafficking in human beings, money laundering, piracy, organized crime and drugs'.[30] They could further share information on how to deal with energy and environmental challenges. The EU has already given substantial support to the ASEAN Energy Centre and the ASEAN Centre for Biodiversity. In implementing its regional strategy for Asia, the European Commission has also pledged to prioritize projects that promote green growth and to establish 'an Asia Investment Facility to facilitate investments relevant to climate change' (MTR Document, 2010, p. 3). The accession of ASEAN members to the Energy Charter Treaty could go a long way towards facilitating regional energy cooperation in the region by providing a stable legal framework for energy trade and investment across borders that is able to 'balance the interests of producer, consumer and transit countries'.[31]

At the international level, an in-depth dialogue between ASEAN and the EU, including within ASEM, could lead to concrete actions in other frameworks such as the G20 and the WTO. Thus, ASEM meetings have led to concerted positions in preparation for G20 meetings. Such a dialogue has also been fruitful in efforts to reform the World Bank and the IMF to give more of a say to developing countries. Yet cooperation between ASEAN and the EU can only work fully if it is rooted in mutual respect and understanding. Only on such basis can an effective strategic partnership be built.

Notes

1. For a comparative perspective on ASEAN, the EU and APEC see Warleigh-Lack (2008).
2. On interregionalism in the EU and East Asia, see Gilson (2005).
3. For more details on ASEM, see A. C. Robles, Jr. (2008).
4. See Chapter 8 by J. W. Blankert in this volume.
5. See also Chapter 9 by O. Keng Yong in this volume.
6. See Introduction and chapters 5 and 10 by N. Chaban, L. Suet-yi and K. Abidat, and X. Nuttin in this volume.
7. See Chapter 5 by N. Chaban, L. Suet-yi and K. Abidat as well as Chapter 9 by O. Keng Yong in this volume.
8. See Chapter 7 by W. Kucera 'The Energy Charter Treaty and the Problem of Energy Security in Southeast Asia' in this volume.
9. See Chapter 9 by O. Keng Yong in this volume.
10. See Chapter 5 by N. Chaban, L. Suet-yi and K. Abidat in this volume.
11. See Chapter 1 by D. Webber in this volume.
12. See chapters 10 and 8 by X. Nuttin and J. W. Blankert in this volume.
13. See Chapter 9 by O. Keng Yong in this volume.
14. See Chapter 8 by J. W. Blankert in this volume.
15. See Chapter 9 by O. Keng Yong in this volume.
16. On ASEAN efforts to understand and adapt EU 'norms and institutions', see Hwee (2008, p.92).
17. See Chapter 2 by N. Maier-Knapp in this volume.
18. See Chapter 3 by M. Clark and J. Pietsch in this volume and Murray (2010, p. 603).
19. See Chapter 5 by N. Chaban, L. Suet-Yi and K. Abidat in this volume.
20. See Chapter 6 by Rachminawati and A. Syngellakis in this volume.
21. See chapters 1 and 8 by D. Webber and J. W. Blankert in this volume.
22. See Chapter 9 by O. Keng Yong in this volume.
23. See Chapter 1 by D. Webber in this volume.
24. See Chapter 3 by M. Clark and J. Pietsch in this volume.
25. See Chapter 6 by Rachminawati and A. Syngellakis in this volume.
26. See Chapter 8 by J. W. Blankert in this volume.
27. See Chapter 5 by N. Chaban, L. Suet-Yi and K. Abidat in this volume; on the involvement of NGOs, see Gilson (2005, p. 316).
28. ASEM has held an Asia—Europe Business Forum since 1996, see Gilson (2005, p. 315).
29. See Chapter 9 by O. Keng Yong in this volume.

30. See Chapter 8 by J.W. Blankert in this volume.
31. See Chapter 7 by W. Kucera in this volume.

Bibliography

ASEAN, 'EU Inaugural Summit Provides Platform for Business and Government Exchanges', ASEAN Statements and Communiqués, Jakarta (2011) 5 May 2011, http://www.aseansec.org/26231.htm, accessed 27 May 2011.

ASEM Public Conference on Europe-Asia Inter-Regional Relations (2010) Closing speech by Vice-Prime Minister and Minister of Foreign Affairs Steven Vanackere, Brussels, 11–13 July 2010.

Beeson M. (2009) *Institutions of the Asia-Pacific. ASEAN, APEC and beyond* (London and New York: Routledge).

Cook M. (2011) 'The East Asia Summit: From Wen to Hu', *The Interpreter*, Lowy Institute for International Policy, 17 May 2011, http://www.lowyinterpreter.org/post/2011/05/17/The-East-Asia-Summit-From-Wen-t..., accessed 27 May 2011.

European Commission, Directorate General External Relations (2007) *'EU/ASEAN 2007: Celebrating 30 Years of Relations. Impressive Achievements – even more Potential'* (Brussels: Publications Office).

European Commission, Directorate-General for Trade (2011) 'Regions, ASEAN' http://ec.europa.eu/trade/creating-opportunities/bilateral-relations/regions/asean/, accessed 6 June 2011.

Foong Khong Y. and Nesadurai H.E.S. (2007) 'Hanging Together, Institutional Design, and Cooperation in Southeast Asia: AFTA and the ARF' in A. Acharya and A. Iain Johnston (eds.), *Crafting Cooperation. Regional International Institutions in Comparative Perspective* (Cambridge: Cambridge University Press).

Gilson J. (2005) 'New Interregionalism? The EU and East Asia', *Journal of European Integration*, 27, No. 3, 307–326.

Hwee Y.L. (2008) 'EU–ASEAN Policy-Learning', in R. Balme and B. Bridges (eds.), *Europe–Asia Relations. Building Multilateralisms* (Basingstoke and New York: Palgrave Macmillan), 92.

Letta C.G.M. (2002) *ASEM's Future. Governance. A Comparative Analysis*, Vol I and II (Bologna: Lo Scarabeo).

Loewen H. (2010) 'ASEM's Enlargement – State-to-State or Region-to-Region Dialogue?' in Y.L. Hwee and W. Hofmeister (eds.), *The Asia-Europe Meeting* (Singapore: EU Centre in Singapore and Konrad Adenauer Stiftung).

MTR Document (2010) Regional Strategy for Asia 2007–2013, Multi-Annual Programme for Asia (MIP) 2011–2013, adopted by Commission Decision C(2010) 7863 of 17 November 2010, http://eeas. europa.eu/asia/rsp/07_13_mtr_annex_en.pdf.

MoD Development, Concepts and Doctrine Centre (DCDC) (2010) *Global Strategic Trends: Out to 2040*, 4th edn (London: Ministry of Defence).

Moeller J.O. (2007) 'ASEAN's Relations with the European Union: Obstacles and Opportunities', *Contemporary Southeast Asia*, 29, 3, 471–472.

P. Murray (ed.) (2008) *Europe and Asia. Regions in Flux* (Basingstoke and New York: Palgrave Macmillan).

Murray P. (2010) 'East Asian Regionalism and EU Studies', *European Integration*, Vol. 32, No. 6, 597–616.

Nguyen T. (2009) 'The Making of the ASEAN Charter in my Fresh Memories' in T. Koh, R. Manolo, and W. Woon (eds.), *The Making of the ASEAN Charter* (Singapore: ISAS).

Parello-Plesner J. (2011) East Asia Summit: Where is Europe?, European Council on Foreign Relations, http://ecfr.eu/content/entry/commentary_east_asia_summit_where_is_europe/, accessed 27 May 2011.
Robles A.C., Jr. (2008) *The Asia-Europe Meeting. The Theory and Practice of Interregionalism* (London and New York: Routledge).
Rüland J. (2006) 'Interregionalism: An Unfinished Agenda', in H. Hänggi, R. Roloff and J. Rüland (eds.), *Interregionalism: An Unfinished Agenda* (London and New York: Routledge).
Simon S. (2008) 'ASEAN and Multilateralism: The Long, Bumpy Road to Community', *Contemporary Southeast Asia*, 30, 2, 264–292.
Warleigh-Lack A. (2008) 'The EU, ASEAN and APEC in Comparative Perspective', in P. Murray (ed.), *Europe and Asia. Regions in Flux* (Basingstoke and New York: Palgrave Macmillan).

Index

'10 minus x' or 'two plus x', 17
1992 project, 13

Aceh Monitoring Mission, 40
acquis communautaire, 17
ASEAN
 ASEAN-USA Summit, 144
 comparisons with EU, 45–6, 52–4, 56, 58, 62, 140–3, 147, 168, 170–1, 185–7
 contingent for peacekeeping, 50
 criticisms/critique of, 47–50, 128, 156
 decision-making mechanism of, 65–6, 78–80, 157, 189
 diversity within, 131, 170–1, 174, 186–7
 East Timor, application for membership of, 145
 economic disparity between member states, 130, 146, 170, 186–7
 economic integration, 62, 133, 139–41, 155–6, 159, 170–1
 EU as an inspiration, 45–6, 53, 56–7, 124–34, 147, 149, 159, 169–71, 173, 184–5, 188
 frictions between member states of, 47, 53, 55, 128, 187
 Inter-parliamentary Assembly, 175–6
 (lack of) democratization of/democratic deficit, 45, 48, 59, 174–6
 maritime versus mainland member states, 128
 Master Plan for Inter-Connectivity (MPIC), 145–7, 161
 most successful outside the EU, 48, 186
 organizational limitations, 46, 170–1
 origins of, 139–40, 177, 179
 political success of, 47
 post-1998 leadership vacuum in, 48
 preferential trade agreements, 126, 141, 144, 148, 162
 quiet diplomacy, 149–50
 Secretariat, 145, 148, 152, 157–9, 170, 185
 'soft' approach to regional integration, 139
 surveillance process, 31
 Swap Arrangements, 31
 territorial disputes, 53, 128, 139, 142, 170, 182, 187
 'Track I', 52
 'Track II', 46, 51, 162
 'Track III', 51–2
ASEAN Charter, 3, 50, 52, 115, 139–40, 143, 151, 159, 170, 175
ASEAN Community (Economic, Political, or Socio-Cultural), 33, 48, 50, 53–4, 62, 108, 133, 143, 156, 159, 170, 186
ASEAN Free Trade Area (AFTA), 15
ASEAN Institutes of Strategic and International Studies (ASEAN ISIS), 46
ASEAN People's Assembly, 51
ASEAN Plus Three (APT) or ASEAN-centered regional architecture, 10, 16, 31, 45, 47, 54, 57, 139–41, 143, 145, 162, 166, 179–83
ASEAN Regional Forum (ARF), 20, 27, 45–6, 140–1, 144, 162, 172, 180–3
 confidence building, 141
 preventive diplomacy, 140–1
ASEAN Security Community (ASC), 48, 50, 143
ASEAN Wayconsensus decision-making and non-interference, 18, 47, 54, 59, 78–9, 140, 170, 175, 181
 destroyed credibility of, 47
Asia
 resilience during global crisis (2008–2009), 166, 179–80
 rise of/key role of, 166–8, 172, 177
Asia-Europe Meeting (ASEM), 29, 162–3, 172, 181–2, 184–5, 188–9
'Asian values', 108, 117

Asia-Pacific Community (APC), 45, 56–9, 145, 167, 186
Asia-Pacific Cooperation (APEC), 180, 182–3
Australia, 7, 10, 49, 56–8, 127–8, 130, 141, 143, 145, 161–3, 182, 186
avian influenza, 36–8

Bangkok Declaration, 115
Bilateral Investment Treaty (BIT), 125
biodiversity, 35
Blair, Tony, 19
borders, 2, 120
Burma, *see* Myanmar/Burma
Bush, George W., 19

Cambodia, 16
Canada, 7
'capability-expectations gap', 99
Charter of Fundamental Rights, 108
Chiang Mai Initiative, 14, 31–2
China, 8, 12, 15, 45, 49, 56–8, 63, 71, 73–5, 77–8, 81, 120, 124, 126–30, 134, 143–4, 150, 161–3, 169–70, 188
 ASEAN's FTA with, 13, 141, 144
 (counter)balancing of, 16, 23, 145–6, 149, 175, 180, 182–3, 185, 187
 the rise of, 11, 50, 54, 56–7, 127, 129, 133, 144–7, 166–7, 173, 180–2, 184, 187
Chirac, Jaques, 19
civil society/NGOs, 50–1, 53, 55, 164, 176, 186–8
'clash of civilisations', 101
climate/environmental change, 36, 57, 128, 162, 163, 176, 184–5
Clinton, Bill, 12
Cologne, 19
colonial rule, 89, 97
Communism
 Eastern Europe, 130
 threat of, 47, 134
Copenhagen criteria, 16
Copenhagen School, 27
corruption, 35
Council of Europe (CoE), 111
crisis
 economic and financial of, 1997, or Asian financial crisis, 26, 31, 47

global financial crisis of 2008–9, 14, 16, 155, 163, 166, 169, 179–80, 188
currency
 single European, 10
 US dollar, 14
Czech Republic, 16

democracy, 16, 100
democratization, 9, 11, 28
Deng Xiaoping, 9
Denmark, 14
Deutsche Gesellschaft für Technische Zusammenarbeit (GTZ), 34
diplomacy, 87ff
 cultural, 87
 public, 87
 quiet, 149–50

East Asia Community, 45, 56–9, 145, 167, 186
East Asia Summit (EAS), 10, 141, 143–4, 150, 162, 166, 180–1, 183, 188
 EU's membership of, 150–1, 167, 182–3
East Timor, 12, 91, 145
energy security
 Agreement on ASEAN Energy Cooperation, 130
 and ASEAN, 124–34, 189
 ASEAN Ministers on Energy Meeting (AMEM), 130–1
 competition from external powers, 124; *see also* ASEAN
 different approaches within ASEAN to, 130–1
 European Energy Charter or Energy Charter Treaty (ECT), 3, 125–33, 189
enlargement, 8, 15ff., 111, 114
EU-ASEAN relations, 62–81, 139–53, 139–53, 155–64, 166–77, 179–90
 ASEAN-EC Cooperation Agreement, 155, 160
 ASEAN Post-Ministerial Conference plus One, 162
 bilateral engagement with ASEAN member states, 63, 80–1, 148, 151, 160–1, 174, 183, 185
 cultural misunderstandings, 186

dialogue partners, 143, 147, 152, 155, 162, 181–4, 186, 188–90
economic/financial interdependence with ASEAN, 63–7, 74, 77
EU-ASEAN Business Summit, 148, 152, 189
EU-ASEAN Ministerial Meeting, 163
EU assistance/aid to ASEAN, 147–8, 151–3, 156–7, 164, 167, 172–3, 185, 189
EU's little interest in Asia/ASEAN, 63, 147, 149–51, 167, 188
EU support for ASEAN integration, 149–53, 156–7, 167, 176, 184–5, 189
foreign direct investment (FDI), 65, 71–4, 81, 185
money/finance, portfolio investment (PI), 74–6, 81
natural partners, 143, 147
preferential trade agreement (FTA), 58, 80, 151, 160, 163, 173, 175, 183, 185
quiet actors, 143
strategic alliance/partnership, 63–5, 77–81, 149, 164, 171, 177, 183–5, 190
trade/economic relations with ASEAN, 13, 62–81, 127, 148, 153, 155, 160–1, 163, 173, 179, 185, 189
European Commission, 17
European Court of Justice, 17, 109
European External Action Service (EEAS), 89, 100
European Forest Institute, 35
European Parliament, 15–16
European Security and Defense Policy (ESDP), 19
European Union (EU)
 ASEAN policy/Asia strategy of, 62, 171–2, 177
 comparison with the U.S., 180–4
 development aid, 142, 185
 economic integration/European Economic Community, 140, 172–3
 economic powerhouse, 143
 EU Constitution, 52, 187
 euro crisis, 142

European Coal and Steel Community (ECSC), 124–5
European Commission's, 2001 Strategic Framework, 66
fire response group (EUFREG), 34
High Representative for CFSP, 167, 169
human rights, 52, 174–5, 188
lack of coherence (of EU foreign policy), 167–8, 173, 181, 188
lack of credibility of, 167, 186
model framework of regionalism, 54, 168
neighborhood policy, 142–3
peacekeeping missions/operations, 142
'people-centered', 46, 53, 58–9, 169, 174, 188
relations with Russia, 141
Treaty of Lisbon, *see* Treaty

flexible engagement, 17
Forrest Law Enforcement, Governance and Trade (FLEGT), 34
France, 16
Free Trade Agreement (FTA), 1

G20, 2, 49, 55–6, 161, 166, 168–9, 182, 184, 190
General Agreement on Tariffs and Trade, 126
Generalized System of Preferences (GSP), 90
geopolitics, 128, 134, 183
 'Asian Meridian', 128–9, 183
 'heartland theory', 129–30
 instability/rivalry, geopolitical, 128–31, 182–4, 187
 pivotal region, 128, 183
 rise of Asia, changing, 166–9, 177
German
 Federal Republic, 9
 reunification, 9
globalization/global challenges, 9, 13, 49, 129, 132, 134, 151, 164, 168–9, 171, 176–7, 183–4

haze, 12, 33
 ASEAN agreement on transboundary haze, 33
 Regional haze action plan (RFAP), 33

haze – *continued*
  Sub-regional ministerial steering committee on transboundary haze pollution, 33
  Technical task force (HTTF), 33
Human rights, 95, 108ff., 117ff
  ASEAN Intergovernmental Commission on Human Rights (AICHR), 50, 52, 115–16, 148, 152, 159–60, 164, 175–6, 186
  human rights body, 3
India, 10, 50, 56, 126–7, 129–30, 141, 143–4, 161–3, 166–7, 179–82, 184, 187

Indonesia, 10, 12, 29, 33, 45–60, 120, 184
  active role/leadership in ASEAN, 46–8, 145–6, 187, 188
  blamed for non-compliance, 48
  Centre for Strategic and International Studies (CSIS), 46, 50–1
  'confrontation' with Malaysia, 46
  consensus decision-making and non-interference, 47
  democratization of, 46–9, 55
  energy security, 128
  foreign policy of, 49–50, 55, 59, 128, 145–6
  and G20, 2, 49, 55, 166
  major regional/global power, 46, 127, 129, 166–7
  perceptions of ASEAN, 46, 48–60, 128
  'Post-ASEAN' regional strategy, 45–6, 55–6, 59
  relations with/attitude to China, 145–6
  Suharto, president (1966–1998), 46
Institutionalism, institutionalisation
  'hard' (or 'strong'), 45, 46, 58–9, 158, 168, 186–7
  'soft' (or 'weak'), 34, 45, 158, 168, 170, 186–7
Interdependence (economic), 63–4, 132–3, 148, 169
International economic coordination, 64–5
International Labour Organisation (ILO), 110

International Monetary Fund (IMF), 12, 31, 47, 169, 190
International Political Economy (IPE), 30
Inter-regionalism, interregional cooperation, 8, 63, 88, 180–1
Ireland, 16

Japan, 7, 15, 45, 54, 56–8, 63, 71, 73–5, 77–8, 81, 124, 126–30, 141, 143–6, 161–3, 167, 179–83, 186–7
  judicial activism, 112

Kohl, Helmut, 9
Korea, North, 8, 12, 20
Korea, South, 8, 15, 45, 56, 58, 63, 71, 73–8, 81, 127–8, 130, 141, 143–4, 161–3, 181–3, 187
Kuala Lumpur, 16, 31

Laos, 12
Lee Kwan Yew, 13
legitimacy, 108
Libya, 19

Malaysia, 10, 35, 120
migrant/overseas workers, 95, 120
Mitterrand, François, 9
Myanmar/Burma
  cyclone Nargis, 51
  democratization/political changes in, 12, 149–50
  military junta, ASEAN's tolerance of, 16, 53, 160, 170, 175
  obstacle to EU-ASEAN relations, 13, 149, 160, 174–5, 186
  political and civil rights violations, 50, 55, 91, 119, 164, 175, 186

Netherlands, 16
New Zealand, 7, 10
non-interference, principle of, 3, 17, 95, 100, 117
North American Free Trade Agreement (NAFTA), 125, 127, 180
North Atlantic Treaty Organization (NATO), 19, 130, 179

Official Development Aid (ODA), 90
one-party rule, 8

orbiter dictum, 112
Organization for Security Cooperation in Europe (OSCE), 130

Partnership and Cooperation Agreement (PCA), 40
perceptions, 88ff
Philippines, 29
Poland, 16
power, 87
 balance of, 18
 big, 19
 disparity, 18
 'soft'/'hard', 87
 'superpower', 18, 91
primus inter pares, 12

regionalism
 EU vis-à-vis US' competing visions of, 180
 participatory, 48–9, 53, 59
religion, 100
remittances, 101
Russia/Soviet Union (USSR), 97, 127, 130, 141, 143, 150, 162–3, 167, 169, 182

Saint Malo Declaration, 19
Sarkozy, Nicolas, 19
Schengen Agreement, 16
security, 46, 49, 50, 55, 58, 132, 144, 158–9, 167–8, 170, 177
 challenges, 56, 129, 148, 162–4, 169, 179, 182, 187–8
 comprehensive, 29
 concerns, 57, 62, 124, 128, 144, 179–80
 EU as a non-traditional security actor, 26ff., 171–2
 'hard', 2, 20
 human, 26
 maritime, 143, 180, 182–3
 non-traditional, 26ff., 171–2, 176, 179, 188–9
 sector reform, 28
 'soft', 2
Shinawatra, Thaksin, 10

Singapore, 21, 23
Single European Act (SEA), 110
Slovenia, 11, 15
state sovereignty, principle of, 117
Strasbourg, 10
Suharto, 12
Sweden, 12, 14

Taiwan, 8
Terrorism, 18, 50
 Al-Qaeda, 18
Thailand, 10, 12, 29
Treaty
 Amity and Cooperation, of (TAC), 140, 183
 Constitutional, 15
 EU's membership of Treaty of Amity and Cooperation, 140, 150–1, 162, 167, 182
 Lisbon Treaty, 16, 52, 114, 151, 168–9, 187–8
 Maastricht Treaty, 110
Turkey, 111

unipolarity, 9, 20
United Kingdom (UK), 14, 97
United Nations Charter, 28
United States, 7, 33, 57–8, 126, 129–30, 132, 141, 143–4, 146, 149–50, 161–3, 166–7, 173, 179–85, 187–8
Universal Declaration of Human Rights (UDHR), 110

Vientiane Action Programme, 33
Vietnam, 7, 10, 12

War
 Cold, 7, 13, 179
 Vietnam, 7
 World War II, 111
World Bank, 47, 169, 190
World Trade Organization (WTO), 120, 125–6, 133, 163, 173, 180, 184–5, 190

Yugoslavia, 11, 18